Take Heed
to
Yourselves!

Paul M. Frane

April 6, 1970

Today in Solemn Assembly in the 140th Annual Conference of the Church, President Joseph Fielding Smith was sustained by the membership of the Church as the Tenth President, Prophet, Seer & Revelator In this Dispensation. There was a great outpouring of the Spirit of the Holy Ghost & all faithful saints rejoyed.

Take Heed to Yourselves!

by

Joseph Fielding Smith

Published by
DESERET BOOK COMPANY
Salt Lake City, Utah
1966

Library of Congress No. 66-25511

Printed by

in the United States of America

Foreword

In the formative years of gospel restoration, the Lord admonished the Prophet Joseph Smith and his brethren associated with him to "say nothing but repentance unto this generation."[1] This theme is repeated frequently throughout the revelations in the Doctrine and Covenants. In harmony with this counsel, President Joseph Fielding Smith has been raising the warning voice as a General Authority for more than fifty-six years.

"I want to raise the warning voice, and I am doing it among the stakes of Zion," President Smith once said. "I want to tell you the judgments have gone forth and they are going forth. . . . Will we escape? When I see, even among the Latter-day Saints the violation of the laws of the Lord, I fear and I tremble. I have been crying repentance among the stakes of Zion, . . . calling upon the people to turn to the Lord, keep his commandments, observe the Sabbath day, pay their honest tithing, do everything the Lord has commanded them to do, to live by every word that proceedeth forth from the mouth of God. . . . So I cry repentance to the Latter-day Saints, and I cry repentance to the people of the United States as well as to the people of all the earth."[2]

Many years ago, as a young boy, I recall an occasion when I attended a sacrament meeting with my father. I remember vividly some of the remarks he made on that occasion. "Who is your friend, or who loves you the most?" he asked the congregation. "The person who tells you all is well in Zion, that prosperity is around the corner or the person who warns you of the calamities and difficulties that are promised unless the principles of the gospel are lived? I want you to know that I love the members of the Church, and I do not want one of them to point an accusing finger at me when we pass beyond the veil of mortal existence and say, 'If you had only warned me I would not be in this predicament.' And so I raise the warning voice in hopes that my brothers and sisters may be prepared for a kingdom of glory."

For President Smith's many years of service to the Church, it seemed only appropriate that a selection of his sermons, warning and pleading with the people, should be published in book form. For this purpose, "Take Heed to Yourselves!" has been compiled for the benefit of members of the Church and others.

Material for this volume has been compiled from the various sources denoted at the end of each discourse. Appreciation is expressed for the use of this material, and also to the Deseret Book Company for making publication of this volume possible.

July 1966 Joseph Fielding Smith, Jr.

---

[1]D&C 6:9; 11:9; 14:8; 18:14, 41; 19:21, 31; 36:6; 44:3; 55:2; 58:47.
[2]*Doctrines of Salvation,* Volume III, pages 33, 35. Read also chapters 1-3.

Contents

I want to tell you, my brothers and sisters, the greatest need in the Church of Jesus Christ today is repentance and more respect for divine authority; more willingness to keep the commandments of the Lord. Who do you think is going to be saved in the kingdom of God? Well, according to the revelation of the Lord—not over half the members of the Church. When I think of the parable of the ten virgins—and that has reference to The Church of Jesus Christ of Latter-day Saints, the kingdom of God, speaking of the last days, the time of his coming—the Lord indicates that about half of them will be ready. When I see the activities of some of the members of the Church, I wonder if even half of them will be ready when the Lord comes.

The commandments of the Lord to the members of the Church constitute the standards of the Church which in every respect should be obeyed faithfully.

The Standards of the Church

The commandments of the Lord to the members of the Church constitute the standards of the Church which in every respect should be obeyed faithfully. In order to obtain the reward of exaltation in the celestial kingdom, every soul must strive to put himself in harmony with and be obedient to every law and ordinance pertaining to that kingdom. In a revelation given September 22 and 23, 1832, the Lord said:

> And I now give unto you a commandment to beware concerning yourselves, to give diligent heed to the words of eternal life.
>
> For you shall live by every word that proceedeth forth from the mouth of God.
>
> For the word of the Lord is truth, and whatsoever is truth is light, and whatsoever is light is Spirit, even the Spirit of Jesus Christ.[1]

Perfect Laws Govern in Celestial Kingdom

James in his epistle said: "For whosoever shall keep the whole law, and yet offend in one point, he is guilty of all." This has appeared to many as a hard saying, yet it is true. The laws which govern in the celestial kingdom are perfect and before we can enter there we must place ourselves in harmony with them all. A person who is in rebellion against any one eternal commandment cannot be justified and cannot enter the celestial kingdom. If he were permitted to do so he would take into that kingdom confusion, and such a condition cannot be justified. The words of the Lord in the Sermon on the Mount are not idle words, "Be ye therefore perfect, even as your Father which is in heaven is perfect." He knew well enough that it is impossible for any man to obtain perfection in this mortal life; but he also knew that it is here that we lay the foundation on which perfection rests. His remark was not limited to this world in its application. Likewise when he said, "But seek ye first the kingdom of God, and his righteousness," he had a broader view than to apply it merely to this temporal existence. However, it is here that we are expected to lay the foundation which will be strong and deep by virtue of our observance of his commandments.

This Life Is a Probationary State

We are taught that this life is a "probationary state," one in which we are tested to see if we will be worthy of salvation through obedience to the divine commandments. We are informed that at one time in the eternity past, we lived in the presence of our Eternal Father. There we were taught correct principles, and the fact that we are here is evidence that we kept those commandments. This earth life is the reward of obedience in that life. Mortality is an advanced step in the path of eternal existence. If we can remain true here, under all the vicissitudes which we find in mortality, then the great reward of eternal life in the celestial kingdom is assured us. It is the way by which we shall become the children of God, his sons and daughters, joint heirs with Jesus Christ, and the fulness, exaltation, will be the reward.[2]

The Prophet Joseph Smith, commenting on the standards governing in the kingdom of God, has said:

We consider that God has created man with a mind capable of instruction, and a faculty which may be enlarged in proportion to the heed and diligence given to the light communicated from heaven to the intellect; and that the nearer man approaches perfection, the clearer are his views, and the greater his enjoyments, till he has overcome the evils of his life and lost every desire for sin; and like the ancients arrives at the point of faith where he is wrapped in the power and glory of his Maker and is caught up to dwell with him. But we consider that this is a station to which no man ever arrived in a moment: he must have been instructed in the government and laws of that kingdom by proper degrees, until his mind is capable in some measure of comprehending the propriety, justice, equality, and consistency of the same.[3]

Without Knowledge We Cannot Be Saved

Again the Prophet said:

As far as we degenerate from God, we descend to the devil and lose knowledge, and without knowledge we cannot be saved, and while our hearts are filled with evil, and we are studying evil, there is no room in our hearts for good, or studying good. Is not God good? Then you be good; if he is faithful, then you be faithful. Add to your faith virtue, to virtue knowledge, and seek for every good thing.[4]

We are only capable of comprehending that certain things exist, which we may acquire by certain fixed principles. If men would acquire salvation, they have got to be subject, before they leave this world, to certain rules and principles, which were fixed by an unalterable decree before the world was.

The disappointment of hopes and expectations would be indescribably dreadful.[5]

We must be familiar with the standards before we can obey them. They embrace far more than the principles which are usually described as ethics: A man may know that it is wrong to steal and that honesty is a just principle without having faith in God or being obedient to his commandments to be baptized for the remission of his sins. Yet honesty in its strictest sense is a fundamental standard of the Church.

The experience gained in life, even among those who do not understand the plan of salvation, may teach a man to be truthful, for he learns that any other course is unsafe and leads to trouble and loss of friends. Truthfulness however, is a fundamental principle of the gospel. There have been peoples in the past, and may be even now, who observe the law of chastity who have no clear conception of the divine command. Chastity is a vital doctrine of the Church and is a standard which we are taught cannot be violated without dire consequences following, which may mean a loss of eternal salvation in the kingdom of God. The Lord has made this principle very plain, and every member of the Church should know that the violation of this law, in the sight of the Lord is second only in its heinous nature to the shedding of innocent blood. The justice of this doctrine is very apparent, for the Lord has centered in the properly organized marriage the right to the sexual relationship, for the family is sacred in his eyes. Therefore, for any person to violate this divine law the punishment must be extremely severe. Those who are guilty of such a sin may think they can hide it; but eventually, if it is not discovered in this life, it will be revealed after, and those who are morally unclean have no place in the kingdom of God.

The Law of Tithing

The law of tithing is a fundamental principle of the gospel and must remain so until the time comes when the Lord will give the law of consecration. Those who cannot keep this law will have no place in the kingdom when it is perfected, for there only the just, the honest, and obedient will dwell. It is written:

> Behold, now it is called today until the coming of the Son of Man, and verily it is a day of sacrifice, and a day for the tithing of my people; for he that is tithed shall not be burned at his coming.
>
> For after today cometh the burning—this is speaking after the manner of the Lord—for verily I say, tomorrow all the proud and

they that do wickedly shall be as stubble; and I will burn them up, for I am the Lord of Hosts; and I will not spare any that remain in Babylon.

Wherefore, if ye believe me, ye will labor while it is called today.[6]

The Word of Wisdom is also one of the fundamental standards of the Church. It is plain enough to be understood by all members of the Church, and there is in it the promise that those who observe it shall have wisdom given to them so that they will know just what the Lord means in relation to its observance. It is the basic law and a standard to guide us and keep us physically, morally, and spiritually clean. Our mortal bodies were given as eternal tabernacles for our spirits. We will never lose them although they may be laid away in the grave for a season. They will then come forth in the resurrection to inherit such degree of glory as we have merited through our deeds performed in mortality.

Laws of Decalogue Are Eternal in Nature

For some reason that is far from clear, there are living persons who maintain that the Decalogue was done away with the law of Moses. This is not so. These laws existed from the beginning and are eternal in their application. Moreover, in this present dispensation the Lord reiterated them. They are standards that must be observed if we expect to receive the blessings of the kingdom. The religious world in the main has rejected some of these commandments, particularly the observance of the Sabbath day. It is a regrettable thing that many members of the Church have followed in their footsteps. Because the peoples of other faiths and those of no faith have shown their contempt for this great commandment is not a reason why members of the Church should follow them. Nor will the Lord hold them guiltless of this sin any more readily than he would had they violated the law of honesty, truthfulness, or chastity.

Peter has given us excellent advice in these words, which will insure our salvation if they are strictly followed:

> Whereby are given unto us exceeding great and precious promises; that by these ye might be partakers of the divine nature, having escaped the corruption that is in the world through lust.
>
> And beside this, giving all diligence, add to your faith virtue; and to virtue knowledge;
>
> And to knowledge temperance; and to temperance patience; and to patience godliness;
>
> And to godliness brotherly kindness; and to brotherly kindness charity.
>
> For if these things be in you, and abound, they make you that ye shall neither be barren nor unfruitful in the knowledge of our Lord Jesus Christ.
>
> But he that lacketh these things is blind, and cannot see afar off, and hath forgotten that he was purged from his old sins.
>
> Wherefore the rather, brethren, give diligence to make your calling and election sure: for if you do these things, ye shall never fall.[7]—(*The Improvement Era*, July, 1957.)

---

[1]D&C 84:43-45.
[2]John 10:34-36; Rom. 8:13-18; Rev. 2:7; D&C 132:19-23.
[3]*Teachings of the Prophet Joseph Smith*, p. 51.
[4]*Ibid.*, p. 217.
[5]*Ibid.*, pp. 324-325.
[6]D&C 64:23-25.
[7]2 Peter 1:4-10.

I know of nothing that is more important or necessary at this time than to cry repentance, even among the Latter-day Saints, and I call upon them as well as upon those who are not members of the Church, to heed these words of our Redeemer. He has stated definitely that no unclean thing can enter his presence. Only those who prove themselves faithful and have washed their garments in his blood through their faith and their repentance—none others shall find the kingdom of God.

Cry Repentance

I wish to read a part of the instruction given by our Redeemer to his disciples on this continent just before he left them.

And my Father sent me that I might be lifted up upon the cross; and after that I had been lifted up upon the cross, that I might draw all men unto me, that as I have been lifted up by men even so should men be lifted up by the Father, to stand before me, to be judged of their works, whether they be good or whether they be evil—

And for this cause have I been lifted up; therefore, according to the power of the Father I will draw all men unto me, that they may be judged according to their works.

And it shall come to pass, that whoso repenteth and is baptized in my name shall be filled; and if he endureth to the end, behold, him will I hold guiltless before my Father at that day when I shall stand to judge the world.

And he that endureth not unto the end, the same is he that is also hewn down and cast into the fire, from whence they can no more return, because of the justice of the Father.

And this is the word which he hath given unto the children of men. And for this cause he fulfilleth the words which he hath given, and he lieth not, but fulfilleth all his words.

And no unclean thing can enter into his kingdom; therefore nothing entereth into his rest save it be those who have washed their garments in my blood, because of their faith, and the repentance of all their sins, and their faithfulness unto the end.

Now this is the commandment: Repent, all ye ends of the earth, and come unto me and be baptized in my name, that ye may be sanctified by the reception of the Holy Ghost, that ye may stand spotless before me at the last day.[1]

Nothing More Important

I know of nothing that is more important or necessary at this time than to cry repentance, even among the Latter-day Saints, and I call upon them as well as upon those who are not members of the Church, to heed these words of our Redeemer. He has stated definitely that no unclean thing can enter his presence. Only those who prove themselves faithful and have washed their garments in his blood through their faith and their repentance—none others shall find the kingdom of God.

We have inducements, enticing features come before us through the press, by television particularly, and in other ways to lead our people and all other people astray and away from keeping the commandments of God. I want to raise a warning voice to the members of the Church, and especially to the youth of the Church. Do not pay heed to the wicked and malicious advertising of tobacco nor of liquor. The advertising of tobacco today is one of the greatest offenses and crimes before our Father in heaven, and those who are guilty of it will one day have to pay the price. They do it now because of greed, but we must not listen to these enticings and to the wicked advertising of things that are detrimental to the body and condemned by our Father in heaven and his Son Jesus Christ, contrary to the gospel they have given to us.

We have those who are among us who are inclined to listen to these pleadings and to the entertainments that are given, all of which are intended to lead us into forbidden fields, to partake of things condemned by the Lord, and which are not for those who have made covenant with him to keep his commandments.

A Warning against Tobacco

I am going to spend a minute or two particularly relative to this filthy tobacco habit. I believe that some of the women of this country are getting to be worse than the men, and those who advertise are seeking to influence the women —the mothers of the children. As I ride through the streets of Salt Lake City in an automobile, I sometimes see women on nearly every street corner or between the blocks with cigarets in their mouths—three or four women to every man. I fear some of them are members of the Church. We cannot afford to turn either to the right nor to the left from the keeping of the commandments of the Lord if we want to enter into his kingdom.

Our bodies must be clean. Our thinking must be clean. We must have in our hearts the desire to serve the Lord and keep his commandments; to remember our prayers, and in humility seek the counsels that come through the guidance of the Spirit of the Lord. That will bring to us our salvation, and we will never get salvation through the violation of the covenants and commandments which will bring to us eternal life.—(*Conference Report*, October 8, 1960.)

---

[1]3 Nephi 27:14-20.

There should not be any doubt in the minds of any of us in regard to the mission of Jesus Christ. Nor should we have any doubts in our minds concerning his second coming and that he will come in his glory, that he will come to establish his work upon the face of the world, setting up his own kingdom which shall have full power over all the peoples on the face of the earth.

The Time Is Short

Years ago when I was a boy and used to read the New Testament about the Savior and the Twelve who traveled with him from place to place and he advised, instructed and counseled them, I thought what a wonderful gift and opportunity it was which was bestowed upon them. Then I also wondered a little about what appeared to be their lack of comprehension. He talked to them plainly, he spoke of his mission, told them the purpose of his earth life, why he was here, of his death and resurrection and yet they seemingly failed to comprehend it. While the accounts of it are very abbreviated yet the Lord spoke to them about his coming, why he was here and the manner of his leaving so far as mortality was concerned, that he was to lay down his life and take it up again and yet they evidently could not comprehend it, except of course on certain occasions, I suppose, when they received inspiration from the Lord as Peter did when he said, "Thou art the Christ, the Son of the Living God."

At the Last Supper he told them he was going to his death, that he would send a Comforter to be with them and to bring to their memory things he had taught them, things that were past. In reading that I would think, "Well, what was the matter with them?" He said these things plainly and yet on the morning of the resurrection they all seemed to be dumbfounded and astonished when the report came to them that he had arisen.

We are into the habit—when I say "we" I will exclude myself, and perhaps I can do the same for you—but our people are in the habit of speaking of Thomas as "doubting Thomas" as though Thomas was standing aloof in his doubt, not comprehending and failing to accept the joint testimonies of the other brethren. I have wondered if it had been Matthew, if it had been Andrew or even Peter or any of the other Apostles who had been absent and the remaining ten would have said, "We have seen the Lord. He has arisen," who perhaps would not have raised the question and said, "Unless I can see, I cannot believe." They did not seem to comprehend the resurrection of the dead and that Christ was to be the first fruits of the resurrection.

Testimony through Guidance of the Spirit

Later when I thought the matter through, that they had not received the inspiration of the Holy Ghost while he was with them, except on one occasion; not understanding the mission of Christ as did Isaiah and the prophets of earlier years who had the Holy Ghost, I felt that I could forgive them for their lack of understanding. They were not dumb men. Here we are, we do not have the experiences that came to them. We do not have the privilege of being with him, of hearing his discourses, seeing him heal the sick and all those wonderful things; but through the guidance of the Spirit of the Lord we can have just as strong a testimony, be just as sure of his mission and resurrection as they had after his resurrection. I am sure there is not a doubt in the minds of the brethren here in regard to any of these things which took place.

I think that throughout the Church those who have been baptized and have been true and faithful have no doubt at all about the resurrection of Jesus Christ, the purpose of his resurrection, what was accomplished by it. We are entitled to the guidance and inspiration that comes through the contacts which we are entitled to have and the guidance of the Holy Ghost so we may understand and comprehend every truth that has been revealed which the Lord intends we should understand, that we may know that just as clearly, just as definitely as we would know it had we stood in his presence.

If there is any member of the Council of the Twelve who does not know that Jesus Christ is the Son of God, and the Redeemer of the world then I would be greatly astonished. We have the right, through our faithfulness, to be guided by that Spirit, to be taught, to have our minds enlightened so we can comprehend the sacred principles of the gospel, matters which have been revealed concerning the plan of salvation and feel and know that these things are true as well as we know we are here in this room. There should not be any doubt in the minds of any of us in regard to the mission of Jesus Christ. Nor should we have any doubts in our minds concerning his second coming and that he will come in his glory, that he will come to establish his work upon the face of the world, setting up his own kingdom which shall have full power over all the peoples on the face of the earth. The Lord has never revealed to us when the day will come, but he has given us knowledge enough by which we may know that that day is not far away. When I say "not far away," I am not setting any definite number of years. I was accused of saying he was coming in twenty years and I have heard the statement made that I said he was coming in forty years. People say all kinds of things but no man knows the day of his coming and no man is going to know and I don't think the Twelve will know it. I have my doubts that the Presidency of the Church will know, because the Lord says he will come when no one is expecting it, but he has given us signs and the world is full of them today, signs of his coming as he draws nigh.

Explanation of Words of Matthew

Many years ago when Brother John H. Taylor was presiding in the Northern States Mission he sent me a letter he received from one of the ministers in Chicago who quoted the words of the Savior as found in the twenty-fourth chapter of Matthew, and other places in which he said, "This generation shall not pass till all these things be fulfilled." The minister said in his letter if we cannot answer that question we might as well quit and close up shop. He said nearly two thousand years have passed and yet he has not come, and yet he says this generation shall not pass. What is the answer to that? If we have no answer to that we might as well throw our Bibles away. Brother Taylor got one of those letters and did not know what to do with it so he sent it on to me. Of course in the Bible it is not translated correctly but the Lord gives us the correct translation.

> And again this Gospel of the Kingdom shall be preached in all the world, for a witness to all nations, and then shall the end come, or the destruction of the wicked.[1]

That is not in the Bible as we have it and the world, in its understanding, thinks something dreadful is going to happen, which will and that the world is going to go to its destruction. What the Lord means is that this telestial order is going to come to an end. He makes an explanation of what is meant by "destruction of the wicked":

> And again shall the abomination of desolation, spoken of by Daniel the prophet, be fulfilled.
>
> And immediately after the tribulation of those days, the sun shall be darkened, and the moon shall not give her light, and the stars shall fall from heaven, and the powers of heaven shall be shaken.
>
> Verily, I say unto you, this generation, in which these things

shall be shown forth, shall not pass away until all I have told you shall be fulfilled.[2]

How Long Is a Generation?

The question is how long is a generation? I don't know and I am not concerned about it. This is the thing that concerns me—the increased calamities, the destruction, the turmoil, the trouble that exists in the world, the fearfulness of nations, their trembling, their hearts failing them. I can remember back in the days of Theodore Roosevelt when one of the powers of Europe intended to enforce some restrictions on a little country in South America. He told them to keep their hands off and keep out "or else," and they kept their hands off. Today we are afraid to say anything. Other nations are afraid. They are preparing for the great final struggle but they do not seem to know it. They have invented or discovered means of making the most terrible weapons of destruction, harnessing the forces, splitting atoms until they have become so fearful that they are all afraid to act. Things have occurred which our country would never have stood for forty or fifty years ago, that other nations would never have stood for.

Now we are having trouble in the Near East, trouble just where the trouble is going to break out according to the revelations. This little nation of Israel is struggling for its existence; they are hemmed in with enemies all around, they are putting up a courageous defense. They have the sympathy of this country and of England and perhaps of France but I don't know about France because they are in bad shape. Russia and her allies on one side are keeping their hands off and we are keeping our hands off. We let the little nation of Egypt, controlled by the followers of Mohammed, step in and we are afraid to do anything. Everyone is afraid and no one will move, their hearts have failed them.

At the last meeting I think I said something about Israel and I want to say a little more. I see things going on in Palestine which are very significant and they have been going on ever since General Allenby went into that country during the war. You brethren, like all the rest, speak of the first and second world wars and look forward to the third world war. I don't. To me it is the same war. I think we have been in the same war since 1914. We speak of the destruction of the Nephites. They and the Lamanites had war with each other for a great period of years before the final destruction. Yet there were years when they were not in conflict, that is in open battle, because they were exhausted and had to go back to their fields, had to prepare themselves, had to make weapons and so forth so they had what could be called, from time to time, armistices, just as we have only we call it a cold war and we have been getting ready all of the time in this country and other countries for the great and final destruction or else I do not understand the scriptures.

Interpretation of Scripture

I do not interpret some things like most people do. I want to read a verse or two.

> Verily, thus saith the Lord concerning the wars that will shortly come to pass, beginning at the rebellion of South Carolina, which will eventually terminate in the death and misery of many souls.
>
> And the time will come that war will be poured out upon all nations, beginning at this place.
>
> For behold, the Southern States shall be divided against the Northern States, and the Southern States will call on other nations, even the nation of Great Britain, as it is called, and they shall also call upon other nations, in order to defend themselves against other nations; and then war shall be poured out upon all nations.[3]

The real beginning of the world war was in 1861. If you will read your histories you will find that from that time on the people began to prepare for the final conflict. What did they have in that war?—wooden vessels, old fashioned guns that could not throw a shot more than a few hundred yards. I don't know exactly how far they would throw them, but strong enough, if they were in close enough quarters, to penetrate a wooden vessel. In that war they made their first iron-clads and then guns had to be made to match the armor. Finally they got to building ships out of steel, very thick steel and then guns that would go through that from miles and miles away. The guns got stronger and larger, the ships got bigger and stronger. As the guns got more powerful, the ships got more strength to resist them and so it has gone on until it has now reached a condition such as we find today. So the next war is going to be largely in the air.

The Time Is Getting Short

All of these things point to the fact that time is getting short. All signs the Lord has given us as recorded in the New Testament we can see; the moon has not been turned to blood and the earth has not reeled to and fro yet as that will be one of the final signs. I heard President Wilford Woodruff say in the Salt Lake Temple, and he also said it in Ogden and a number of other times before his death following the dedication of the Salt Lake Temple, that the angels who were waiting, as spoken of in the thirteenth chapter of Matthew, have now been loosed and sent on their mission. You can read what their mission is and he has said that they had been loosed and sent on their mission to prepare the earth for the harvest. The wheat and the tares were to grow together until the harvest was ripe. President Woodruff said that time had started, these angels have been sent on their mission.

About 1916 I got a little curious and I spoke to my father. I told him the calamities and the destructions on the face of the earth were increasing year by year and I thought

I would go through the current magazines that recorded world events and note these events year by year and to my astonishment they increased each year. The destructions became more frequent. If you will make a record of that you will find it is true. Someone else got the same idea, someone connected with the Smithsonian Institution, and I was surprised but that is a fact. Tornadoes and all the things the Lord has promised are coming, we are in the midst of them, so I think we should raise a warning voice to our people and call upon them to repent and make them understand that the Lord wants them to keep his commandments and prepare themselves for events to come and sever themselves from the foolishness of this world. We are getting pretty much like the rest of the world and it is time we should be crying repentance.—(Quarterly Meeting of the Council of the Twelve, April 10, 1957.)

---

[1]Joseph Smith 1:31.
[2]*Ibid.*, 1:32-34.
[3]D&C 87:1-3.

We should be missionaries of the Church by the manner of our living. Our lives should speak. The testimony of the truth should be borne through our faithfulness, the purity of our lives, the integrity and devotion of our souls.

"Entangle Not Yourselves in Sin"

The Mutual Improvement organizations were very happy in their choice of a theme for the young people of the Church in adopting this one taken from the eighty-eighth section of the Doctrine and Covenants:

> Abide ye in the liberty wherewith ye are made free; entangle not yourselves in sin, but let your hands be clean, until the Lord comes.[1]

This is taken from a revelation, one of the greatest given to the Church, known as "The Olive Leaf." The Prophet so described it in sending the revelation to the brethren who were dwelling at that time in Zion, as it was called, " 'The Olive Leaf,' which we have plucked from the Tree of Paradise." In the main, this revelation was given for the guidance of missionaries. We have heard that we are all missionaries. Every member of the Young Women's and every member of the Young Men's Mutual Improvement Associations is or ought to be a missionary, and we are all set apart, not by the laying on of hands; we have not had a special calling; we have not been singled out to do missionary labor, but as members of the Church, having pledged ourselves to the advancement of the gospel of Jesus Christ we become missionaries. That is part of the responsibility of every member of the Church. That does not mean that we have to go into a foreign field; we can be missionaries at home, nor is it necessary that we be called to be stake missionaries, for in this very revelation the Lord has something to say about it, and I am going to read those verses; in fact, I may want to read a good many of these verses, and then if the Spirit of the Lord directs me, maybe from some other revelations.

A Warning to All

Now, this that I will read was said to those who were called and appointed to go into the mission field, but you will see that the Lord applied it not only to all the members of the Church, but also to everybody else, whether in the Church or out of the Church:

> That ye may be prepared in all things when I shall send you again to magnify the calling whereunto I have called you, and the mission with which I have commissioned you.
>
> Behold, I sent you out to testify and warn the people, and it becometh every man who hath been warned to warn his neighbor.
>
> Therefore, they are left without excuse, and their sins are upon their own heads.[2]

So here is a command from our Father in heaven that is so broad that it is not confined to those who are set apart and commissioned and sent forth into the world to teach the world the gospel, but the Lord commands every soul to whom this message comes that it is his responsibility, not only to receive it, but also to carry it to his neighbor; and they who hear it and refuse to carry it, to warn their neighbors, shall be left without excuse before the judgment seat of God. Now as the Lord requires that of those who are not in the Church, then how much more so is it required of us who are members of the Church?

We should be missionaries of the Church by the manner of our living. Our lives should speak. The testimony of the truth should be borne through our faithfulness, the purity of our lives, the integrity and devotion of our souls.

I am happy to know that this work of the Mutual Improvement organizations is going to go on through the whole year. I think it was Brother Stevenson who made the remark that the devil will be busy this summer. Well, did you ever hear of the devil taking a vacation? For six thousand years he has never laid off a day, nor an hour, nor a minute, and in all these years since he was cast out of heaven and placed upon the earth he has been determined to destroy faith, to lead away the innocent, to bind their souls through unrighteousness, teaching them wickedness, and always in the most clever manner. No, he does not rest.

Strengthen Our Minds and Bodies

I do not mean to say that we who are mortals should not take a few days off if we want to, to rest and build up our bodies, strengthen them, give our minds a chance perhaps to repair themselves and be prepared for the energies that will be required of them, but we should not lie down and forget the responsibilities which the Lord has placed upon us.

Whether we are engaged in softball, basketball, or in any other kind of sport, in dancing, or whatever it may be, it should all be done in the spirit of building up and strengthening the kingdom of God.

I am very grateful for the opportunities that come to our young people to engage in these sports under proper direction and to have this recreation. I think it is a part of the gospel plan, but whatever it is that we do should be done in the Spirit of the Lord, and if we cannot do it that way, it should not be done. I think that this is the spirit in which these contests, whatever they may be, are carried on. I commend our good brethren throughout the Church who conduct these exercises, and the sisters, too, in drama, in art, in music, whatever it is, as well as in the athletic field.

This wonderful revelation, I say, was intended mostly, not all of it, but most of it, for missionaries, but there is in it much that is intended for members of the Church at large. There are things in it intended for the brethren holding the priesthood. The Lord has pointed out how they should meet in their solemn assemblies, the spirit in which they should meet, how these meetings should be conducted.

The members of the Church are taught to inform themselves in regard to all principles of truth, and much of this responsibility has been assigned to the Mutual Improvement organizations. I want to read these verses:

> Also, I give unto you a commandment that ye shall continue in prayer and fasting from this time forth.
>
> And I give unto you a commandment that you shall teach one another the doctrine of the kingdom.
>
> Teach ye diligently and my grace shall attend you, that you may be instructed more perfectly in theory, in principle, in doctrine, in the law of the gospel, in all things that pertain unto the kingdom of God, that are *expedient* for you to understand.[3]

Now I emphasize that, because I want to come back to it.

> Of things both in heaven and in the earth, and under the earth; things which have been, things which are, things which must shortly come to pass; things which are at home, things which are abroad; the wars and the perplexities of the nations, and the judgments which are on the land; and a knowledge also of countries and of kingdoms.[4]

I say this is counsel given to missionaries; it is counsel that is good for all the members of the Church. We should make ourselves acquainted with all these things, but I am very glad that the Lord put in this counsel that expression, that in our seeking for knowledge, we seek for those things which are expedient for our understanding.

We Are Living in a Troubled World

We are living in a very troubled world, and I am going to talk plainly: we are living in a world that has discarded

God or is rapidly doing so. We are living in a world where the Christian ministers of various denominations have been frightened by the philosophies of men and, therefore, because they lack the Spirit of the Lord, have tried to modify the scriptures, or, the meaning of the scriptures, so that they can make them harmonize with the false theories so prevalent in the world today, theories which are in absolute conflict with divine revelation; and yet these people, afraid, dominated by the influence of false philosophy, are modifying the doctrines to make them conform to these theories and ideas which are godless in their foundation. We cannot afford to do that.

I picked up a book that is being used in a great many high schools throughout the United States, published by three gentlemen of renown, noted in their certain fields of science. This book was one that was in the possession of one of my grandsons who does not live here in Salt Lake City, but it is in his possession, and it is being used in the schools. In it some of these theories, damnable in their nature, are placed before these children in a very enticing form to lead them away from a belief in God.

You cannot see what I have in my hand, but it is showing to these students in the school, where man came from. I wish we had a blackboard here, and I were an artist, but it does not take an artist to do this. I am going to tell you just what there is here.

Details of a False Theory

Here is a V-shaped diagram showing on one side the descent of animals, on the other side the descent of plants, or ascent, whichever way you want to look at it, from a little speck. At one time, according to the theory, this came to life all of itself, spontaneously, and presently it became an amoeba, and then a worm, and then an insect, and here is the amoeba, here is the worm, here is a grasshopper representing the insect, then a reptile, and finally they put a cow. I do not know why they picked a cow, because Mr. Darwin says that we are related to the horse, but that does not matter. That is on one side. Then from this same side of the V and from the same source we get the algae that we find in the water, then the fungi, like the toadstools, then the mosses, then the ferns, and after a while, we get the trees, all coming from the same source.

That is the kind of stuff that that book is filled with. Then it shows on one page the leg of a man and opposite it the leg of a grasshopper, showing how much they are alike. The one thing they overlook is that the grasshopper's leg works just opposite to the way the man's leg works, so far as the joint is concerned.

You can see the effect that has upon the youth, and they add other pictures, scores of them, and all of this is being taught to your sons and your daughters, your children's children when they get old enough to have children in public schools, and you cannot get a textbook, anywhere that I know of, on the "ologies," except theology, and many of these carry you the same way, along this same course of nonsense—that is all it is.

So I think the Lord was wise here in saying that in our studying we must study those things that are expedient, things that are useful, that will not destroy our faith in God.

We Are the Sons and Daughters of God

Now, we believe we are the sons and daughters of God, do we not? The Lord has revealed it. He has taught us that in our own day. You will find it so recorded in Section 76 in the Doctrine and Covenants. The Savior taught his disciples that we are the offspring of God, and he said to Mary, when she met him after his resurrection, ". . . go to my brethren, and say unto them, I ascend unto my Father, and your Father; and to my God, and your God,"[5] and that he would then come and visit with them.

We have just surrendered, I think, and now these silly things are dominating the teaching of the peoples of the world in what are called civilized countries.

Now, a few more things from this revelation which concern us, one and all:

> Behold, that which you hear is as the voice of one crying in the wilderness—in the wilderness, because you cannot see him—my voice, because my voice is Spirit; my Spirit is truth; truth abideth and hath no end; and if it be in you it shall abound.
>
> And if your eye be single to my glory, your whole bodies shall be filled with light, and there shall be no darkness in you; and that body which is filled with light comprehendeth all things.
>
> Therefore, sanctify yourselves that your minds become single to God, and the days will come that you shall see him; for he will unveil his face unto you, and it shall be in his own time, and in his own way, and according to his own will.
>
> Remember the great and last promise which I have made unto you; cast away your idle thoughts and your excess of laughter far from you.
>
> Tarry ye, tarry ye in this place, and call a solemn assembly, even of those who are the first laborers in this last kingdom.
>
> And let those whom they have warned in their traveling call on the Lord, and ponder the warning in their hearts which they have received, for a little season.
>
> Behold, and lo, I will take care of your flocks, and will raise up elders and send unto them.
>
> Behold, I will hasten my work in its time.[6]

Faithful Will Behold the Lord's Face

Here the Lord promises that if we are faithful and true we will behold his face. There is not anyone here this afternoon who has not seen his face. Every one of you, we all dwelt in his presence, we have all seen him, but for a wise purpose that knowledge was taken away, and the Lord intends that we should walk by faith, not by sight. Here is what the Lord says himself about it in this same revelation:

> Behold, all these are kingdoms, and any man who hath seen any or the least of these hath seen God moving in his majesty and power.

I say unto you, he hath seen him; nevertheless, he who came unto his own was not comprehended.

The light shineth in darkness, and the darkness comprehendeth it not; nevertheless, the day shall come when you shall comprehend even God, being quickened in him and by him.

Then shall ye know that ye have seen me, that I am, and that I am the true light that is in you, and that you are in me; otherwise ye could not abound.[7]

This is a wonderful revelation. It covers so many things of vital importance to every member of the Church. I wonder how many of us have read Section 88? Do not stop by just reading this one section. Take it as your theme, there is none better, but read the whole revelation. No! read the whole book. The Lord commanded in the very first section of the Doctrine and Covenants, which is the preface of this book, the Lord's preface:

Search these commandments, for they are true and faithful, and the prophecies and promises which are in them shall all be fulfilled.[8]

"Search these commandments." How much do we love the Lord? What is the greatest of all the commandments? The Lord has told us here in Section 59 of the Doctrine and Covenants what it is, as he applies it to the members of The Church of Jesus Christ of Latter-day Saints in this dispensation of the fulness of times:

Wherefore, I give unto them [the members of the Church] a commandment, saying thus: Thou shalt love the Lord thy God with all thy heart, with all thy might, mind, and strength; and in the name of Jesus Christ thou shalt serve him.

Thou shalt love thy neighbor as thyself. Thou shalt not steal; neither commit adultery, nor kill, nor do anything like unto it.

Thou shalt thank the Lord thy God in all things.[9]

First Commandment Is to Love God

So, the first of all the commandments is to love God with all our soul, and in the name of Jesus Christ, serve him, and he has commanded us to make ourselves familiar with these truths which have been revealed to us in the dispensation of the fulness of times.

How many of us have done it? So I say to you, and all the members of the Church, for that matter, do not let your understanding rest upon one verse, which is a very excellent theme, but search the scriptures that you may not be deceived by false theories and practices and doctrines so prevalent in the world today. If you will do this, if you will have in your hearts the guidance of the Spirit of the Lord which every member of the Church has a right to have, the companionship of the Holy Ghost, you will not be led astray by the theories of men because the Spirit of the Lord will tell you they are false, and you will have the spirit of discernment that you may understand.

Now I was going to read two passages from the Bible, because they are so closely connected with this theme. The Savior was speaking to the Jews. They marveled at his doctrine, and

> Jesus answered them, and said, My doctrine is not mine, but his that sent me.
>
> If any man will do his will, he shall know of the doctrine, whether it be of God, or whether I speak of myself.[10]

"If any man will do his will, he shall know of the doctrine—"

Why, we ought to be able to understand the doctrine of Jesus Christ; we ought to have within us the power, aided by the Spirit of the Lord, to discern between the doctrines that come from our Father in heaven, through his Son, Jesus Christ, and the doctrines of men.

Do Not Believe Theories of Men

When you go to school, and you are told all these theories and have to pass an examination on them, all right, write it down and say, "This is what my teacher says," and

"This is what the textbook says." You do not have to say you believe it.

Here is the other passage: He had been preaching to the Jews, and many of them believed on him.

> As he spake these words, many believed on him.
>
> Then said Jesus to those Jews which believed on him, If ye continue in my word, then are ye my disciples indeed;
>
> And ye shall know the truth, and the truth shall make you free.[11]

Now if you understand the gospel of Jesus Christ, it will make you free. If your softball, your volleyball, your basketball, your foot racing, your dancing, your other entertainments are devoid of the Spirit of the Lord, they will be of no value to you. Let everything be done in the spirit of prayer and in faith. I think that is the case, maybe it is unnecessary for me to say it, but so let it be. Do everything with an eye single unto the glory of God, and let us teach to build up and strengthen ourselves and The Church of Jesus Christ of Latter-day Saints.

May the Lord bless all of us and be with you people who are leading and directing in this Mutual Improvement work that you may teach and guide the youth in the truth that will make them free.—(Address delivered at June Conference of Mutual Improvement Associations, June 12, 1953.)

---

[1]D&C 88:86.
[2]*Ibid.*, 88:80-82.
[3]*Ibid.*, 88:76-78.
[4]*Idem.*, v. 79.
[5]John 20:17.
[6]D&C 88:66-73.
[7]*Ibid.*, 88:47-50.
[8]*Ibid.*, 1:37.
[9]*Ibid.*, 59:5-7.
[10]John 7:16-17.
[11]*Ibid.*, 8:30-32.

The missionary effort cannot be stopped. It must and will go forth that the inhabitants of the earth may have the opportunity of repenting and receive the remission of their sins and come into the Church and kingdom of God.

Missionaries Labor to Fulfil Promise

Yesterday, with my brethren, I was in session with some thirty mission presidents. We heard a report from all in relation to their work and the work of the missionaries who labor under them. At the close of the meeting, and all through the meeting, we felt to rejoice because of the glowing reports that they were able to give to us.

There is one reason why these missionaries go forth and that is to fulfil the promise that was made by our Redeemer that his gospel of the kingdom should be preached in all the world as a witness before the time of his second coming. In his discourse as recorded in the twenty-fourth chapter of Matthew which came in response to the request of his disciples to know concerning his second coming, and the events that would take place before his coming, he told them of the calamities, the distress among the nations, the wars, the rumors of wars, the commotions, men's hearts failing them, and that they would turn away from the truth. Then speaking of the latter days he said to them:

> And again, because iniquity shall abound, the love of many shall wax cold; but he that shall not be overcome, the same shall be saved.

And again, this Gospel of the Kingdom shall be preached in all the world, for a witness unto all nations, and then shall the end come, or the destruction of the wicked.[1]

Fulfilling that prediction that the gospel would again be preached, inferring that there would be a time when it would not be preached and it would have to be restored, these missionaries are going forth and spending their time which is appointed among the nations of the earth.

More Missionaries Needed

Unfortunately, because of conditions which cannot be controlled by the Church, our missionary forces are reduced. We need missionaries. It is true today, as it was one hundred years ago, that the field is white; the harvest is great; but the laborers are few. Likewise the field is white and ready for the harvest. In a revelation given to the Church November 1, 1831, the Lord said he would send forth his missionaries, or his servants.

And the voice of warning shall be unto all people, by the mouths of my disciples, whom I have chosen in these last days.

And they shall go forth and none shall stay them, for I the Lord have commanded them.

Behold, this is mine authority, and the authority of my servants, and my preface unto the book of my commandments, which I have given them to publish unto you, O inhabitants of the earth.

Wherefore, fear and tremble, O ye people, for what I the Lord have decreed in them shall be fulfilled.[2]

Now the Lord has said that his missionaries shall not be stayed and that they shall go forth until he says the work is finished. In this same revelation he also says this:

For they [the people of the earth] have strayed from mine ordinances, and have broken mine everlasting covenant;

They seek not the Lord to establish his righteousness, but every man walketh in his own way, and after the image of his own God, whose image is in the likeness of the world, and whose substance is that of an idol, which waxeth old and shall perish in Babylon, even Babylon the great, which shall fall.

Wherefore, I the Lord, knowing the calamity which should come upon the inhabitants of the earth, called upon my servant Joseph Smith, Jun., and spake unto him from heaven, and gave him commandments:

And also gave commandments to others, that they should proclaim these things unto the world; and all this that it might be fulfilled, which was written by the prophets—

The weak things of the world shall come forth and break down the mighty and strong ones, that man should not counsel his fellow man, neither trust in the arm of flesh—

But that every man might speak in the name of God the Lord, even the Savior of the world;

That faith also might increase in the earth;

That mine everlasting covenant might be established;

That the fulness of my gospel might be proclaimed by the weak and the simple unto the ends of the world, and before kings and rulers.[3]

Missionary Effort Will Continue

And so in fulfilment of these promises to the world, our missionaries go forth. No power has been able to stay their hands. It has been tried. Great efforts were made in the very beginning when there was only a handful of missionaries, but the progress of this work could not be stopped. It cannot be stopped now. It must and will go forth that the inhabitants of the earth may have the opportunity of repenting of their sins and receive the remission of their sins and come into the Church and kingdom of God, before these final destructions come upon the wicked, for they have been promised.

There is in the world today distress, turmoil, trouble, commotion, and contention among the nations. There is no peace. There will be no peace until the Prince of Peace comes to bring it. And his warning is to the world to repent. This I might have read, for it is the first verse of this revelation I have been quoting. The righteous have been called on to come out of Babylon, or the world, to receive the gospel of

Jesus Christ as it has been restored, and find a place in the kingdom of God.

And these missionaries, mostly young men, untrained in the ways of the world, go forth with this message of salvation and confound the great and the mighty, because they have the truth. They are proclaiming this gospel; the honest and sincere are hearing it and are repenting of their sins and coming into the Church. The ungodly will not repent. This truth is also stated in this revelation. They will not repent because today, as in times of old, men love darkness more than light.

Heavens Are Never Closed Against Righteous

I wish to testify to you, my brethren and sisters, and to all the world, that God lives, that he has spoken again from the heavens, and the heavens have never been closed against those who are honest and true, who earnestly seek the guidance of the Lord. The Lord never closed the heavens. Men closed the heavens and said there should be no more revelation, no more commandments, only those which are in the canon of scripture. It was men who said that, not God. Men have said that the Lord finished his work. They have said there could be no more coming of angels, no more scripture, and that we would have to depend on the dead letter of the law as it is recorded in the books contained within the lids of the Bible. Men are saying that—God did not say it.

And he has restored to us the everlasting gospel and has given us revelation and made known to us many of the plain and important things pertaining to his kingdom—things revealed anciently, and also in the day in which we live, and he will give revelation to this Church from time to time according to the needs of the people, for the heavens are not sealed, only as men have sealed them against themselves.

Let us seek to know his will, hearken to the counsels of the First Presidency of this Church, and the President, who is the mouthpiece, the servant of God, with the authority to receive revelation for the guidance not only of the Latter-day Saints, but also for the people of all the world if they will only hearken to it.—(*Conference Report,* April, 1953.)

[1]Joseph Smith 1:30-31.
[2]D&C 1:4-7.
[3]*Ibid.,* 15-23.

We have the means of escape through obedience to the gospel of Jesus Christ. . . . I have been crying repentance among the stakes of Zion, calling upon the people to turn to the Lord, . . . to live by every word that proceedeth forth from the mouth of God.

Solemn Warning to the World

And again this gospel of the kingdom shall be preached in all the world for a witness unto all nations; and then shall the end come or the destruction of the wicked.[1]

These words were spoken by our Savior to his disciples shortly before his crucifixion. They have reference to the day in which we live. In fulfilment of that prediction the elders of this Church have been preaching the gospel in the nations of the earth since 1830. They have been raising the warning voice and crying repentance. It was not only expedient, but it was inspirational that the Presidency of this Church, at the opening of this conference should send forth a petition or an epistle not only to the Latter-day Saints, but to the people of the earth calling them to repentance and giving unto them a warning.

From the very beginning the Lord has called upon the elders of the Church to raise the warning voice, and we read:

Hearken, O ye people of my church, saith the voice of him who dwells on high, and whose eyes are upon all men; yea, verily I say: Hearken ye people from afar; and ye that are upon the islands of the sea, listen together.[2]

That is the call from the Lord to every soul upon the

face of the earth, to give heed to his warning. Then continuing he says:

For verily the voice of the Lord is unto all men, and there is none to escape; and there is no eye that shall not see, neither ear that shall not hear, neither heart that shall not be penetrated.

And the rebellious shall be pierced with much sorrow; for their iniquities shall be spoken upon the housetops, and their secret acts shall be revealed.

And the voice of warning shall be unto all people, by the mouths of my disciples, whom I have chosen in these last days.

And they shall go forth and none shall stay them, for I the Lord have commanded them.[3]

And so they have gone forth, bearing witness of the restoration of the gospel, preaching repentance, warning the people of the calamities that were to follow their preaching.

A Warning to the World

Wherefore, fear and tremble, O ye people, for what I the Lord have decreed in them—(that is, in the elders)—shall be fulfilled.

And verily I say unto you, that they who go forth, bearing these tidings unto the inhabitants of the earth, to them is power given to seal both on earth and in heaven, the unbelieving and rebellious;

Yea, verily, to seal them up unto the day when the wrath of God shall be poured out upon the wicked without measure—

Unto the day when the Lord shall come to recompense unto every man according to his work, and measure to every man according to the measure which he has measured to his fellow man.

Wherefore the voice of the Lord is unto the ends of the earth, that all that will hear may hear:

Prepare ye, prepare ye for that which is to come, for the Lord is nigh.[4]

Then again the Lord gave this instruction:

Wherefore, I the Lord, knowing the calamity which should come upon the inhabitants of the earth, called upon my servant Joseph Smith, Jr., and spake unto him from heaven, and gave him commandments;

And also gave commandments to others, that they should proclaim these things unto the world; and all this that it might be fulfilled, which was written by the prophets—

The weak things of the world shall come forth and break down the mighty and strong ones, that man should not counsel his fellow man, neither trust in the arm of flesh—

But that every man might speak in the name of God the Lord, even the Savior of the world;

That faith also might increase in the earth;

That mine everlasting covenant might be established;

That the fulness of my Gospel might be proclaimed by the weak and the simple unto the ends of the world, and before kings and rulers.[5]

That proclamation was given in the very beginning of this Church; it is found in the Preface which the Lord himself wrote to this book of commandments.

Further, again the Lord says:

For I am no respecter of persons, and will that all men shall know that the day speedily cometh; the hour is not yet, but is nigh at hand, when peace shall be taken from the earth, and the devil shall have power of his own dominion.

And also the Lord shall have power over his saints, and shall reign in their midst, and shall come down in judgment upon Idumea, or the world.[6]

That was said more than a hundred years ago. Peace has been taken from the world, the devil does have power over his own dominion today, and the Lord has not yet come to dwell with his Saints, but that also shall be fulfilled.

The Judgments to Come

Let me present another petition to the nations of the earth and to the elders of the Church:

Hearken ye, for, behold, the great day of the Lord is nigh at hand.

For the day cometh that the Lord shall utter his voice out of heaven; the heavens shall shake and the earth shall tremble, and the trump of God shall sound both long and loud, and shall say to the sleeping nations: Ye saints arise and live; ye sinners stay and sleep until I shall call again.

Wherefore gird up your loins lest ye be found among the wicked.

Lift up your voices and spare not. Call upon the nations to repent, both old and young, both bond and free, saying: Prepare yourselves for the great day of the Lord;

For if I, who am a man, do lift up my voice and call upon you to repent, and ye hate me, what will ye say when the day cometh when the thunders shall utter their voices from the ends of the earth, speaking to the ears of all that live, saying—Repent, and prepare for the great day of the Lord?

Yea, and again, when the lightnings shall streak forth from the east unto the west, and shall utter forth their voices unto all that live, and make the ears of all tingle that hear, saying these words—Repent ye, for the great day of the Lord is come?

And again, the Lord shall utter his voice out of heaven, saying: Hearken, O ye nations of the earth, and hear the words of that God who made you.

O, ye nations of the earth, how often would I have gathered you together as a hen gathereth her chickens under her wings, but ye would not!

How oft have I called upon you by the mouth of my servants, and by the ministering of angels, and by mine own voice, and by the voice of thunderings, and by the voice of lightnings, and by the voice of tempests, and by the voice of earthquakes, and great hailstorms, and by the voice of famines and pestilences of every kind, and by the great sound of a trump, and by the voice of judgment, and by the voice of mercy all the day long, and by the voice of glory and honor and the riches of eternal life, and would have saved you with an everlasting salvation, but ye would not!

Behold the day has come, when the cup of the wrath of mine indignation is full.

Behold, verily I say unto you, that these are the words of the Lord your God.

Wherefore, labor ye, labor ye in my vineyard for the last time—for the last time call upon the inhabitants of the earth.[7]

Again speaking to the missionaries in an early day the Lord said:

Behold, I sent you out to testify and warn the people, and it becometh every man who hath been warned to warn his neighbor.

Therefore, they are left without excuse, and their sins are upon their own heads.

He that seeketh me early shall find me, and shall not be forsaken.

Therefore, tarry ye, and labor diligently, that you may be perfected in your ministry to go forth among the Gentiles for the last time, as many as the mouth of the Lord shall name, to bind up the law and seal up the testimony, and to prepare the saints for the hour of judgment which is to come;

That their souls may escape the wrath of God, the desolation of abomination which awaits the wicked, both in this world and in the world to come. Verily, I say unto you, let those who are not the first elders continue in the vineyard until the mouth of the Lord shall call them, for their time is not yet come; their garments are not clean from the blood of this generation.

Abide ye in the liberty wherewith ye are made free; entangle not yourselves in sin, but let your hands be clean, until the Lord comes.

For not many days hence and the earth shall tremble and reel to and fro as a drunken man; and the sun shall hide his face, and shall refuse to give light; and the moon shall be bathed in blood; and the stars shall become exceedingly angry, and shall cast themselves down as a fig that falleth from off a fig-tree.

And after your testimony cometh wrath and indignation upon the people.

For after your testimony cometh the testimony of earthquakes, that shall cause groanings in the midst of her, and men shall fall upon the ground and shall not be able to stand.

And also cometh the testimony of the voice of thunderings, and the voice of lightnings, and the voice of tempests, and the voice of the waves of the sea heaving themselves beyond their bounds.

And all things shall be in commotion; and surely, men's hearts shall fail them; for fear shall come upon all people.

And angels shall fly through the midst of heaven crying with a loud voice, sounding the trump of God, saying: Prepare ye, prepare ye, O inhabitants of the earth; for the judgment of our God is come. Behold, and lo, the Bridegroom cometh; go ye out to meet him.[3]

These are the words of the Lord to his servants, and to the nations of the earth. As I look into your faces I see before me hundreds, thousands, who have been gathered out from the nations of the earth, either you or your parents, but you heard the gospel in foreign lands. In obedience to this call you are here today. Nations have refused to hear the testimony of the elders of Israel as it has been proclaimed, and the Lord has withdrawn them from among the nations, that is, many of them. He has done that because they have rejected the truth, and because of their wickedness. War comes because of wickedness; it never comes because of righteousness, but through the violation of the laws of God.

The Word of the Lord Has Gone Forth

Now, the Lord has predicted all these things. We have known this, it has been taught to us for a hundred years. We have been informed that it is necessary to keep the commandments of the Lord, for us to repent of our sins, for us to walk in ways of righteousness, and do the thing that the Lord would have us do. The nations have had proclamations made to them from time to time. In the early days of this Church it was very customary for the Presidency of the Church to send forth a proclamation, not only to the Saints, but to the inhabitants of the earth, calling upon them to repent, to turn from their ways of wickedness to ways of righteousness, accepting the fulness of the gospel as it has been revealed.

It is nothing new—should not be—to us to see these calamities and these destructions taking place upon the face of the earth. We have been warned; the Authorities of the Church have spoken from the very beginning calling attention to these things. We have seen and we have read in the records the Lord has given us, the Doctrine and Covenants, the Book of Mormon, and the Pearl of Great Price, that all these things were due to come in the dispensation of the fulness of time.

Now let me read this other scripture:

Therefore, verily, thus saith the Lord, let Zion rejoice, for this is Zion—THE PURE IN HEART; therefore, let Zion rejoice, while all the wicked shall mourn.

For behold, and lo, vengeance cometh speedily upon the ungodly as the whirlwind; and who shall escape it?

The Lord's scourge shall pass over by night and by day, and the report thereof shall vex all people; yea, it shall not be stayed until the Lord come;

For the indignation of the Lord is kindled against their abominations and all their wicked works.

Nevertheless, Zion shall escape if she observe to do all things whatsoever I have commanded her.

But if she observe not to do whatsoever I have commanded her, I will visit her according to all her works, with sore affliction, with pestilence, with plague, with sword, with vengeance, with devouring fire.

Nevertheless, let it be read this once to her ears, that I, the Lord, have accepted of her offering; and if she sin no more none of these things shall come upon her.[9]

We have the means of escape through obedience to the gospel of Jesus Christ. Will we escape? When I see, even among the Latter-day Saints the violation of the laws of the Lord, I fear and tremble. I have been crying repentance among the stakes of Zion, calling upon the people to turn to the Lord, keep his commandments, observe the Sabbath day, pay their honest tithing, do everything the Lord has commanded them to do, to live by every word that proceedeth forth from the mouth of God.

By doing this we shall escape the calamities.

I am going to repeat what I have said before, for which I have been severely criticized from certain quarters, that even in this country we have no grounds by which we may escape, no sure foundation upon which we can stand, and by which we may escape from the calamities and destruction and the plagues and the pestilences, and even the devouring fire by sword and by war, unless we repent and keep the commandments of the Lord, for it is written here in these revelations.

So I cry repentance to the Latter-day Saints, and I cry repentance to the people of the United States, as well as to the people of all the earth. May we turn to live in accordance with divine law, and keep the commandments the Lord has given, I humbly pray, in the name of Jesus Christ. Amen. —(*Conference Report*, October, 1940.)

---

[1]Matt. 24:32 (Inspired Version), Matt. 24:14, Joseph Smith 24:31.
[2]D&C 1:1.
[3]*Ibid.*, 1:2-4.
[4]*Ibid.*, 1:7-12.
[5]*Ibid.*, 1:17-23.
[6]*Ibid.*, 1:35-36.
[7]*Ibid.*, 43:17-28.
[8]*Ibid.*, 88:81-92.
[9]*Ibid.*, 97:21-27.

We who live in the present day should take heed and profit by the experiences of those who have gone before and not fall into their grievous errors. . . . Let us not forget that the Lord said that it should be in this day as it was in the days of Noah.

"Take Heed to Yourselves"

After Adam and Eve were driven from the Garden of Eden an angel came to them and gave them commandments stating that they should worship the Lord their God and do all things in the name of the Son. The angel further said Adam should call upon God in the name of the Son forevermore. Obedient to this charge Adam and Eve "blessed the name of God, and they made all things known unto their sons and their daughters."

At that time Satan came among Adam's children saying:

> . . . I am also a son of God; and he commanded them, saying: "Believe it not; and they believed it not, and they loved Satan more than God. And men began from that time forth to be carnal, sensual and devilish.[1]

This is the account as it was revealed to Moses. The Lord confirmed these teachings in a revelation given to the Church in April, 1830, wherein he said:

> By these things (the restoration of divine truth) we may know that there is a God in heaven, who is infinite and eternal, from *everlasting to everlasting* the same *unchangeable* God, the framer of heaven and earth, and all things which are in them;

And that he created man, male and female, after his own image and in his own likeness, created he them;

And gave unto them commandments that they should love and serve him, the only living and true God, and that he should be the only being whom they should worship.

But by the transgression of these holy laws man became sensual and devilish, and became fallen man.[2]

Noah Called to Cry Repentance

In course of time, so the scriptures say, "God saw that the wickedness of men had become great in the earth; and every man was lifted up in the imagination of the thoughts of his heart, being only evil continually."[3]

Noah was called on to cry repentance and to warn the wicked world of its destruction unless mankind repented of their wickedness; but all Noah got for his trouble was abuse and ridicule by the great and the mighty who said, "Behold, we are the sons of God . . . and they hearkened not to the words of Noah." But Noah "found grace in the eyes of the Lord, for Noah was a just man, and perfect in his generation; and he walked with God, as did also his three sons, Shem, Ham, and Japheth." Now, the record states, "The earth was corrupt before God, and it was filled with violence. And God looked upon the earth, and, behold, it was corrupt, for all flesh had corrupted its way upon the earth." And God said unto Noah: "The end of all flesh is come before me, for the earth is filled with violence, and behold I will destroy all flesh from off the earth." It should be remembered that the Lord said *he* would do it![4]

So the Lord commanded Noah to build an ark into which he was to take his family and the animals of the earth to preserve seed after the flood, and all flesh that was not in the ark perished according to the Lord's decree. Of course this story is not believed by the wise and the great among the children of men, any more than was Noah's story in his day.

Then after this new start man again became carnal, sensual and devilish upon the earth and drastic punishment had to be meted out to some of the earth's inhabitants once more according to the Lord's decree. In the days of Abraham there were two cities known as Sodom and Gomorrah in which wickedness was without measure and the Lord said to Abraham that he was going to destroy these cities. Abraham plead with the Lord to spare them, which the Lord promised to do, if ten righteous souls could be found therein. Since this could not be done "the Lord rained upon Sodom and upon Gomorrah brimstone and fire from the Lord out of heaven," and these cities with all their inhabitants were destroyed. And again the Lord said *he* did it! But the self-righteous and the wise of this present day say this is not a true record, for a merciful God would not do such a thing even if the people were wicked.[5]

Land Promised to Abraham

About this time the Lord promised to give to Abraham for an everlasting inheritance all of this land where Sodom and Gomorrah were and all of the land from "the river of Egypt unto the great river, the river Euphrates"; but Abraham was told that his posterity could not possess the land for four hundred years, because "the iniquity of the Amorites is not yet full." When the time came, and the wickedness of the Amorites was full, the Lord commanded Israel to take their armies and cleanse the land of the wickedness, and take possession of the inheritance which had been promised their father Abraham.

And thus, down through the ages, we discover, if we are willing to believe what is written in the scriptures, that judgments and destructions had to be poured out upon the wicked because they would not repent. Even the kingdoms of Israel and Judah were destroyed and the people scattered because of the anger of the Lord which was kindled against them for their transgressions. At least this is the case if we are willing to believe the word of the Lord given through his prophets.

Not only were these punishments meted out to the inhabitants of the so-called old world, but destructions awaited the inhabitants of this western world for the same cause. Through their prophets they were constantly reminded that this land is "choice above all other lands, which the Lord God had preserved for a righteous people." And he (the Lord) had "sworn in his wrath unto the brother of Jared, that whoso should possess this land of promise, *from that time henceforth and forever,* should serve him, the true and only God, or they should be swept off when the *fulness of his wrath should come upon them.*"[6] When these people refused to worship the true and living God, then his wrath came upon them—if we are willing to believe the record—and they were swept off. Then another people came to possess the land under all the blessings of protection and guidance of the Lord.

Same Promises Made to Others

These same promises and warnings were made to the second group of inhabitants, and the prophets who were raised up among them constantly warned them of these promises the Lord had made. But these people also fell from grace and the wrath of the Almighty came upon them.

So wicked had they become at the time of the crucifixion of our Lord that it became necessary for him to destroy many of their cities by earthquake, flood, fire and other forms of destruction. Yes, it is true, the same meek and lowly Nazarene, who came into the world and offered himself a sacrifice for sin because of the great love his Father and he had for the human family; he "who is infinite and eternal, from everlasting to everlasting the same unchangeable God," who loves little children and suffered them to come unto him, found himself under the necessity of meting out punishment to the inhabitants of this choice land and that too in a most drastic fashion. Hearken to his words which he uttered after his resurrection:

> Wo, wo, wo unto this people; wo unto the inhabitants of the *whole earth* except they shall repent; for the devil laugheth, and his angels rejoice, because of the slain of the fair sons and daughters of my people; and *it is because of their iniquity and abomination that they are fallen!*
>
> Behold that great city Zarahemla *have I burned with fire,* and the inhabitants thereof.
>
> And behold, that great city Moroni *have I caused to be sunk in the depths of the sea,* and the inhabitants thereof to be drowned.
>
> And behold, that great city, Moronihah *have I covered with earth,* and the inhabitants thereof, to hide their iniquities and their abominations from before my face, that the blood of the prophets and the Saints shall not come any more unto me against them.[7]

Similar expressions did the Lord utter against the cities of Gilgal, Onihah, Mocum, Jerusalem, Gadiandi, Gadiomnah, Jacob, Gimgimno, Jacobugath, Laman, Josh, Kishkumen and others. But, says the self-righteous modernist, such things could not be, for God is "a God of love," and the Savior "a man of peace," and the God I worship does not "decree death upon farmers, factory hands," and "women and children, regardless of who has sinned"!

We Should Take Heed

But we who live in the present day should take heed and profit by the experiences of those who have gone before and not fall into their grievous errors. We should remember that the same warnings have been given to us and "to all the inhabitants of the earth," that destruction awaits this age unless they refrain from wickedness and abominations. Let us not forget that the Lord said that it should be in this day as it was in the days of Noah. We should remember also that he is still a "God of wrath" as well as a "God of love," and that he has promised to pour out his wrath upon the ungodly, and "take vengeance upon the wicked" who will not repent.

Not only did the ancient prophets predict that such should be the case in these latter days, but the Lord has spoken it in our own dispensation. Let us give ear to the following which are a few of the warnings which have been given to the world through the prophets of the present day:

> The plain fact is this, the power of God begins to fall upon the nations . . . and the nations of the Gentiles are like the waves of the sea, casting up mire and dirt, are all in commotion, and they are hastily preparing to act the part allotted them, when the Lord rebukes the nations, when he shall rule them with a rod of iron, and break them in pieces like a potter's vessel. The Lord declared to his servants, some eighteen months since, that he was then withdrawing his Spirit from the earth; and we can see that such is the fact, for not only the churches are dwindling away, but there are no conversions, or but a very few; and this is not all, the governments of the earth are thrown into confusion and division; and *destruction*, to the eye of the spiritual beholder, seems to be written by the finger of an invisible hand, in large capitals, upon almost everything we behold.[8]

> You must make yourselves acquainted with those men who like Daniel pray three times a day toward the House of the Lord. Look to the Presidency and receive instruction. Every man who is afraid, covetous, will be taken in a snare. The time is soon coming, when no man will have any peace but in Zion and her stakes.

> I saw men hunting the lives of their own sons, and brother murdering brother, women killing their own daughters, and daughters seeking the lives of their mothers. I saw armies arrayed against armies. I saw blood, desolation, fires. The Son of Man has said that the mother shall be against the daughter, and the daughter against the mother. These things are at our doors. They will follow the Saints of God from city to city. Satan will rage, and the spirit of the devil is now enraged. I know not how soon these things will take place; but *with a view of them, shall I cry peace?* No! *I will lift up my voice and testify of them.* How long you will have good crops, and the famine be kept off, I do not know; when the fig tree leaves, know then that summer is nigh at hand.[9]

Nations to Rise Against Nations

We see nation rising against nation; we hear of the pestilence destroying its thousands in one place and its tens of thousands in another; the plague consuming all before it, and we witness this terror that reigns in the hearts of the wicked, and we are ready to exclaim, The Lord is certainly about bringing the world to an account of its iniquity. Let us reflect, then, in the last days, that there was to be great tribulations; for the Savior says, nation shall rise against nation, kingdom against kingdom, and there shall be famine, and pestilence, and earthquake in divers places, and the prophets have declared that the valleys should rise; that the mountains should be laid low; that a great earthquake should be, in which the sun should become black as sackcloth of hair, and the moon turn into blood; yea, the Eternal God hath declared that the great deep shall roll back into the north countries and that the land of Zion and the land of Jerusalem shall be joined together, as they were before they were divided in the days of Peleg. No wonder the mind starts at the sound of the last days.[10]

Do you think there is calamity abroad now among the people? . . . All we have yet heard and all we have experienced is scarcely a preface to the sermon that is going to be preached. When the testimony of the elders ceases to be given, and the Lord says to them, '*come home; I will now preach my own sermons to the nations of the earth,*' all you now know can scarcely be called a preface to the sermon that will be preached with fire and sword, tempests, earthquake, hail, rain, thunders and lightnings, and fearful destruction. What matters the destruction of a few railway cars? You will hear of magnificent cities, now idolized by the people, sinking in the earth, entombing the inhabitants. The sea will heave itself beyond its bounds, engulfing mighty cities. Famine will spread over the nations, and nation will rise up against nation, kingdom against kingdom, and states against states, in our own country and in foreign lands; and they will destroy each other, caring not for the blood and lives of their neighbors, of their families, or for their own lives. They will be like the Jaredites who preceded the Nephites upon this continent, and will destroy each other to the last man, through the anger that the devil will place in their hearts, because they have rejected the words of life and are given over to Satan to do whatever he listeth to do with them. You may think that the little you hear of now is grievous; yet the faithful of God's people will see days that will cause them to close their eyes because of the sorrow that will come upon the wicked nations. The hearts of the faithful will be filled with pain and anguish for them.[11]

One of the marked signs of the last days is the blindness of the people; we are told they would have eyes and see not, and ears but hear not, and hearts but understand not. If in the days of Jesus this was true of the Jews and surrounding nations, it is doubly so now in relation to the nations with which we are acquainted.

Fulfilment of Words of the Prophets

Though the fulfilment of the words of the prophets is clear and visible to us as the noonday sun in its splendor, yet the people of the world are blinded thereto; they do not comprehend nor discern the hand of the Lord. The Saints who live in the Spirit, walk by the Spirit, and are governed by the counsels of the Almighty, can see the working of the Lord, not only in our midst . . . but we let our minds stretch abroad to creation's utmost extent, and we see the hand of the Lord in all the events of the earth.

We see it in the revolutions of our own continent; we see it in the scattering and scourging of the house of Israel; in the fading away of nations, on the right and on the left. . . . We see it in the preparations of war, and the framing of treaties of peace among strong nations. The world is in commotion and the hearts of men fail them for fear of the impending storm that threatens to enshroud all nations in its black mantle. Treaties of peace may be made, and war will stop for a season, but there are certain decrees of God, and certain bounds fixed, and laws and edicts passed the high courts of heaven beyond which the nations cannot pass; and when the Almighty decrees the wicked shall slay the wicked, strong nations may interfere, peace conventions may become rife in the world and exert their influence to sheath the sword of war, and make treaties of peace to calm the troubled surface of all Europe, to no effect; the war cloud is still booming o'er the heavens, darkening the earth, and threatening the world with desolation.

This is a fact the Saints have known for many years—that the Gods in yonder heavens have something to do with these revolutions; the angels, those holy beings who are sent from the heavens to the earth to minister in the destiny of nations, have something to do in these mighty revolutions and convulsions that shake creation almost to its center.

Consequently, when we see nation stirred up against nation, and on the other hand see other nations exerting a powerful influence to bring about negotiations of peace, shall we say they can bring it about? Do we expect they can stay the onward course of war? The

Prophet of God has spoken it all, and we expect to see the work go on —and see all things fulfilled as the prophets have declared by the spirit of prophecy in them.

Three days before the Prophet Joseph started for Carthage, I well remember his telling us we should see the fulfilment of the words of Jesus upon the earth, where he says the father shall be against the son, and the son against the father; the mother against the daughter, and the daughter against the mother; the mother-in-law against the daughter-in-law, and the daughter-in-law against the mother-in-law; and when a man's enemies shall be those of his own household.

The Prophet stood in his own house when he told several of us of the night the visions of heaven were opened to him, in which he saw the American continent drenched in blood, and he saw nation rising against nation. He also saw the father shed the blood of the son, and the son the blood of the father; the mother put to death the daughter, and the daughter the mother; and natural affection forsook the hearts of the wicked; for he saw that the Spirit of God should be withdrawn from the inhabitants of the earth, in consequence of which there should be blood upon the face of the whole earth, except among the people of the Most High. The Prophet gazed upon the scene his vision presented, until his heart sickened and he besought the Lord to close it up again.[12]

Latter-day Saints Were Warned

Were we surprised when the last terrible war took place here in the United States? No! Good Latter-day Saints were not, for they had been told about it. Joseph Smith had told them where it would start, that it should be a terrible time of bloodshed and that it should start in South Carolina. But I tell you today the end is not yet. You will see worse things than that, for God will lay his hand upon the nations, and they will feel it more terribly than ever they have done before; there will be more bloodshed, more ruin, more devastation than ever they have seen before. *Write it down!* You will see it come to pass; it is only just starting in. And would you feel to rejoice? No! I would feel sorry. I knew very well myself when this last war was commencing, and could have wept and did weep over this nation; but there is yet to come a sound of war, trouble and distress in which brother will be arrayed against brother, father against son, son against father, a scene of desolation and destruction that will permeate our land until it will be a vexation to hear the report thereof. Would you help to bring it about? No! I would stop it if I could. I would pour in the oil and the wine and balm and try to lead people in the right path that will be governed by it, *but* they won't![13]

I refer to these things because I know not how long I may have the privilege of bearing my testimony of the gospel of Christ on the earth. The revelations that are in the Bible the predictions of the patriarchs and prophets who saw by vision and revelation the last dispensation and fulness of times plainly tell us what is to come to pass. The 49th chapter of Isaiah is having its fulfilment. I have often said in my teachings, if the world want to know what is coming to pass, let them read the revelations of St. John. Read of the judgments of God that are going to overtake the world in the last dispensation. Read the papers and see what is taking place in our own nation and in the nations of the earth, and what does it all mean? It means the commencement of the fulfilment of what the prophets of God have predicted. In the Doctrine and Covenants there are many revelations given through the mouth of the prophet of God; these revelations will all have their fulfilment, as the Lord lives, and no power can hinder it. In one of the revelations the Lord told Joseph Smith: Behold, Verily I say unto you, the angels are crying unto the Lord day and night, who are ready and waiting to be sent forth to reap down the fields. . . .

I want to bear testimony to this congregation, and to the heavens and the earth, that the day is come when those angels are privileged to go forth and commence their work. They are laboring in the United States of America; they are laboring among the nations of the earth; and they will continue. We need not marvel or wonder at anything that is transpiring in the earth. The world do not comprehend the revelations of God. They did not in the days of the Jews; yet all that the prophets had spoken concerning them came to pass. So in our day these things will come to pass. I heard the Prophet Joseph bear his testimony to these events that would transpire in the earth. . . . We cannot draw a veil over the events that await this generation. *No man that is inspired by the Spirit and power of God can close his ears, his eyes or his lips to these things.*[14]

Many Other Warnings Given

And thus we might quote indefinitely from the ancient prophets as well as from the prophets of this dispensation and even from the Lord himself, in relation to the troubles, destructions, wars and plagues, which are to come upon the inhabitants of the earth—yes even Zion also—unless the people repent. "The Lord's scourge," so he says, "shall pass over by night and by day, and the report thereof shall vex all people; yea, it shall not be stayed until the Lord come; for the indignation of the Lord is kindled against their abominations and all their wicked works." But the promise has been made to Zion and the pure in heart, that they shall escape *if* they "observe to do all things whatsoever I (the Lord) have commanded."[15]

What is here given will suffice as a warning to a "perverse generation" and to remind the members of the Church that the Lord has said:

> Even so it shall be in that day when they shall see all these things, then shall they know that the hour is nigh.
>
> And it shall come to pass that he that feareth me shall be looking forth for the great day of the Lord to come, even for the signs of the coming of the Son of Man.
>
> And they shall see signs and wonders, for they shall be shown forth in the heavens above, and in the earth beneath.
>
> And they shall behold blood, and fire, and vapors of smoke.[16]
>
> And take heed to yourselves, lest at any time your hearts be overcharged with drunkenness, and cares of this life, and so that day come upon you unawares.
>
> For as a snare shall it come on all them that dwell on the face of the whole earth.
>
> Watch ye therefore, and pray always, that ye may be accounted worthy to escape all these things that shall come to pass, and to stand before the Son of Man.[17]—(Church Section, *The Deseret News*, Feb. 10, 1940.)

---

[1]Moses 5:13.
[2]D&C 20:17-20.
[3]Gen. 6:5.
[4]Read Gen. 6:1-13.
[5]Read Gen., chapter 18-19.
[6]Ether 2:8.
[7]3 Nephi 9:2-5. Read also verses 6-12.
[8]*Teachings of the Prophet Joseph Smith*, pp. 11-12.
[9]*Ibid.*, p. 161.
[10]Joseph Smith, February, 1845.

[11]President Brigham Young, *J. of D.,* 8:123.
[12]President Jedediah M. Grant, *J. of D.,* 2:146-147.
[13]President John Taylor, *J. of D.* 20:318.
[14]President Wilford Woodruff, *M. S.* 58:738-739.
[15]D&C 97:23-24.
[16]*Ibid.,* 45:38-41.
[17]Luke 21:34-36.

The matter of teaching is one of greatest importance. We cannot estimate its value when it is properly done; neither do we know the extent of the evil that may result if it is improperly done. The greatest qualification of a teacher is that she have faith in the principles of the gospel; that she believe in the principles of revealed truth as they have come through inspired prophets in our own day as well as in times of old; and that she shall exercise their privilege as a teacher in the spirit of prayer and faith.

Teaching the Gospel

The Church has two great responsibilities. That is, the members of the Church have these responsibilities. It is our individual duty to preach the gospel by precept and by example among our neighbors. In Section 88 of the Doctrine and Covenants, we are informed that even those who are warned are under the obligation to receive the message and also to warn their neighbors.

The people who are living are entitled to hear the message, so this responsibility to teach the world is an outstanding one. We cannot get away from the obligation. The Lord declared that his coming is nigh at hand. It is our duty, then, to do all we can, and the Lord will bring to our aid other forces besides our missionaries, that his work may be advanced and his words be fulfilled.

I speak of this responsibility at this time for fear there may be some who think the work they are doing is the great work of this dispensation. The people engaged in the Relief Society and other auxiliaries feel that they have great responsibility and they have, but their work does not overshadow this great duty of preaching the gospel to the world.

Many Debts We Owe the Lord

There are many debts which we owe the Lord. There is the debt of preaching this gospel to a wicked and perverse generation, and those are the words of the Lord, so do not accuse me of calling the world wicked. It is. I can testify to that from what I have seen of it, and I have seen of the wickedness but a small part, I assure you. The world today is filthy, drunken, saturated and stinking with tobacco. The world is full of immorality. It is a fallen world. It has been a fallen world since Adam was driven from the Garden of Eden, and yet we are in it, and the Lord has given us the mission of assisting him, of being agents in this world, to regenerate it, as far as it is possible to bring to pass that regeneration. It will never be fully accomplished, so far as we are concerned. We are not going, by our preaching, to save very many souls.

The Lord has given unto us our agency. We may act for ourselves, we may choose to do good or we may choose to do evil. The Lord said that men love darkness rather than light because their deeds are evil. Yet our mission, I say, so far as it is within our power, is to regenerate, to bring to repentance, just as many of the children of our Father in Heaven as it is possible for us to do. That is one of our debts; that is an obligation the Lord has placed upon the Church. *It is the duty of every member of this Church to preach the gospel by precept and by example.*

Purpose and Duties of the Relief Society

The purpose and duties of the Relief Society are many. I am going to repeat myself again because there may be some here today who were not here when I made this statement before, and I also have the backing of my father, President Joseph F. Smith. "This is an organization that was established by the Prophet Joseph Smith. It is, therefore, the oldest auxiliary organization of the Church, and it is of the first importance. It has not only to deal with the necessities of the poor, the sick and the needy, but a part of its duty—and the larger part, too—is to look after the spiritual welfare and salvation of the mothers and daughters of Zion; to see that none is neglected, but that all are guarded against misfortune, calamity, the powers of darkness, and the evils that threaten them in the world. It is the duty of the Relief Societies to look after the spiritual welfare of themselves and of all the female members of the Church. It is their duty to collect means from those who have in abundance, and to distribute it wisely unto those in need. It is a part of their duty to see that there are those capable of being nurses, as well as teachers and exemplars in Zion, and that they have an opportunity to become thoroughly prepared for this great labor and responsibility.

Harmony Must Exist

"I have heard of a disposition on the part of some of our sisters to become a law unto themselves in relation to these things. I would like to say that it is expected of the Relief Society, especially the general authorities of that great organization, that they will have a watchcare over all its organizations among the women of Zion. They stand at the head of all such; they ought to stand at the head, and they should magnify their calling, and see to it that error is not permitted to creep in, that cabals are not formed, that secret combinations may not get a foothold, to mislead the sisters. They should see to it that the other organizations of women in the Church correspond and are in harmony with their organizations.

"Why should this be? In order that the women of Zion may be united, that their interests may be in common, and not conflicting or segregated, and that the purpose of this organization may be realized and the organization itself be effective for good in every part of the Church throughout the world, wherever the gospel is preached. . . . I commend the Relief Societies to the bishops and say, be friendly to these organizations, because they are auxiliary organizations and a great help to the bishops. . . ."

It is the duty of the Relief Society "to look after the interests of all the women of Zion and of all the women that may come under their supervision and care, irrespective of religion, color or condition. . . . Today it is too much the case that our young, vigorous, intelligent women feel that only the aged should be connected with the Relief Society. This is a mistake. We want the young women, the intelligent women, women of faith, of courage and of purity to be associated with the Relief Societies of the various stakes and wards of Zion. We want them to take hold of this work with vigor, with intelligence, and unitedly, for the building up of Zion and the instruction of women in their duties—domestic duties, public duties, and every duty that may devolve upon them."

Teaching Is of Great Importance

The matter of teaching is one of the greatest importance. We cannot estimate its value when it is properly done; neither do we know the extent of the evil that may result if it is improperly done. The greatest qualification required of a teacher is that she have faith in the principles of the gospel; that she believes in the principles of revealed truth as they have come through inspired prophets in our own day as well as in times of old; and that he or she shall exercise their privilege as a teacher in the spirit of prayer and faith.

I am in full accord with the commandment as it is written in this revelation. Unless a man (or woman) does have a knowledge of the truth, has faith in the word of the Lord and his power, and is guided by the Spirit of the Lord, he should not teach. We are commanded "to give diligent heed to the words of eternal life." For we "shall live by every word that proceedeth forth from the mouth of God.

For the word of the Lord is truth, and whatsoever is truth is light, and whatsoever is light is Spirit, even the Spirit of Jesus Christ."[1]

I was handed a poem the other day by Sister Pauline Marie Bell which fits in with Relief Society and I would like to give it to you now:

Ancient mothers, God has blessed you
With a hope so mighty strong
Thou didst give a glorious pattern,
Courage filled our hearts with song—
Relief Society in faith united
Walking where the Savior trod,
Gazing upward to that Giver,
Praising ever Israel's God.
Daughters of those faithful Marys,
Sharing woe with Christ so true,
Faith undaunted, God has given—
Blessings are fulfilled in you.
Zion's daughters, meek and loyal,
Children of that chosen band,
True and faithful, God has called you,
To assist his mighty hand.

May we all strive to keep the commandments, and the Lord will bless us in our work, and may he bless each of you with a desire to follow in paths of righteousness, I humbly pray in the name of Jesus Christ, our Redeemer. Amen. —(Address, Relief Society General Conference, Sept. 29, 1965.)

---

[1]D&C 84:43-45.

I have realized for a long time the need of spiritual protection, protection in the teachings that we give to our young people in our organizations, to save them from the false doctrines and teachings of the world.

"... And if Ye Receive Not the Spirit Ye Shall Not Teach"

My dear brethren and sisters, I realize my weakness and the need of your faith and prayers and the help of the Spirit of the Lord. I am grateful for the nature of the remarks made by President McKay in the opening session of this conference and for the prayer that has just been offered by President Pugmire[1] in which a plea to our Father in heaven was made in behalf of the faith of the young people of the Church.

I, too, am concerned over the faith of our young people, for that matter, of all the members of the Church in this day when there are so many prevailing notions, ideas, and philosophies. I have realized for a long time the need of spiritual protection, protection in the teachings that we give to our young people in our organizations, to save them from the false doctrines and teachings of the world.

About three days ago I received a letter from one of my very dearest friends, a brother who is a teacher and who has been a teacher for nearly a half century, one who sat in the councils of the Church in stakes of Zion and in whom I have a great deal of confidence. He expressed in his letter his solicitation for our young people, and in fact, for all the members of the Church and the need of giving them proper protection and guidance in the teachings that are placed before them.

Not All Are Prepared to Teach

I copied from his letter one paragraph, and asked him if I might use it. He said I might, and I am going to read it to you:

> There are in our community, and I suspect in other places, men who are instructing in our quorums and other organizations who teach false doctrine, and the craziest imaginations, and almost invariably they are brethren who are *not in line.*[2] They have brilliant, trained minds, sometimes with pleasing, influential personalities, but lacking the spirit of truth that comes by obedience. You cannot give what you do not possess. In my humble opinion only those who believe in, and can prove their teachings by their works, should be instructing in our quorums and other organizations.

That remark of his I fully endorse, and so I am expressing these thoughts particularly to our bishops, presidents of stakes, superintendents of Sunday Schools and Mutuals, and those who have charge of priesthood quorums, and the other organizations of the Church, to see to it that in the choosing of teachers they use wisdom and seek for the guidance of the Spirit of the Lord that these men spoken of here in this communication, brilliant, outstanding personalities, but without faith, are not called to teach in our Sunday Schools, our Mutual Improvement Associations, and in the priesthood quorums of the Church. We want men who are trained in the principles of the gospel and who have faith and a testimony of the truth. We have them.

Great Schooling Is Not Sufficient

Because a man has great schooling, is educated according to the ideas of the world, is not sufficient reason why he should be called to take charge of a class in any of the organizations or priesthood quorums within the Church. Now, if he has scholastic ability and training, and along with it has faith in the principles of the gospel and in the mission of the Lord Jesus Christ, and of the Prophet Joseph Smith, all well and good. But if he is filled with all kinds of philosophy and notions and cannot accept the doctrines in the standard works of the Church, we do not want him, whether it is in our auxiliaries or the priesthood, or in our seminaries or institutes, that are given for the teaching of religious principles and to instil faith in the hearts of our young people.

> Remember, [the Lord has said], the worth of souls is great in the sight of God;
>
> For, behold, the Lord your Redeemer suffered death in the flesh; wherefore he suffered the pain of all men, that all men might repent and come unto him.
>
> And he hath risen again from the dead, that he might bring all men unto him, on conditions of repentance.
>
> And how great is his joy in the soul that repenteth!
>
> Wherefore, you are called to cry repentance unto this people.
>
> And if it so be that you should labor all your days in crying repentance unto this people, and bring, save it be one soul unto me, how great shall be your joy with him in the kingdom of my Father![3]

In the early days of the Church men came out of the world and received the testimony of the gospel, but they had been trained in the traditions of the world, the religious world, and they brought in with them some of those religious notions. The Lord had to correct them, and he said:

> Let us reason even as a man reasoneth one with another face to face.
>
> Now, when a man reasoneth he is understood of man, because he reasoneth as a man; even so will I, the Lord, reason with you that you may understand.
>
> Wherefore, I the Lord ask you this question—unto what were ye ordained?
>
> To preach my gospel by the Spirit, even the Comforter which was sent forth to teach the truth.

And then received ye spirits which ye could not understand, and received them to be of God; and in this are ye justified?

Behold ye shall answer this question yourselves; nevertheless, I will be merciful unto you; he that is weak among you hereafter shall be made strong.

Verily I say unto you, he that is ordained of me and sent forth to preach the word of truth by the Comforter, in the Spirit of truth, doth he preach it by the spirit of truth or some other way?

And if it be by some other way it is not of God.

And again, he that receiveth the word of truth, doth he receive it by the Spirit of truth or some other way?

If it be some other way it is not of God.

Therefore, why is it that ye cannot understand and know, that he that receiveth the word by the Spirit of truth receiveth it as it is preached by the Spirit of truth?

Wherefore, he that preacheth and he that receiveth, understand one another, and both are edified and rejoice together.

And that which doth not edify is not of God, and is darkness.[4]

It makes no difference who the teacher is, if he teaches false doctrine, if he teaches that which has been condemned by the Lord, that is contrary to what is written in the revelations given to the Church, then he should not teach.

He Who Hath Not Spirit Shall Not Teach

In the forty-second section of the Doctrine and Covenants the Lord declares that he who hath not the Spirit shall not teach. I call upon you brethren in the stakes and in the wards to be alert to find men who have faith in their hearts and a love of the truth of the gospel of Jesus Christ and do not choose men simply because they have a personality or worldly wisdom. Find if they have in their hearts a love of divine truth. If a man cannot accept the revelations in the Bible, in the Book of Mormon, the Doctrine and Covenants, the Pearl of Great Price, which we have received as standards, if he has reservations in his mind in regard to the things that are there recorded, which have come to us by the word of the Lord, then he ought not be teaching in any organization, any class, anywhere in The Church of Jesus Christ of Latter-day Saints.

May the Lord bless us one and all, guide us in righteousness, help us through the study of the scriptures to know his will, I humbly pray in the name of Jesus Christ. Amen. —(*Conference Report*, October, 1954.)

---

[1]President L. Burdette Pugmire of Bear Lake Stake.
[2]Italics used in various articles are for author's emphasis.
[3]D&C 18:10-15.
[4]*Ibid.*, 50:11-23.

No matter how much a man may learn, no matter how long he may study, should it be through all eternity, he will never come to the fulness of truth and light—that which is pure intelligence and which has no part or lot with that evil one—only by continuing in God and through full and complete obedience to his commandments.

Knowledge and Pure Intelligence

I have always taken an interest in the Brigham Young University and its wonderful achievements. It has been a great source of pleasure and pride to me to observe the measure of success which has come to its graduates. Many have gone forth from this great university to attain great distinction both in the Church, the nation, and various other fields. I expect many others to go forth from this institution of learning to make equal progress and to achieve equal renown.

I shall take for my theme, or text, tonight, an old but true saying: "Knowledge is power." And now, having given this text, I will straightway lay it aside, at least for the present and consider other things.

It is my hope and prayer that those who have finished the prescribed course of study in the various schools of arts and sciences, will not leave this institution feeling that the greatest accomplishment has been to meet the necessary requirements of this school for graduation. It is to be hoped that they have kept in mind the need of higher and better understanding than they have received in the regular courses of study which entitles them to graduation and a place in the world among their fellow men. It is the case too frequently in our great institutions of learning that the students go forth after graduation having lost sight of the most important things in life and with their minds trained and prepared to make their place among their fellows concerned alone in worldly things.

A few years back it was my privilege to visit Stanford University and there written on the panels in the church were engraved many sayings intended to impress the minds of the students with the importance of life. One of these sayings impressed me beyond the others and I made a copy of it. It is as follows:

> There is no narrowing so deadly as the narrowing of man's horizon of spiritual things. No worse evil could befall him in his course on earth than to lose sight of heaven; and it is not civilization that can prevent this; it is not civilization that can compensate for it. No widening of science, no possession of abstract truth, can indemnify for an enfeebled hold on the highest and central truths of humanity.
>
> What shall a man give in exchange for his soul?

Good Doctrine

This is good sound "Mormon" doctrine. There is no knowledge, no learning that can compensate the individual for the loss of his belief in heaven and in the saving principles of the gospel of Jesus Christ. An education that leads a man from these "central truths" cannot compensate him for the great loss of spiritual things. Members of the Church, and especially those who are engaged in the teaching of the youth of the Church, are very fond of quoting the following inspired sayings of the Prophet Joseph Smith:

> Whatever principle of intelligence we attain unto in this life, it will rise with us in the resurrection.
>
> And if a person gains more knowledge and intelligence in this life through his diligence and obedience than another, he will have so much the advantage in the world to come.[1]

> It is impossible for a man to be saved in ignorance.[2]

I think these passages have been at times misapplied. It is true that the knowledge we attain to in this life will be beneficial to us in the life to come, no matter what may be the nature of that knowledge. But when giving expression to these thoughts the Prophet Joseph Smith had certain things definitely in mind. I have regretted that the expression: "It is impossible for a man to be saved in ignorance," was not coupled with other sayings of the Prophet which give us a clearer meaning of this statement. What kind of knowledge was he speaking of? It was the knowledge of the saving principles of the gospel of Jesus Christ. Permit me to quote some of his thoughts on this question:

> It is not wisdom that we have all knowledge at once presented before us; but that we should have a little at a time; then we can comprehend it.[3]

Process of Learning

How true this is! The individual seeking knowledge goes to school for several years. He learns line upon line and precept upon precept. There is no other way. Perhaps he may think it would be an excellent thing could he go to school, say for one year, and accomplish everything, but all knowledge comes in the same way, that is, gradually through study and by faith. In the establishment of the Church, Joseph Smith had to be instructed a little at a time. If the Lord had revealed to him the fulness of the plan of salvation with all its covenants and obligations at one time, he would have been overwhelmed as with a flood and could not have endured. So it is with us in all other matters of learning. We must plod along growing in understanding and power day by day.

Now to continue the quotation:

> Add to thy faith knowledge. The principle is the principle of salvation. This principle can be comprehended by the faithful and diligent; and every one that does not obtain knowledge sufficient to

be saved will be condemned. The principle of salvation is given us through the knowledge of Jesus Christ.

Salvation is nothing more nor less than to triumph over all our enemies and put them under our feet. And when we have power to put all enemies under our feet in this world, and a knowledge to triumph over all evil spirits in the world to come, then we are saved, as in the case of Jesus, who was to reign until he had put all enemies under his feet, and the last enemy was death.

Perhaps there are principles here that few men have thought of. No person can have this salvation except through a tabernacle. . . .

Then knowledge through our Lord and Savior Jesus Christ is the grand key that unlocks the glories and mysteries of the kingdom of God.[4]

Quotes Brigham Young

The enemies spoken of here are our sins and imperfections and ignorance of eternal truths. These we must overcome if we would attain to salvation and exaltation in the kingdom of God. Permit me to continue my quotations. This is from President Brigham Young.

Every man and woman that has talent and hides it will be called a slothful servant.

Improve day by day upon the capital you have. In proportion as we are capacitated to receive so it is our duty to do. . . . .

I shall not cease learning while I live, nor when I arrive in the spirit world; but shall there learn with greater facility; and when I again receive my body, I shall learn a thousand times more in a thousand times less time; and then I do not mean to cease learning.

All truth is for the salvation of the children of men—for their benefit and learning—for their furtherance in the principles of divine knowledge, and divine knowledge is any matter of fact—truth and all truth pertains to divinity.

But we should all live so that the Spirit of revelation could dictate and write on the heart and tell us what we should do. . . . Jesus says if we do not we cannot enter the kingdom of heaven. . . .

We are all the children of Adam and Eve, and they are the offspring of him who dwells in the heavens, the highest Intelligence that dwells anywhere that we have any knowledge of. Here we find ourselves, and when infants, the most helpless and needing the most care and attention, of any creatures that come into being on the face of the earth. Here we find in ourselves the germ and the foundation, the embryo of exaltation, glory, immortality and eternal lives. As we grow up we receive strength, knowledge and wisdom, some more, some less; but only by keeping the commands of the Lord Jesus can we have the privilege of knowing the things pertaining to eternity and our relationship to the heavens.[5]

So we see from these quotations that the truth that saves in the kingdom of God is that which comes in the form of gospel principles and ordinances. As the Prophet says, "Then knowledge through our Lord and Savior Jesus Christ is the grand key that unlocks the glories and mysteries of the kingdom of heaven." This being true, then it is necessary that we do not forget the spiritual things and lose sight of heaven.

True Education

Discoursing on true education, President Joseph F. Smith has also given us this excellent advice.

The knowledge of truth, combined with proper regard for it and its faithful observance, constitutes true education.

The mere stuffing of the mind with a knowledge of facts is not education. The mind must not only possess a knowledge of truth, but the soul must revere it, cherish it, love it as a priceless gem; and this human life must be guided and shaped by it in order to fulfil its destiny. The mind should not only be charged with intelligence, but the soul should be filled with admiration and desire for pure intelligence which comes of a knowledge of the truth. The truth can only make him free who hath it, and will continue in it. And the word of God is truth, and it will endure forever.

Educate yourself not only for time, but also for eternity. The latter of the two is the more important. Therefore, when we shall have completed the studies of time, and enter upon the commencement ceremonies of the great hereafter, we will find our work is not finished, but just begun, we may then say with the poet:

"Lay this aside—say not your work is done.
No deed of love or goodness ever dies.
But in the lives of others—multiplies.
Say it has just begun."

There is no science, nor philosophy, that can supersede God Almighty truth. The Lord has said, "My word is truth," and indeed it is; and I believe that the Latter-day Saints know enough about the word of God to know it is his word when they see it and shun whatever is not; and that they will abide by the word of God, for it is truth. As the Savior said, "If ye continue in my word, then are ye my disciples indeed; and ye shall know the truth, and the truth shall make you free." I believe that the Latter-day Saints, and especially the leading men in Israel, have sufficient knowledge and understanding of the principles of the gospel that they know the truth, and they are made free by its possession—free from sin, free from error, free from darkness, from traditions of men, from vain philosophy, and from untried, unproved theories of scientists, that need demonstration beyond the possibility of a doubt. We have had science and philosophy through all the ages and they have undergone change after change. Scarcely a century has passed but they have introduced new theories of science and philosophy that supersede the old traditions and the old faith and the old doctrines entertained by philosophers and scientists. These things may undergo continuous changes, but the word of God is always true, is always right. I want to say to you that the principles of the gospel are always true—the principle of faith in God, of repentance from sin, of baptism for the remission of sins by authority of God, and the laying on of hands for the gift of the Holy Ghost; these principles are always true and are always absolutely necessary for the salvation of the children of men, no matter who they are or where they are. These principles are always true and you cannot get away from them. No other name, under heaven, is given, but that of Jesus Christ, by which you can be saved or exalted in the kingdom of God. . . .

If the Lord has revealed to the world the plan of salvation and redemption from sin, by which men may be exalted again into his presence and partake of eternal life with him, I submit, as a proposition that cannot be controverted, that no man can be exalted in the presence of God and attain to a fulness of glory and happiness in his kingdom and presence, save and except he will obey the plan that God has devised and revealed.[6]

Intelligence

Since I have been speaking of intelligence, perhaps it would be well to give President Smith's definition of intelligence—no, it is the Lord's definition, as I shall presently show. President Smith once said:

> Christ inherited his intelligence from his Father. There is a difference between knowledge and pure intelligence. Satan possesses knowledge, far more than we have, but he has not intelligence or he would render obedience to the principles of truth and right. I know men who have knowledge, who understand the principles of the gospel as well as you do, who are brilliant, but who lack the essential qualification of pure intelligence. They will not accept and render obedience thereto. Pure intelligence comprises not only knowledge, but also the power to properly apply that knowledge.[7]

It has been a regret to me that our Mutual Improvement Associations, and practically all members of the Church, have quoted the expression: "The glory of God is intelligence," as though this was the complete thought, and we have lost sight of the rest of the expression. What the Lord said was this: "The glory of God is intelligence, or, in other words, light and truth." Then he adds: "Light and truth forsake that evil one." A man with pure intelligence will not follow in paths of evil. Ofttimes men turn their knowledge to the committing of evil, but this could not be if they were possessed of intelligence, for then they would walk in light and truth and forsake that evil one.

Ultimate View

This brings me back to my text: "Knowledge is power." While this is a true saying and we see it on every side made manifest, even where those who revel in wickedness have knowledge they have obtained the power, yet as I desire to discuss it this expression has reference to ultimate knowledge and truth. In Section 50 of the Doctrine and Covenants I find a passage which has impressed me as much as any other passage of scripture. If this saying were the only truth revealed through the Prophet Joseph Smith, it would be sufficient to stamp him with the power of prophetic vision. It is one of the outstanding truths revealed for the salvation of man. It has been the means of helping me to be humble and to rejoice in the eternal truth of exaltation as that truth has been revealed. It has caused me to rejoice and thank the Lord for his mercy and goodness and for the hope of eternal life which has come to me. Here is what the Lord revealed:

> And that which doth not edify is not of God, and is darkness.
>
> That which is of God is light; and he that receiveth light, and continueth in God, receiveth more light; and that light groweth brighter and brighter until the perfect day.[8]

What a glorious promise is here given unto us! All light, all truth comes from God. That which is not from him does not edify but brings darkness. If we will continue in God, that is, keep his commandments, worship him and love his truth, then the time will come when we shall be bathed in the fulness of truth, which shall grow brighter and brighter unto the perfect day. Here then, we find power, wisdom, advancement, the knowledge which is perfect and which can only be obtained through continuing in God through obedience unto him.

I like to associate with this wonderful passage another equal unto it found in Section 93. Before I quote it, however, let me comment for a moment on another saying in this same revelation. We are informed that the Lord gave to the Church and to the world, if they will receive it, the commandments which are contained in this volume of scripture, that we might know his will, and as he has expressed it:

> I give unto you these sayings that you may understand and know how to worship, and know what you worship, that you may come unto the Father in my name, and in due time receive of his fulness.
>
> For if you keep my commandments you shall receive of his fulness and be glorified in me as I am in the Father; therefore, I say unto you, you shall receive grace for grace.
>
> And now, verily I say unto you, I was in the beginning with the Father, and am the Firstborn;

And all those who are begotten through me are partakers of the glory of the same and are the church of the Firstborn.[9]

Church of the Firstborn

As I understand it, those who become members of the Church of the Firstborn are those who have kept the commandments of the Lord in their fulness. I do not understand that every member of The Church of Jesus Christ of Latter-day Saints is to become a member of the Church of the Firstborn; for there are many who are not willing to walk in the light of truth and continue in God obedient to every ordinance and commandment. These will fall short of this great glory for they have not overcome by faith. Then again you see from this scripture that the promise is made that if we will walk in the light, learn how and what to worship, we become begotten sons and daughters of God and hence are partakers of his glory.

The passage, then, that I had in mind, and which I delight to couple with that in Section 50, is as follows:

The Spirit of truth is of God. I am the Spirit of truth, and John bore record of me, saying: He received a fulness of truth, yea, even of all truth.

And no man receiveth a fulness unless he keepeth his commandments.

He that keepeth his commandments receiveth truth and light, until he is glorified in truth and knoweth all things.[10]

Only Way

We have discovered, then, from these glorious revelations, that the only way that a person can learn all things and receive the fulness of the Spirit of truth, is through the Church and obedience to the gospel of Jesus Christ in its fulness. No matter how much a man may learn, no matter how long he may study, should it be through all eternity, he will never come to the fulness of truth and light—that which is pure intelligence and which has no part or lot with that evil one—only by continuing in God and through full and complete obedience to his commandments.

Here, then, we discover the full significance of the saying that "Knowledge is power." The Father has promised through the Son that all that he has shall be given to those who are obedient to his commandments. They shall increase in knowledge, wisdom and power, from grace to grace, until the fulness of the perfect day shall burst upon them. They shall, through the glory and blessing of the Almighty, become creators. All power and dominion and might shall be given to them, and they shall be the only ones upon whom this great blessing shall be bestowed. All others, no matter how much learning, wisdom and power, they may obtain, shall nevertheless be restricted in their several spheres, for they cannot attain to the fulness which is held in reserve for those who are permitted to pass by the angels and the Gods who are set to guard the way to this great exaltation.

"If ye continue in my word, then are ye my disciples indeed; and ye shall know the truth, and the truth shall make you free."[11] These are the words of our Master, and it is obedience to him and his word that "unlocks the glories and mysteries of the kingdom of heaven." It cannot be unlocked in any other way.—(Synopsis of Baccalaureate sermon given at BYU, Sunday, June 6, 1937.)

---

[1]D&C 131:18-19.
[2]*Ibid.*, 131:6.
[3]*Teachings of the Prophet Joseph Smith,* p. 297.
[4]*Ibid.*, pp. 297-298.
[5]*J. of D.*, Volume 8, p. 10.
[6]*Gospel Doctrine,* p. 269.
[7]*Ibid.*, p. 58.
[8]D&C 50:23-24.
[9]*Ibid.*, 93:19-22.
[10]*Ibid.*, 93:26-28.
[11]John 8:31-32.

Every person baptized into this Church has made a covenant with the Lord to keep his commandments. We are told that we are to serve the Lord with all the heart and all the mind, and with all the strength that we have, and that too in the name of Jesus Christ.

Keep Covenants of the Lord, Be Guided by Prayer

I have been extremely happy because of the nature of the remarks that have been made by those who have spoken. I feel very humble, and pray that the Spirit of the Lord will lead me this afternoon in the remarks that I may make, for I have only one desire and that is to say the things the Lord would have me say.

I am going to read from Section 59 of the Doctrine and Covenants:

> Wherefore I give unto them (meaning the members of the Church) a commandment, saying thus: Thou shalt love the Lord thy God with all thy heart, with all thy might, mind, and strength; and in the name of Jesus Christ thou shalt serve him.
>
> Thou shalt love thy neighbor as thyself. Thou shalt not steal; neither commit adultery, nor kill, nor do anything like unto it.
>
> Thou shalt thank the Lord thy God in all things.[1]

Covenants to Be Kept

Every person baptized into this Church has made a covenant with the Lord to keep his commandments, and in this commandment, reiterated in the dispensation in which we live, we are told that we are to serve the Lord with all the heart and all the mind, and with all the strength that we have, and that too in the name of Jesus Christ. Everything that we do should be done in the name of Jesus Christ.

In the waters of baptism we covenanted that we would keep these commandments; that we would serve the Lord; that we would keep this first and greatest of all the commandments, and love the Lord our God; that we would keep the next great commandment, we would love our neighbor as ourselves; and with all the might that we have, with all the strength, with all our hearts we would prove to him that we would "live by every word that proceedeth forth from the mouth of God"; that we would be obedient and humble, diligent in his service, willing to obey, to hearken to the counsels of those who preside over us and do all things with an eye single to the glory of God.

We should not forget these things, for this commandment is binding upon us as members of the Church.

Now may I read you another commandment:

> But ye (again having reference to the members of the Church) are commanded in all things to ask of God, who giveth liberally; and that which the Spirit testifies unto you even so I would that ye should do in all holiness of heart, walking uprightly before me, considering the end of your salvation, doing all things with prayer and thanksgiving, that ye may not be seduced by evil spirits, or doctrines of devils, or the commandments of men; for some are of men, and others of devils.
>
> Wherefore, beware lest ye are deceived; and that ye may not be deceived seek ye earnestly the best gifts, always remembering for what they are given.[2]

Now, my good brethren and sisters, if we are humble, if we are diligent in the service of the Lord, if we seek to serve him with an eye single to the glory of our Father in heaven, keeping in mind that he has asked for that service with a full heart, with all our might, with all our mind, and with all our strength, we will not go astray, we will not be seduced by evil spirits nor by the spirits of men, but we will be led and directed by the Spirit of God.

Guidance Comes through the Holy Ghost

Every member of the Church has had hands laid upon his head for the gift of the Holy Ghost. He has a right to receive the revelations that are expedient and necessary for his guidance individually; not for the Church, but for himself. He has a right through his obedience, through his humility, to receive light and truth as it shall be revealed through the Spirit of truth, and he who will hearken to that Spirit and seek for the gift of the Spirit in humility and faith shall not be deceived.

Now there are some of our people who are being deceived. Why? Because they lack knowledge, because they lack understanding, and because they are not in tune with the Holy Spirit, which they have a right to receive through their faithfulness and obedience.

President Lorenzo Snow's Counsel Regarding Tithing

I would like briefly to call attention to a few things that have been mentioned here, and some that have not. I would like to say a word or two about tithing. It has been mentioned, and I am very grateful to know that it has. I want to read to you a few words that were uttered by President Lorenzo Snow when he was pleading with the people to be honest with the Lord. Now we are not faithful Latter-day Saints if we are dishonest with the Lord, we are not serving him with all our hearts, with all our might, with all our strength if we are dishonest in the payment of our tithes and our offerings, and we shall stand before the Lord condemned and not entitled to the guidance of his Holy Spirit, and likely will be deceived by these spirits that lie in wait to deceive, if we are guilty of failing to keep this great commandment or any other of the commandments that the Lord has given us.

These are the words of President Snow to the Church:

Teach the children to pay tithing so that it may be properly observed. If we observe this law, no matter what our enemies may do the Lord will preserve us. Because we are his sons and daughters he loves us, and he has forgiven our forgetfulness of this holy law in the past, but he will not forgive you and me any longer, should we continue in this dilatory way of paying tithing. We shall be scattered just as the people in Jackson County were. This is true as the Lord is true. The Lord has blessed us wonderfully and preserved us in the land and yet we have refused to pay our honest debt unto him. A great many people have not paid one cent of tithing, and yet they have gone into the temples of the Lord.

Then speaking to the officers of the stakes and wards he said:

How do you feel when you give a recommend to a person to come into our temples who pays no tithing, who only pays half a tithing? How will you feel after this? You will feel that you are taking a sacred responsibility in doing that which God does not approve. He has said that the man who fails to pay his tithing shall have no place among the people of God. Yet here are these temples erected by the sacrifice of the poor, and to give recommends to parties who pay little or no tithing, how can you feel to take this responsibility? I could not. Part of a tithing is not tithing at all in the eyes of the law that the Lord has revealed.

President Brigham Young's Advice to Bishops

I have another statement here from President Brigham Young, given to the bishops of the Church:

These men and women whom you recommend must be individuals who pay their tithing from year to year; that is, those who are recommended to go to the temple should pray and not speak against the Authorities of the Church, against the kingdom of God, nor steal, nor lie, nor interfere with their neighbors' things, nor their neighbors' wives or husbands, but attend strictly to meetings, and prayer meetings, and those who pay due respect to their presiding officers and bishops, and those who do not swear.

People who are guilty of these offenses, according to President Young, should not be recommended to go to the temple to receive the ordinances of the House of the Lord.

Fast Day Requirements

Let me say a word or two now in regard to fasting and fast offerings. This morning in the meeting that was held—the welfare meeting we had portrayed before us the gradual rise of the percentage of fast offerings paid by the Church. Now, my good brethren and sisters, the amount that has been paid up to this present year is not by any means the amount that we ought to pay. We have not kept this commandment, for fasting and prayer in faith and the payment of offerings are commandments of the Lord. We have been called upon to fast. I do not know when we have heard a discourse on fasting; not very often, and I am sure that we are not observing this law of fasting as members of the Church as we ought to do. We have made it easy for the people, that is, easy to break this commandment because we have moved the fast service up so high on the fast day that we can get all through and home again by one o'clock, or 12:30. That is a good time to eat, isn't it? And yet according to the commandment that the Lord has given to us through his servants we should abstain from food and water for one day, counting twenty-four hours, or from sunset to sunset. Now if you want to fast from twelve o'clock noon until twelve o'clock noon I suppose it would be just as well if that is what you wish to do, but many of us are not observing the fast day now.

I want to say to you, my good brethren, we cannot have that guidance of the Holy Spirit as we ought to have it if we do not fast as the Lord has required it of us; not extensive fasts, but the fast which has been set apart which we should do in wisdom. Now the Lord says we should do all things in wisdom, but we are not fasting, hence, we are not paying our fast offerings; we are not praying, I fear, as we should. I wonder if we are praying in our secret closets. I wonder if we are teaching our families to pray; if the spirit of prayer is among us as it ought to be.

I commend to your reading, and I shall not take time to do it, the words of an ancient prophet, found in the thirty-fourth chapter of Alma in the Book of Mormon. Amulek says that we should cry unto the Lord over our flocks, over our herds, over our goods, in our fields, and in our secret chambers, that we should do nothing but that we present the matter before the Lord and ask for his guidance and his blessing. We should go on our knees a little more and then we will have more faith. We need to be more humble in the service of the Lord. We need to spend less time in the criticism of those who preside.

Joseph Smith's Teachings Regarding Perfection

I am going to read to you a statement from the Prophet Joseph Smith that I think is important. I have a number of statements here that I should like to read, but I shall not take the time to do so, but this is worthy of our consideration:

> We consider that God has created man with a mind capable of instruction, and a faculty which may be enlarged in proportion to the heed and diligence given to the light communicated from heaven to the intellect; and that the nearer man approaches perfection, the clearer are his views, and the greater his enjoyments, till he has overcome the evils of his life and lost every desire for sin; and like the ancients, arrives at that point of faith where he is wrapped up in the power and glory of his Maker and is caught up to dwell with him. But we consider that this is a station to which no man ever arrived in a moment; he must have been instructed in the government and laws of that kingdom by proper degrees, until his mind is capable in some measure of comprehending the propriety, justice, equality, and consistency of the same. . . .
>
> If God should speak from heaven, he would command you not to steal, not to commit adultery, not to covet, nor deceive, but be faithful over a few things. As far as we degenerate from God, we descend to the devil and lose knowledge, and without knowledge we

cannot be saved, and while our hearts are filled with evil, and we are studying evil, there is no room in our hearts for good, or studying good. Is not God good? Then you be good; if he is faithful, then you be faithful. Add to your faith virtue, to virtue knowledge, and seek for every good thing.[3]

Faithfulness a Protection Against Evil

The nearer we approach God, the better we endeavor to keep his commandments, the more we will search to know his will as it has been revealed, the less likely it will be for us to be led astray by every wind of doctrine, by these false spirits that lie in wait to deceive, and by the spirits of men, as the Lord has stated in the revelations which I have read to you. We will be protected, and we will have the power to understand, to segregate truth from error, we will walk in the light and we will not be deceived. Now the man who is dilatory, the man who is unfaithful, the man who is not willing to keep the commandments of the Lord in all things lays himself open to deception because the Spirit of the Lord is not with him to lead and direct him and to show him the way of truth and righteousness, and therefore some error comes along and he absorbs it because he cannot understand and realize the difference between truth and error. I want to tell you there is much error in this world that is passed off as truth, and it behooves every man of us to seek God, and, as stated by the prophet, draw near unto him, and the nearer we draw unto him, and the more we seek to do his will the more light we shall receive and the less shall be the danger of our deception.—(*Conference Report,* April, 1940.)

---

[1]D&C 59:5-7.
[2]*Ibid.,* 46:7-8.
[3]*Teachings of the Prophet Joseph Smith,* pp. 51, 217.

The Lord offers us what? A place in his kingdom, where we can be heirs, in other words sons and daughters, possessing and receiving the fulness of that kingdom, through obedience to the principles and ordinances of the gospel as we are required to take that obedience upon us in the temple of the Lord.

The Pearl of Great Price

> Again, the kingdom of heaven is like unto treasure hid in a field; the which when a man hath found he hideth, and for joy thereof goeth and selleth all that he hath, and buyeth that field.
>
> Again, the kingdom of heaven is like unto a merchant man, seeking goodly pearls:
>
> Who, when he had found one pearl of great price, went and sold all that he had, and bought it.[1]

A great many of the members of the Church evidently do not realize the importance of the blessings we receive in the temples of the Lord. I wish we all loved the gospel to the extent that we would be willing to do anything the Lord asks of us irrespective of what the world thinks or does. Why cannot the Latter-day Saints uphold the standards and the regulations of the Church with united effort notwithstanding what the world might do or think? With some of us it is the custom to do very much as the world does. We dress as the world does. We seek its pleasures; we follow its customs; and there is no question in my mind that these things do bring us somewhat in conflict with things the Lord has taught and commanded us to do.

Blessings Come Through Obedience to Law

The Lord says that when we obtain any blessing it is based upon obedience to the law upon which that blessing is predicated.[2] We cannot get a blessing from him in any other way and this is according to that which was "decreed in heaven before the foundation of this world." I wonder if we have thought of this seriously?

The Lord, when speaking to some of the elders of the Church in the beginning, said: "And they who remain"—when rewards are given and men are assigned to the place where they belong—"shall be quickened; nevertheless they shall return again to their own place, to enjoy that which they are willing to receive, because they were not willing to enjoy that which they might have received."[3]

He has revealed to us things pertaining to the celestial kingdom, the terrestrial kingdom and the telestial kingdom, and how those who inherit these kingdoms will come forth in the resurrection to receive their rewards; then he says, "And they who remain shall also be quickened"—those who do not belong to any of these kingdoms—"to enjoy that which they are willing to receive, because they were not willing to enjoy that which they might have received. For what doth it profit a man if a gift be bestowed upon him, and he receive not the gift? Behold, he rejoices not in that which is given unto him, neither rejoices in him who is the giver of the gift."

Heirs of the Kingdom

The Lord offers us what? A place in his kingdom, where we can be heirs, in other words sons and daughters, possessing and receiving the fulness of that kingdom, through obedience to the principles and ordinances of the gospel as we are required to take that obedience upon us in the temple of the Lord. If we will not receive these blessings then we do not rejoice in them, neither in the Giver of this great gift.

In one of the parables by the Savior he likens the kingdom of God to a treasure of great price which a man discovered in a field and, who, when he discovered it, sold all that he had and purchased that field. In other words, he was willing to forsake all for the kingdom of God. *So we should be willing to give up everything in this world for the sake of the kingdom of God.* This doctrine Jesus taught emphatically, saying that we are not worthy of him if we are not willing to do so for his sake.

He has offered us the fulness of his kingdom and to make us heirs to receive all that the Father has, if we will receive it through obedience to his commandments. The Lord said to John, "He that overcometh shall inherit all things; and I will be his God, and he shall be my son."[4] There are other expressions of similar nature in the Bible, but the people of the world do not understand them. In the revelations given to the Prophet Joseph Smith this promise is enlarged upon, or made more clear. For instance, in that wonderful revelation known as "The Vision" we read:

> And again, we bear record, for we saw and heard, and this is the testimony of the gospel of Christ, concerning them who come forth in the resurrection of the just:
>
> They are they who received the testimony of Jesus, and believed on his name and were baptized after the manner of his burial, being buried in the water in his name, and this according to the commandment which he has given—
>
> That by keeping the commandments they might be washed and cleansed from all their sins, and receive the Holy Spirit by the laying on of the hands of him who is ordained and sealed unto this power;
>
> And who overcome by faith, and are sealed by the Holy Spirit of promise, which the Father sheds forth upon all those who are just and true.
>
> They are they who are the church of the Firstborn.
>
> They are they into whose hands the Father has given all things—

They are they who are priests and kings, who have received of his fulness, and of his glory;

And are priests of the Most High, after the order of Melchizedek, which was after the order of Enoch, which was after the order of the Only Begotten Son.

Wherefore, as it is written, they are gods, even the sons of God—

Wherefore all things are theirs, whether life or death, or things present, or things to come, all are theirs and they are Christ's and Christ is God's.

And they shall overcome all things.[5]

All Things Are Theirs

These are the promises the Lord makes to all those who come into his Church in the waters of baptism and then, by keeping his commandments, remain washed and cleansed from all their sins, and receive the Holy Spirit of Promise by obedience to the requirements made in the temples of the Lord. "All things are theirs." They become sons and daughters of God and are made heirs in that kingdom. That is what salvation means to us. I am using the term "salvation" in the full sense of exaltation. The world has a very vague idea of salvation. The great majority of men most everywhere believe that you are either saved in heaven or you are in an extremely bad place. If you get into heaven there is nothing much for you to do. You rest from your labors, being saved; no work to perform; no responsibility upon your shoulders, only to sing, or play a harp. If you are damned you are in eternal torment where you are to remain forever. They have very little idea of the exaltation which the Lord has prepared for the faithful in the mansions of the Father. The Lord has revealed it to us, and these are our privileges on conditions of faithfulness according to the law decreed in the heavens upon which these blessings are predicated.

No Exaltation without Fulness of Priesthood

There is no exaltation in the kingdom of God without the fulness of priesthood. How could a man be an heir in that kingdom without priesthood? While the sisters do not hold the priesthood, they share in the fulness of its blessings in the celestial kingdom with their husbands. These blessings are obtained through obedience to the ordinances and covenants of the House of the Lord. The Prophet Joseph Smith once said: *"If a man gets a fulness of the priesthood of God, he has to get it . . . by keeping all the commandments and obeying all the ordinances of the house of the Lord."* To obtain the fulness of the priesthood does not mean that a man must become president of the Church. Every man who is faithful and will receive these ordinances and blessings obtains a fulness of the priesthood, and the Lord has said that "he makes them equal in power, and in might, and in dominion." Only one man at a time on the earth holds the keys of the priesthood; only one man at a time has the power to receive revelations for the Church; but the Lord has made it possible for every man in this Church, through his obedience, to receive the fulness of the priesthood through the ordinances of the temple of the Lord. This cannot be received anywhere else.

So being ordained an elder, or a high priest, or an apostle, or even president of the Church, is not the thing that brings the exaltation, but obedience to the laws and the ordinances and the covenants required of those who desire to become members of the Church of the Firstborn as these are administered in the House of the Lord. *To become a member of the Church of the Firstborn, as I understand it, is to become one of the inner circle.* We are all members of The Church of Jesus Christ of Latter-day Saints by being baptized and confirmed, and there are many who seem to be content to remain such without obtaining the privileges of exaltation. *The Lord has made it possible for us to become members of the Church of the Firstborn by receiving the blessings of the House of the Lord, and "overcoming all things."* Thus we become heirs, "priests and kings, who have received of his fulness, and of his glory," who shall "dwell in the presence of God and his Christ forever and ever," with full exaltation. Are such blessings worth having?

I have said that only one man at a time on the earth holds the keys of this sealing power of priesthood, but he may, and does, delegate power to others and they officiate under his direction in the temples of the Lord. No man can officiate in these sealing ordinances until he receives the authority to do so by being set apart by the one who holds the keys, notwithstanding he may hold the priesthood. All the authority exercised in the temples, is then, after all, the authority centered in one man. He has the power and calls upon others to officiate and they *seal upon us the keys and powers which, through our obedience, entitle us to become sons and daughters, and members of the Church of the Firstborn, receiving all things in the kingdom.* This is what we can get in the temple, so that we become *members of the family, sons and daughters of God, not servants.*

Sons and Daughters of God

You know what it says about servants in the scriptures. Those who become servants are those who are not willing to receive these blessings in the House of the Lord and abide in them. They are not sons, they are not daughters. They are children of God, it is true, for all men are his children. But they do not inherit, and therefore remain servants throughout all eternity because they were not willing to receive that which they might have received, and the gift which was bestowed upon them or offered to them. They not only rejected the gift, but the Giver of the gift. There will be a great many servants, but there will not be many heirs, "Because strait is the gate, and narrow is the way, which leadeth unto life, and few there be that find it."[6]

Having put this matter before you in this way, endeavoring to impress you with the importance of these blessings obtained in the temples, I would like to ask you a question.

Are these blessings to be desired? The question answers itself. Now let me ask another. When the Lord offers us these great blessings, are we justified in saying, "It is all right, we want them, but we want to put them off just as long as we can before we receive them, so that we can live as the world lives"? Is there any sincerity in that? Is there any spirit of humility or repentance, or faith in such an attitude? I have known of mothers saying to their daughters, "I do not want you to go to the temple now. Wait a little while. When you get older you may go to the temple, but now have a good time while you are young." Well, of course, if a girl is going to enter into covenants in the temple which she does not intend to keep, it is better for her not to go there. Far better for her to stay out. But is there any blessing the Lord offers us that we are justified in postponing because we feel that it will interfere with our having a good time, or indulging in the customs and fashions of the world? Is it right for us to feel that we are justified in seeking the things of the world until we are along in years and then we will repent and turn unto the Lord? Should we not seek to obtain these important blessings just as soon as we can, consistently and in reason?

The Pearl of Great Price

Children should not go to the temple until they are old enough to understand the purpose of their going. They should be taught the principles of the gospel and to have faith in God and in the mission of Jesus Christ, and should gain a testimony of the truth before they receive the blessings of the temple. I believe that a young man or woman should seek after these blessings in the temple and just as soon as they are old enough to understand the meaning of temple ordinances they should have them. Moreover, they should not go to the temple until they do have a testimony of the truth and a knowledge of the gospel, no matter how old they may be. It is not intended that these sacred covenants should be given to those who do not have faith and who have not proved themselves worthy by obedience to the gospel.

After we have received these covenants we should sacredly observe them even if it should cost us the association and good will of all the world. Why? *Because we have found the pearl of great price, the kingdom of God.* We are on the road to receive all that the Father has, all that he can give—exaltation. If others are not willing to receive these blessings let them take their course, but for us, let us walk in the light of the truth and forsake the world.

I do not think because girls go through the temple they will necessarily be ostracized socially by friends and companions. I know of mothers, however, who have made their daughters feel that they would be, and that they could not make themselves attractive if they went to the temple and kept the covenants made there, for they would not be able to dress according to the fashion. Such a doctrine may mean the damnation of that precious daughter in whose welfare you have such an interest if you feel that way.

Power from on High

The Lord has not offered us these blessings that we might receive them just before we die or when we are old or crippled. What are these blessings for? Not only for eternity, but to be a guide to us and a protection through the struggle of life. Do you understand why our missionaries go to the temple before they are set apart for their mission fields? This is a requirement made of them whether they are eighteen years of age, or twenty, or older, because the Lord has said it should be done. He called all the missionaries to Kirtland in the early days of the Church to receive endowments in the temple erected there. He said this was so that they could go out with greater power from on high and with greater protection. Zion was not to be redeemed until endowments were given. These are the words of the Lord:

> Therefore in consequence of the transgression of my people, it is expedient in me that mine elders should wait for a little season for the redemption of Zion—
>
> That they themselves may be prepared, and that my people may be taught more perfectly, and have experience, and know more perfectly concerning their duty, and the things which I require at their hands.
>
> And this cannot be brought to pass until mine elders are endowed with power from on high.
>
> For behold, I have prepared a great endowment and blessing to be poured out upon them, inasmuch as they are faithful and continue in humility before me.[7]

Speaking of the building of the temple at Kirtland the Lord further said:

> Yea, verily I say unto you, I gave unto you a commandment that you should build a house, in the which house I design to endow those whom I have chosen with power from on high.
>
> For this is the promise of the Father unto you; therefore I command you to tarry, even as mine apostles at Jerusalem.[8]

The endowment received now is greater than that given in Kirtland, for the Lord has revealed additional covenants and obligations for us to keep. If we go into the temple we raise our hands and covenant that we will serve the Lord and observe his commandments and keep ourselves unspotted from the world. If we realize what we are doing then the endowment will be a protection to us all our lives —a protection which a man who does not go to the temple does not have.

I have heard my father say that in the hour of trial, in the hour of temptation, he would think of the promises, the covenants that he made in the House of the Lord, and they were a protection to him. He was but fifteen years of age when he received his endowments and went forth into the mission field. This is exceptional, I know, and I do not recommend that our sons and our daughters go to the temple as young as that, but that they go as soon as they are prepared. This protection is what these ceremonies are for, in part. They save us now and they exalt us hereafter, if we will honor them. I know that this protection is given for I, too, have realized it, as have thousands of others who have remembered their obligations.

The Greatest Blessing of Life

And yet mothers and fathers will say: "Oh, let the children have a good time, let them do as the world does and when their charms are gone, then they can go to the temple." Therefore many procrastinate the day of their repentance, which is a very dangerous thing to do. These blessings insure to us, through our faithfulness, the pearl of great price the Lord has offered us, for *these are the greatest blessings we can receive in this life.* It is a wonderful thing to come into the Church, but you cannot receive an exaltation until you have made covenants in the House of the Lord and received the keys and authorities that are there bestowed and which cannot be given in any other place on the earth today.

You have read what the Prophet has written in the Pearl of Great Price. He has given us some of the interpretations of the Egyptian characters in the writings of Abraham and we learn that Abraham wrote things and sealed them up that they cannot be read, saying: "They cannot be revealed unto the world but are to be had in the holy temple of God." They are certain keys and blessings that are obtained in the house of the Lord that we must have if we are to obtain exaltation.

The Need of Repentance

What we need in the Church, as well as out of it, is repentance. We need more faith and more determination to serve the Lord. Do not get the impression from what I have said that I feel that we should keep aloof from everybody outside of the Church and not associate with them. I have not said that, but I do want us to be consistent Latter-day Saints, and if the people of the world walk in darkness and sin and contrary to the will of the Lord, there is the place for us to draw the line. Why should we not uphold the standards of our faith? Why should we not walk in strict accord with the regulations of the Church notwithstanding what the world may think? The Lord has revealed the fulness of his gospel. We have been fully informed regarding all of its principles pertaining to salvation. Is it worthwhile for us to maintain our integrity and prove faithful to every trust? *Is the pearl of great price—the fulness of the glory, honor and eternal life in the presence of the Father and the Son—worth the sacrifice we may be called upon to make? Are we, as the man spoken of in former times, willing to sell all that we have in order that we may buy this field which will bring to us everlasting joy and exaltation as sons and daughters of God?* I pray that we are, in the name of our Redeemer. Amen.—(Remarks at a meeting of the high priests quorum of the Salt Lake Stake, Sunday, October 20, 1920, in the Seventeenth Ward Meetinghouse.)

---

[1]Matt. 13:44-46.
[2]D&C 131:20-21.
[3]*Ibid.,* 88:32.
[4]Rev. 21:7.
[5]D&C 76:50-60.
[6]Matt. 7:14.
[7]D&C 105:9-12.
[8]*Ibid.,* 95:8-9.

Baptism is not merely a door into the kingdom, which entitles us to enter, bringing with us a trail of sins unrepented of. It is not that at all. We must not enter that door until our hearts are humble, our spirits contrite, and we give the assurance that we will serve the Lord in faithfulness and righteousness to the end.

Obedience Held Greatest Virtue

The theme of this conference seems to be obedience. I know of nothing that is of greater importance to members of the Church, and if I may be so led I would like to add a few words in regard to this important topic.

Those Who May Be Baptized

A few months ago, when I was in one of the mission fields, meeting with a group of missionaries, one of them asked me this question: Shall we baptize men into this Church when they say they believe that Joseph Smith was a prophet of God and they believe that the Lord appeared to him, and that The Church of Jesus Christ of Latter-day Saints is indeed the Church of Christ upon the earth, and yet they have not forsaken all of their sins?

He stated that this question had been discussed among the elders. Some took one view, some another. Some held that if we accepted a man who so expressed himself, that eventually he would repent of all his sins. I said in answer to him: "I shall read to you what the Lord himself has said, and we will see if that will not answer your question." I am going to read those words here this afternoon:

And again, by way of commandment to the Church concerning the manner of baptism—All those who humble themselves before God, and desire to be baptized, and come forth with broken hearts and contrite spirits, and witness before the Church that they have truly repented of all their sins, and are willing to take upon them the name of Jesus Christ, having a determination to serve him to the end, and truly manifest by their works that they have received of the Spirit of Christ unto the remission of their sins, shall be received by baptism into his church.[1]

Then I asked if that did not answer the question. The missionaries concluded that it did. But yet this question arose: We keep the man out who has not forsaken all his sins and yet confesses that this is the Church of Christ; but think of the great many who are in the Church, the great number who violate the commandments of the Lord, and yet we do nothing about it.

Church Membership Will Not Escape Judgment

I answered: True, unless it is a grievous sin we do not excommunicate people from the Church. We try to teach them their duty. We try to bring them to repentance. We try to make them understand the truth. But after they are in the Church, if they will not do these things and will not hearken to our counsels, you may be assured that they are going to be judged according to their works.

The fact that they are members of the Church will not save them. Every man and every woman will have to answer for the deeds done in the body.

Then again an ancient prophet said:

Wo unto him that has the law given, yea, that has all the commandments of God, like unto us, and that transgresseth them, and that wasteth the days of his probation, for awful is his state.[2]

Now, when people come into this Church they should, by all means, subscribe to the regulations which the Lord himself has laid down by commandment. But does that mean that after we are in the Church, after we have confessed our sins and have forsaken them, that we can return to them after membership has been secured? That would not be consistent. Wo unto all those who are disobedient after they have made the preparation which is expressed in this commandment which I have read to you—wo unto them. Mark you, the Lord says before a man comes into the Church he must have a desire; he must come with a broken heart and a contrite spirit.

What is a broken heart? One that is humble, one that is touched by the Spirit of the Lord, and which is willing to abide in all the covenants and the obligations which the gospel entails.

Baptism a Covenant to Continue Faithful

Further we read that he must forsake all of his sins. Does that mean merely until he gets into the Church, and then he may return to them again? I call your attention to the words of Paul, speaking himself in regard to baptism and membership, and rather rebuking some of the members of the Church when he said:

> How shall we, that are dead to sin, live any longer therein?[3]

Every baptized person who has fully repented, who comes into the Church with a broken heart and a contrite spirit, has made a covenant to continue with that broken heart, with that contrite spirit, which means a repentant spirit. He makes a covenant that he will do that.

Then again we read here, in this admonition and commandment, that he is to endure to the end. It is essential that we endure to the end. In the revelation that was given to the Church, this same revelation, at the time the Church was organized, the Lord said this:

> And we know that all men must repent and believe on the name of Jesus Christ, and worship the Father in his name, and endure in faith on his name to the end, or they cannot be saved in the kingdom of God.[4]

Now, I believe the Lord meant what he said. I think this is true. Baptism is not merely a door into the kingdom, which entitles us to enter, bringing with us a trail of sins unrepented of. It is not that at all. We must not enter that door until our hearts are humble, our spirits contrite, and we give the assurance that we will serve the Lord in faithfulness and righteousness to the end.

Again:

> And we know that justification through the grace of our Lord and Savior Jesus Christ, is just and true."[5]

That is, if we come into this Church with a broken heart and a contrite spirit, with a determination to forsake all our sins and live faithfully to the end, then we are justified, and the sanctification of the blood of Jesus Christ is efficacious, and we receive the blessings.

> We know also that sanctification through the grace of our Lord and Savior, Jesus Christ, is just and true, to all those who love and serve God with all their mights, minds and strength.[6]

Again here we are involved: it is our duty as members of this Church, to serve the Lord our God with all our mights, with all our minds, with all our strength, and as it is stated in another revelation, with all our hearts. That is our duty—not to serve him half-heartedly, not to accept a portion of the commandments—only, not to receive only those things which appeal to us, and refuse to accept those principles which do not appeal to us. We should be converted in full to the gospel of Jesus Christ.

"Take Heed and Pray Always"

Now let me read this:

> But there is a possibility that man may fall from grace and depart from the living God;
>
> Therefore let the Church take heed and pray always, lest they fall into temptation—(not only the Church collectively, but you and me; let us take heed.)[7]

Never in the history of the world, that is, in the history of the Church, have there been so many temptations, so many pitfalls, so many dangers, to lure away the members of the Church from the path of duty and from righteousness, as we find today. Every day of our lives we come in contact with these temptations, these dangers. We should continue in the spirit of prayer and faith, remembering that there is this possibility that we may turn from the grace of the living God, and fall, unless we continue in that humility, in the exercise of faith and obedience to every principle of truth.

The Word of the Lord Should Be Revered

In another of these revelations the Lord says—I think I will read it, instead of attempting to quote it:

> And I now give unto you a commandment to beware concerning yourselves, to give diligent heed to the words of eternal life.
>
> For you shall live by every word that proceedeth forth from the mouth of God.
>
> For the word of the Lord is truth, and whatsoever is truth is light, and whatsoever is light is Spirit, even the Spirit of Jesus Christ.
>
> And the Spirit giveth light to every man that cometh into the world; and the Spirit enlighteneth every man through the world, that hearkeneth to the voice of the Spirit.[8]

So we are commanded here to give heed concerning ourselves, each of us individually, as to the words of eternal life, how we hold them. We should hold them sacred. It is just as much my obligation, and yours, after baptism, to be humble, to have that contrite spirit, that broken heart, and the desire to forsake all sin, as it was before we came into this Church through the waters of baptism.

Mortality, the Foundation for Perfection

I often think, and I suppose you do, too, of that great and wonderful discourse—the greatest that was ever preached, so far as we know—which we call the Sermon on the Mount, in which instructions of various kinds were given by our Lord for the benefit of the members of the Church of all ages, by which, if we will only hearken to those teachings, we may come back again into the presence of God, the Father, and his Son Jesus Christ.

I often think of that which is really a summation:

> Be ye therefore perfect, even as your Father which is in heaven is perfect.[9]

I have heard many discourses upon that, with which I could not agree, not fully, because I believe the Lord meant just what he said, that we should be perfect, as our Father in heaven is perfect. That will not come all at once, but line upon line and precept upon precept, example upon example, and even then not as long as we live in this mortal life, for we will have to go even beyond the grave, before we reach that perfection and shall be like God.

But here we lay the foundation. Here is where we are taught these simple truths of the gospel of Jesus Christ, in this probationary state, to prepare us for that perfection. It is my duty, it is yours, to be better today than I was yesterday, and for you to be better today than you were yesterday, and better tomorrow than you were today. Why? Because we are on that road, if we are keeping the commandments of the Lord, we are on that road to perfection, and that can only come through obedience and the desire in our hearts to overcome the world. That is all.

Weaknesses Conquered Through Concentrated Effort

There should be no sin in The Church of Jesus Christ of Latter-day Saints. No man should attempt to excuse himself because he has this failing or that. If we have a failing, if we have a weakness, there is where we should concentrate, with a desire to overcome, until we master and conquer. If a man feels that it is hard for him to pay his tithing, then that is the thing he should do, until he learns to pay his tithing. If it is the Word of Wisdom, that is what he should do, until he learns to love that commandment.

May the Lord bless and guide the members of the Church, and protect us from evil. We know that the world is full of evil. It is a wicked world. The Lord has said that. We have come out of it. We don't belong to it, although we are in it. If we are keeping the commandments of the Lord we have no right and we should have no desire to partake of those things which belong to the world, which are contrary to the kingdom of God.—(*Conference Report*, October, 1941.)

---

[1]D&C 20:37.
[2]2 Nephi 9:27.
[3]Rom. 6:2.
[4]D&C 20:29.
[5]*Ibid.*, 20:30.
[6]*Ibid.*, 20:31.
[7]*Ibid.*, 20:32-33.
[8]*Ibid.*, 84:43-46.
[9]Matt. 5:48.

We have no right to transgress the law of the Sabbath or any of the other laws that are so fundamental to our exaltation, and how can the members of the Church expect to receive salvation and exaltation in the celestial kingdom of God, and show contempt for his sacred commandments?

The Sabbath–A Day of Rest

In his remarks this morning President Clark stated that there are those who would destroy the Constitution of the United States, and there are those who would destroy the Decalogue, or the Ten Commandments. I would like to speak on the Ten Commandments, if time would permit, but since it will not I shall center on one of them—that of keeping the Sabbath day holy.

These commandments have not been abrogated nor annulled, and they are in force as much today, although not observed, as they were when they were thundered from Mount Sinai. The Sabbath day has become a day of pleasure, or revelry, anything but a day of worship, from one border of the country to the other; and I regret to say that too many—one would be too many—members of The Church of Jesus Christ of Latter-day Saints have joined that procession, and the Sabbath day to some members of the Church is looked upon as a day of revelry, of pleasure, rather than one in which we can serve the Lord our God with all our hearts, with all our mights, mind, and strength.

We Have No Right to Transgress

The Lord cannot forgive us when we know better and

we violate his commandments. He has given unto us a law, a commandment, saying that we are to accept the words of the Lord as he has revealed them unto us. We have no right to transgress this law or any one of the other laws that are so fundamental to our exaltation, and how can the members of the Church expect to receive salvation and exaltation in the celestial kingdom of God, and show contempt for his sacred commandments?

I want to read to you a condemnation that the Lord pronounced upon Israel because they refused to keep this commandment.

Wherefore I caused them to go forth out of the land of Egypt, and brought them into the wilderness.

And I gave them my statutes, and shewed them my judgments, which if a man do, he shall even live in them.

Moreover also I gave them my sabbaths, to be a sign between me and them, that they might know that I am the Lord that sanctify them.

But the house of Israel rebelled against me in the wilderness: they walked not in my statutes, and they despised my judgments, which if a man do, he shall even live in them; and my sabbaths they greatly polluted: then I said, I would pour out my fury upon them in the wilderness, to consume them.

But I wrought for my name's sake, that it should not be polluted before the heathen, in whose sight I brought them out.

Yet also I lifted up my hand unto them in the wilderness, that I would not bring them into the land which I had given them, flowing with milk and honey, which is the glory of all lands;

Because they despised my judgments, and walked not in my statutes, but polluted my sabbaths: for their heart went after their idols.

Nevertheless mine eye spared them from destroying them, neither did I make an end of them in the wilderness.

But I said unto their children in the wilderness, Walk ye not in the statutes of your fathers, neither observe their judgments, nor defile yourselves with their idols:

I am the Lord your God; walk in my statutes, and keep my judgments, and do them;

And hallow my sabbaths; and they shall be a sign between me and you, that ye may know that I am the Lord your God.[1]

Lord Still Pleads with Backsliders

Those are the words of the Lord to Ezekiel. Notwithstanding all their backsliding and their wickedness and their violation of his commandments, the Lord still pleaded with them; and in the days of Ezekiel, after the greatest number of the tribes of Israel had been carried off because of their rebellion, the Lord pleaded with those who still remained to keep his sabbaths, to walk in his statutes—and even then they refused. Yet he said if they would do these things, it was a covenant with him, and by keeping that covenant he would bless them.

Now, this is the law to the Church today just as it was the law to ancient Israel, and some of our people get rather disturbed because they feel that observing the Sabbath day curtails their activities. So I want to read to you now the commandment the Lord has given to modern Israel, and this we ought to learn to keep.

> Wherefore, I give unto you a commandment, saying thus: Thou shalt love the Lord thy God, with all thy heart, with all thy might, mind, and strength; and in the name of Jesus Christ thou shalt serve him.
>
> Thou shalt love thy neighbor as thyself. Thou shalt not steal; neither commit adultery, nor kill, nor do anything like unto it.
>
> Thou shalt thank the Lord thy God in all things.
>
> Thou shalt offer a sacrifice unto the Lord thy God in righteousness, even that of a broken heart and a contrite spirit.
>
> And that thou mayest more fully keep thyself unspotted from the world, thou shalt go to the house of prayer and offer up thy sacraments upon my holy day;
>
> For verily this is a day appointed unto you to rest from your labors, and to pay thy devotions unto the Most High;
>
> Nevertheless thy vows shall be offered up in righteousness on all days and at all times;
>
> But remember that on this, the Lord's day, thou shalt offer thine oblations and thy sacraments unto the Most High, confessing thy sins unto thy brethren, and before the Lord.
>
> And on this day thou shalt do none other thing, only let thy

food be prepared with singleness of heart that thy fasting may be perfect, or, in other words, that thy joy may be full.

Verily, this is fasting and prayer, or in other words, rejoicing and prayer.

And inasmuch as ye do these things with thanksgiving, with cheerful hearts and countenances, not with much laughter, for this is sin, but with a glad heart and a cheerful countenance—

Verily I say, that inasmuch as ye do this, the fulness of the earth is yours, the beasts of the field and the fowls of the air, and that which climbeth upon the trees and walketh upon the earth;

Yea, and the herb, and the good things which come of the earth, whether for food or for raiment, or for houses, or for barns, or for orchards, or for gardens, or for vineyards.

Yea, all things which come of the earth, in the season thereof, are made for the benefit and the use of man, both to please the eye and to gladden the heart;

Yea, for food and for raiment, for taste and for smell, to strengthen the body and to enliven the soul.

And it pleaseth God that he hath given all these things unto man; for unto this end were they made to be used, with judgment, not to excess, neither by extortion.

And in nothing doth man offend God, or against none is his wrath kindled, save those who confess not his hand in all things, and obey not his commandments.[2]

We Must Stop Violating the Sabbath

Now, my good brethren and sisters, when you go home from this conference, you cannot go home and say, "The brethren have praised us for our welldoing; they have commended us because we have come into The Church of Jesus Christ of Latter-day Saints." We cannot say this when we remember our shortcomings in regard to the keeping of some of these commandments which the Lord has given us, and which pertain to his celestial kingdom.

We must stop violating the Sabbath day. We must stop the violation of other commandments, should we be violating them, and I promise you that if you will observe the Sabbath day, you who are opening your stores on the Sabbath day, if you will close them and tend to the duties that the Lord has given to you, and keep his commandments, that you will prosper and he will bless you more abundantly, for he has made that promise. You will not be blessed by showing your contempt for the commandments which he has given unto us.—(*Conference Report,* April 6, 1957.)

---

[1]Ezek. 20:10-20.
[2]D&C 59:5-21.

We all have the right to know the truth. It is a requirement the Lord makes of every member of the Church that he know for himself and have a testimony of the truth in his own heart and not be under the necessity of depending upon anyone else to know that Jesus Christ is the Son of God or that Joseph Smith is a prophet of God.

Be Not Deceived

I shall take for my text a few verses from the forty-sixth section of the Doctrine and Covenants:

> But ye are commanded in all things to ask of God, who giveth liberally; and that which the Spirit testifies unto you even so I would that ye should do in all holiness of heart, walking uprightly before me, considering the end of your salvation, doing all things with prayer and thanksgiving, that ye may not be seduced by evil spirits, or doctrines of devils, or the commandments of men; for some are of men, and others of devils.
>
> Wherefore, beware lest ye are deceived; and that ye may not be deceived seek ye earnestly the best gifts, always remembering for what they are given.[1]

President Clark said we are a singing people, but I am inclined to think, while that is true, we are not a studious people, that as members of the Church we have not taken advantage of our opportunities to learn, to make ourselves acquainted with the plan of salvation, the commandments of the Lord pertaining to our exaltation. We have not considered the Book of Mormon and the Doctrine and Covenants and the Pearl of Great Price as thoroughly as we should have done, and that is also true of the Bible.

The Lord Revealed the Gospel

The Lord in his mercy and kindness sent angels from his presence to reveal the gospel and to make known the record of the ancient inhabitants of this continent, the Jaredites and the Nephites and Lamanites. Likewise by the inspiration and guidance of his Spirit, he revealed to the Prophet Joseph Smith many of the precious things that were taken out of the writings of the prophets, and we have them restored again. But are we reading them? Are we making ourselves acquainted with these commandments, these precious truths which have been made known for our salvation? Have we ever stopped to think of the great advantage that we have over the rest of the Christian world in this fact, that they maintain that the Bible contains the full word of God, that revelation from him ceased nearly two thousand years ago? Men are left now to depend upon that written word. But the Lord has revealed to us the history of these other ancient peoples. He has given unto us the commandments and the revelations that were given to them, and so earnestly did he feel the responsibility of giving to us this additional information that he sent an angel from his presence to reveal it.

Are we, who profess to believe in the mission of the Prophet Joseph Smith, to testify that angels came to him, and through them that the gospel was restored, the priesthood again revealed and given to men? Do we feel that we are under any responsibilities to search these scriptures and make ourselves familiar with them? I wonder. It is my understanding, I hope I am wrong, that a great multitude of members of this Church have never read the Book of Mormon, are not acquainted with the Doctrine and Covenants, who have not taken the time to consider the commandments that have been revealed for our eternal good, and that to our detriment.

Many Spirits Abroad in the Land

Now we know that there are many spirits abroad in the land, and as the Lord says, some of their doctrines are doctrines of devils; some are the commandments of men. Are we prepared by our knowledge and understanding to segregate these doctrines which are of men and which are of devils, from the truth? Are we living near enough unto the Lord to have that spirit of discernment, that we are entitled, as we would be through our humility and faith, to know the truth that would make us free?

In an earlier revelation, the Lord said:

> And whoso having faith you shall confirm in my church, by the laying on of the hands, and I will bestow the gift of the Holy Ghost upon them.[2]

We have the right to the guidance of the Holy Ghost, but we can't have that guidance if we wilfully refuse to consider the revelations that have been given to help us to understand and to guide us in the light and truth of the everlasting gospel. We can't hope to have that guidance when we refuse to consider these great revelations which mean so much to us both temporally and spiritually. Now if we find ourselves in this condition of unbelief or unwillingness to seek for the light and the knowledge which the Lord has placed within our reach, then we are liable or in danger of being deceived by evil spirits, the doctrine of devils, and the teachings of men. And when these false influences are presented before us, we will not have the distinguishing understanding by which we can segregate them and know that they are not of the Lord. And so we may become prey unto the ungodly, to the vicious, to the cunning, to the craftiness of men.

We all have a right to know the truth. It is a requirement the Lord makes of every member of the Church that he know for himself and have a testimony of the truth in his own heart and not be under the necessity of depending upon anyone else to know that Jesus Christ is the Son of God or that Joseph Smith is a prophet of God. If there is any person in the sound of my voice, a member of this Church, who does not know in his heart that the Father and the Son appeared to Joseph Smith, revealed themselves, and made known again the true doctrine concerning God, then that person has not lived up to his or her requirements, the commandments the Lord has placed upon us, for we should know that fact. We should know that John the Baptist came and restored the Aaronic Priesthood. We ought not to have to depend upon any other source, only the light of truth which is planted in our hearts by the Holy Spirit through our faithfulness. We should know that Peter, James, and John came and restored the Melchizedek Priesthood with all its powers, so that the gospel again could be preached, the knowledge of God declared, and righteousness again be found in the earth, for the salvation of all those who would repent of their sins and turn unto God.

I have in my pocket an invitation sent to me personally; it may be many of you have received one that was sent to you personally, inviting me to attend one of the churches to make myself familiar with the doctrines. Now the man who sent this had a perfect right to send it. He has a right to send this to you and to give you that invitation, but do you have faith enough, knowledge enough of the gospel of Jesus Christ that you would not be deceived if you should accept the invitation, and go and listen to the doctrines of the church to which this man belongs? Do you know the truth?

I have a testimony, definitely, positively that our Father in heaven restored the gospel of Jesus Christ, that Joseph Smith told the truth. I know that the Father and the Son appeared to him, just as well as I know I am here. I know that Jesus Christ is the Son of God, the Redeemer of the world, the Savior of men who will repent and receive his gospel. Are we all prepared so that we will not be subject to the cunning craftiness of men, to the false doctrines that are in the world, the teachings that are contrary to the plan of eternal salvation? If we are not, then we need to repent.

I am going to read to you a statement that I made sometime ago which I think is true, and which is a guide to me and I hope may be to you.

So far as the philosophy and wisdom of the world are concerned, they mean nothing unless they conform to the revealed word of God. Any doctrine, whether it comes in the name of religion, science, philosophy, or whatever it may be, if it is in conflict with the revealed word of the Lord, will fail. It may appear plausible. It may be put before you in language that appeals and which you may not be able to answer. It may appear to be established by evidence that you cannot controvert, but all you need to do is to abide your time. Time will level all things. You will find that every doctrine, every principle, no matter how universally believed, if it is not in accord with the divine word of the Lord to his servants, will perish. Nor is it necessary for us to try to stretch the word of the Lord in a vain attempt to make it conform to these theories and teachings. The word of the Lord shall not pass away unfulfilled, but these false doctrines and theories will all fail. Truth, and only truth, will remain when all else has perished. The Lord has said,

> And truth is knowledge of things as they are, and as they were, and as they are to come.[3]—(*Conference Report,* October, 1952.)

---

[1]D&C 46:7-8.
[2]*Ibid.,* 33:15.
[3]*Ibid.,* 93:24.

Why should a man in idleness partake of the industry of the industrious—provided that this man who is idle, is in a physical condition that he can work? I am not at all in sympathy with any kind of movement that tends to destroy manhood by encouraging men to be idle, and I don't care what age that is. It doesn't matter how old he gets, if a man is physically strong and is able to perform services, he should take care of himself; that the Lord expects him to do.

"The Idler Shall Not Have Place in the Church"

On the second day of January, in the year 1831, the Lord gave a revelation to the Church and in that revelation commanded them to move from the headquarters then established in New York to the Ohio. He gives the reason for it:

> And that ye might escape the power of the enemy, and be gathered unto me a righteous people, without spot and blameless—
>
> Wherefore, for this cause I gave unto you the commandment that ye should go to the Ohio; and there I will give unto you my law; and there you shall be endowed with power from on high.[1]

In obedience to this commandment the people moved to the Ohio. The law the Lord gave, spoken of here in this promise, is found in Section 42, in large part at least, of the Doctrine and Covenants. In this revelation many things are recorded for our benefit. I am only sorry that we have not always adhered strictly to these commandments. Of course, I cannot mention all of the things recorded in this revelation, for there are many, but I desire to speak of one or two that were given for the benefit of the Church. First of all, let me say that when Adam was driven out of the Garden of Eden, the Lord passed a sentence upon him. Some people have looked upon that sentence as being a dreadful thing. It was not; it was a blessing. I don't know that it can truthfully be considered even as a punishment in disguise. The Lord said to him: "In the sweat of thy face shalt thou eat bread,"[2] and all down through the ages the Lord has called upon his people to be diligent, to serve him in faithfulness, to work. And here in verses forty to forty-two in this revelation I read:

> And again, thou shalt not be proud in thy heart; let all thy garments be plain, and their beauty the beauty of the work of thine own hands;
>
> And let all things be done in cleanliness before me.
>
> Thou shalt not be idle; for he that is idle shall not eat the bread nor wear the garments of the laborer.[3]

And to this I wish to speak.

Stress Placed upon Industry

In the early days of the Church in these valleys, great stress was placed upon industry by President Brigham Young and the other brethren, and it was necessary because our forefathers came here with nothing. They had to work. They had to be industrious. It was essential that they produce the things they needed, and therefore counsel to that extent and in that direction was given to them constantly that they should be industrious. They were taught not to be proud in their hearts. They came out here where they could worship the Lord their God and keep his commandments. They were told to be humble as well as to be diligent. They were to make their own garments, and they were to be plain. Oh, I wish we could remember that. I am sorry that we have forgotten. And President Brigham Young, Heber C. Kimball, and others of the brethren in those early days taught the people and prevailed upon them to start industries throughout this country, to raise sheep, to gather the wool, to make their own clothes out of that wool, to plant cotton that they might have cotton also to make clothing, to plant flax that they might get linen, to build tanneries that they might tan the hides and make themselves leather, and a thousand other things.

We used to have some of these industries here among us, and would still have them if we had been willing to adhere to these counsels that had been given to us in those early days by the authorities of the Church, which we would not do. I used to wear suits that were made at Provo, in the woolen mills. I did that as long as I could get them. The suit I have on now was not made at Provo, nor was it made in Utah—that is the cloth—but the tailor made it here. Last week at a stake conference, I made the statement that I did not believe there was in that building an individual born in this country who knew how to make a suit of clothes. If there was one there, would he please make himself manifest, and nobody made himself manifest. Then I said, "If there's a cobbler in this room, he was not born in this country. If there is a cobbler here, let him stand up." Nobody stood. There was no cobbler. And so we might go on.

Let No Man Be Idle

Now, the Lord said, "Let all things be done in cleanliness before me." I could spend some time on that, but time will not permit; so I continue, the Lord said, "Thou shalt not be idle for he that is idle shall not eat the bread, nor wear the garments of the laborer." That is good sound sense, isn't it? Why should a man in idleness partake of the industry of the industrious—provided that this man who is idle, is in a physical condition that he can work? I am not at all in sympathy with any kind of movement that tends to destroy manhood by encouraging men to be idle, and I don't care what age that is. It doesn't matter how old he gets, if a man is physically strong and is able to perform services, he should take care of himself; that the Lord expects him to do.

The Lord said in another revelation:

And again, verily I say unto you, that every man who is obliged to provide for his own family, let him provide, and he shall in nowise lose his crown; and let him labor in the church.

Let every man be diligent in all things. And the idler shall not have place in the church, except he repent and mend his ways.[4]

So that is the counsel the Lord has given the Church today. And this is not merely to be applied to plowing fields, or to reaping and harvesting and engaging in industry, but it means likewise that a man should be industrious in spiritual things as well as in the temporalities by which he makes his living.

Again, here is another commandment the Lord gave:

And the inhabitants of Zion also shall remember their labors, inasmuch as they are appointed to labor, in all faithfulness; for the idler shall be had in remembrance before the Lord.

Now, I, the Lord, am not well pleased with the inhabitants of Zion, for there are idlers among them; and their children are also growing up in wickedness; they also seek not earnestly the riches of eternity, but their eyes are full of greediness.[5]

If the Lord were speaking to us today, I wonder if he would not put even more emphasis upon this commandment.

And again, the Lord said of his servants who preach the gospel:

. . . I give unto them a commandment, thus: Thou shalt not idle away thy time, neither shalt thou bury thy talent that it may not be known.[6]

And that means whatever that talent may be, the man should not bury it. If he is a mechanic, if he is skilled in some other direction, if he has the power and ability to preach the gospel, whatever it is, the Lord expects him to use that talent in his service.

Words of President Joseph F. Smith

Let me present a statement here from President Joseph F. Smith:

> There should be no idlers in Zion. Even the poor who have to be assisted should be willing to do all in their power to earn their own living. Not one man or woman should be content to sit down and be fed, clothed, or housed without an exertion on his or her part to compensate for these privileges. All men and women should feel a degree of independence of character that would stimulate them to do something for a living and not be idle; for it is written that the idler shall not eat the bread of the laborer in Zion, and he shall not have place among us. Therefore, it is necessary that we should be industrious, that we should intelligently apply our labor to something that is productive and conducive to the welfare of the human family.[7]

And then, President Brigham Young: out of all the many things that he has said, let me present this:

> We want you henceforth to be a self-sustaining people. Hear it, O Israel! hear it, neighbors, friends and enemies, this is what the Lord requires of this people. . . . Ye Latter-day Saints learn to sustain yourselves, produce everything you need to eat, drink or wear; and if you cannot obtain all you wish for today, learn to do without that which you cannot purchase and pay for; and bring your minds into subjection that you must live within your means. . . . Who are deserving of praise? The persons who take care of themselves or the ones who always trust in the great mercies of the Lord to take care of them? It is just as consistent to expect that the Lord will supply us with fruit when we do not plant the trees; or that when we do not plow and sow and are saved the labor of harvesting, we should cry to the Lord to save us from want, as to ask him to save us from the consequences of our own folly, disobedience and waste. . . .
>
> Brethren, learn. You have learned a good deal, it is true, but learn more; learn to sustain yourselves; lay up grain and flour and save it against a day of scarcity. Sisters, do not ask your husbands to sell the last bushel of grain you have to buy something for you out of the stores, but aid your husbands in storing it up against a day of want, and always have a year's, or two, provision on hand.[8]

I hope the time will come when we will not feel restricted and will be able to lay up in store for a year or two in advance.—(*Conference Report,* April, 1945.)

---

[1]D&C 38:31-32.
[2]Gen. 3:19.
[3]D&C 42:40-42.
[4]*Ibid.,* 75:28-29.
[5]*Ibid.,* 68:30-31.
[6]*Ibid.,* 60:13.
[7]*Gospel Doctrine,* pp. 235-236.
[8]*Discourses of Brigham Young,* p. 293.

To know the way to eternal life is far more important than all the learning that the world can give.

The Way to Eternal Life

Near the close of a discourse by our Lord and Savior, many believed on him. It is written:

> Then said Jesus to those Jews which believed on him, If ye continue in my word, then are ye my disciples indeed;
>
> And ye shall know the truth, and the truth shall make you free.[1]

The only truth that makes us free is the truth of the gospel of Jesus Christ. In fact, all truth belongs to the gospel of Jesus Christ. When our Savior was brought before Pilate, Pilate questioned him and asked him if he were a king. Jesus answered,

> Thou sayest that I am a king. To this end was I born, and for this cause came I into the world, that I should bear witness unto the truth. Every one that is of the truth heareth my voice.[2]

Then Pilate asked him, "What is truth?" Perhaps the Savior had no time given him to answer. Perhaps he was silent, and from that time until now volumes have been written asking that question. The only true answer that has been given was given by the Lord to the Prophet Joseph Smith.

And truth is knowledge of things as they are, and as they were, and as they are to come.[3]

In other words, truth is that which endures. All else must perish. This being true, it behooves us to search for truth—this truth the Savior spoke of that makes us free.

Not All Truth Is of Same Value

Not all truth is of the same value or importance. Some truths are greater than others. The greatest truth, or the greatest truths, we find in the fundamentals of the gospel of Jesus Christ. First of all, that Jesus Christ is the Son of God, the Redeemer of the world, who came into this world to die that men might live. That truth we should know. It is far more important to know that Jesus Christ is our Redeemer, that he has given unto us the principles of eternal life, than it is to know all that can be obtained in secular education.

It is far more important to know that baptism is for the remission of sins, and when properly performed by one who has the authority, remission of sins will come, and through the baptism following, of the Holy Ghost, we come back into the presence of God our Father, at last, through the guidance of the Holy Ghost.

To know the way to eternal life is far more important than all the learning that the world can give. We find that in the sacred principles which have been revealed for the last time, and in these ordinances which are being performed for the last time—that is, in the dispensation of the fulness of times—for the gospel will never be restored again. It has been restored to remain. The Lord has ordained his servants, and has given them authority to execute his laws, to preach his gospel, to cry repentance, to call upon men to humble themselves and receive these fundamental principles of eternal life.

The way of eternal life is here. The covenants that were promised that lead to that great gift are here. All men on the face of the earth have now the privilege not only of repentance, but also of remission of sins through the waters of baptism, and the gift of the Holy Ghost by the laying on of hands, and to receive the covenants and obligations which were promised anciently that will bring them back into the presence of God, our Father.

These blessings are free. They are the most important truths in all the world. Brethren and sisters, we have received them. Let us be true and faithful, turning neither to the right nor to the left in the keeping of the commandments of the Lord, and by example as well as by precept, serve him.—(*Conference Report,* April, 1955.)

[1]John 8:31-32.
[2]*Ibid.,* 18:37.
[3]D&C 93:24.

[illegible] not only at [illegible] through the waters of [illegible] the Holy Ghost by the laying on of hands [illegible] which [illegible] bring them back into the [illegible]

[illegible] the most important [illegible] we have [illegible] commandments of [illegible] as well as [illegible] (C[illegible] 1895.)

We are all aware that we are in imminent danger—danger because Satan rages in the hearts of the people. This has all been predicted and the predictions are coming true. Antichrist is gaining power, and Satan has put into the hearts of the people—the majority of them—greed, and the desire to dominate and take advantage of those who are weak.

Fulfilment of Prophecy

I am very grateful for the meeting that was held this morning and for the good counsel that was given to the members of the Church. I pray that we will heed it and remember that we are living in a wicked world where men's hearts have turned from truth to untruth, from righteousness to wickedness; when men are unrighteously ambitious, seeking for power; when the liberties of the people are in danger. It behooves us as members of the Church to heed the counsels that are given by those who stand as our leaders under Jesus Christ.

I am grateful for the gospel, for all the privileges which are mine to give service, for the privilege that is mine to honor my Maker and be a true servant to our Master, the Savior and Redeemer of the world.

We are all aware that we are in imminent danger—danger because Satan rages in the hearts of the people. This has all been predicted, and the predictions are coming true. Antichrist is gaining power, and Satan has put into the hearts of the people—the majority of them—greed, and the desire to dominate and take advantage of those who are weak.

Our Duty Is to Keep the Commandments

Our duty is to keep the commandments of the Lord, to walk uprightly, to defend every principle of truth, to sustain and uphold the Constitution of this great country, to remember the Declaration of Independence, for, as we heard this morning from our President, upon these principles our country was based. They stand at the foundation, the cornerstones of the liberty that our fathers fought for, and which brought to pass according to the word of the Lord, the redemption of this land by the shedding of blood.

There is no other course for us to take but the course of righteousness and truth. An ancient prophet on this continent said, ". . . the natural man is an enemy to God."[1] The world today has become carnal, as much so now as in the beginning when Adam attempted to teach his children the principles of eternal truth, and Satan came among them and commanded them to believe it not.

And we read, "From that time forth man became carnal, sensual, and devilish."[2]

Surely we see these indications prevalent in our own land and in foreign lands. Men have become carnal. They have become enemies to God. They are seeking for their own advancement and not for the advancement of the kingdom of God.

Let me call your attention to this fact which you, of course, all know, that we are living in the last days, the days of trouble, days of wickedness, spoken of as days of wickedness several hundred years before the coming of Christ by Nephi, as it is recorded in the twenty-seventh chapter of Second Nephi.

> But, behold, in the last days, or in the days of the Gentiles—yea, behold all the nations of the Gentiles and also the Jews, both those who shall come upon this land and those who shall be upon other lands, yea, even upon all the lands of the earth, behold, they will be drunken with iniquity and all manner of abominations.

And when that day shall come they shall be visited of the Lord of Hosts, with thunder and with earthquake, and with a great noise, and with storm, and with tempest, and with the flame of devouring fire.[3]

The Days of the Gentiles

That was said many hundreds of years before the birth of Christ. We are living in the days of the Gentiles when this prediction was to be fulfilled. We see it being fulfilled, and we must remember, my good brethren and sisters, that members of the Church are not members of, and do not belong to the world.

In the wonderful prayer of our Redeemer, as recorded in the seventeenth chapter of John—I can hardly read this chapter without tears coming to my eyes—wherein our Lord, in praying to his Father in the tenderness of all his soul because he knew the hour had come for him to offer himself as a sacrifice, prayed for his disciples. In that prayer he said,

I pray not that thou shouldest take them out of the world, but that thou shouldest keep them from the evil.

They are not of the world, even as I am not of the world.

Sanctify them through thy truth: thy word is truth.[4]

If we are living the religion which the Lord has revealed and which we have received, we do not belong to the world. We should have no part in all its foolishness. We should not partake of its sins and its errors—errors of philosophy and errors of doctrine, errors in regard to government, or whatever those errors may be—we have no part in it.

The only part we have is the keeping of the commandments of God. That is all, being true to every covenant and every obligation that we have entered into and taken upon ourselves.

Brother Kimball in his remarks this morning spoke of a man who could not quite understand when he paid his tithing and kept the Word of Wisdom, was prayerful, and tried to be obedient to all the commandments the Lord had given him, and yet he had to struggle to make a living; while his neighbor violated the Sabbath day, I suppose he smoked and drank; he had what the world would call a good time, he paid no attention to the teachings of our Lord and Savior Jesus Christ, and yet he prospered.

You know, we have a great many members of the Church that ponder that over in their hearts and wonder why. Why this man seems to be blessed with all the good things of the earth—incidentally, many of the bad things that he thinks are good—and yet so many members of the Church are struggling, laboring diligently to try to make their way through the world.

The Answer Is Simple

The answer is a simple thing. If I sometimes, and once in a while I do, go to a football game or a baseball game or some other place of amusement, invariably I will be surrounded by men and women who are puffing on cigarets or cigars or dirty pipes. It gets very annoying, and I get a little disturbed. I will turn to Sister Smith, and I will say something to her, and she will say, "Well, now, you know what you have taught me. You are in *their* world. This is their world." And that sort of brings me back to my senses. Yes, we are in their world, but we do not have to be of it.

So, as this is their world we are living in, they prosper, but, my good brethren and sisters, their world is coming to its end. It will not be many years. I can say that. I do not know how many years, but Elijah said when he bestowed his keys: ". . . by this ye may know that the great and dreadful day of the Lord is near, even at the doors."[5] I am sure that over a hundred years later I can say that this world is drawing to its end.

The day will come when we will not have *this* world. It will be changed. We will get a better world. We will get one that is righteous, because when Christ comes, he will cleanse the earth.

Read what is written in our scriptures. Read what he himself has said. When he comes, he will cleanse this earth from all its wickedness, and speaking of the Church, he has said that he would send his angels and they would gather out of his kingdom, which is the Church, all things that offend. Then we are going to have a new earth, a new heaven. The earth will be renewed for a thousand years, and there shall be peace, and Christ, whose right it is, shall reign. Afterwards will come the death of the earth, its resurrection, its glorification, as the abode of the righteous or they who belong to the celestial kingdom, and they only shall dwell upon the face of it.

Let us be true and faithful, keep our covenants, be true to every obligation the Lord has given us.—(*Conference Report,* April, 1952.)

[1]Mosiah 3:19.
[2]Moses 5:13.
[3]2 Nephi 27:1-2.
[4]John 17:15-17.
[5]D&C 110:16.

We may safely say that today the anger of the Lord is kindled against this generation for its wickedness and the earth again groans under the weight of iniquity which is practiced upon its face. The Almighty has not forgotten his promise made to Enoch, and the day is soon at hand when the earth again will be cleansed of all iniquity and shall rest for a thousand years.

"Watch Therefore"

During the past two years the question has constantly arisen and been discussed in priesthood classes, Sunday Schools and in private conversations—"Is this great war which has cast its evil shadow over a large portion of the world, and which threatens to engulf all the rest of mankind, the great last war to precede the second coming of our Lord, as predicted by the prophets?"

We may answer this question by saying we truly hope that it is; but the Lord definitely informed his disciples that not even the angels in heaven knew the day nor the hour when he should make his appearance, but his Father only. Therefore unless the Lord sees fit to reveal to us the information, we do not know when or where this great conflict will end.

Great Day Near

This much we may know, for the Lord has revealed it very explicitly: The distress and perplexity, bloodshed and terror, selfish ambition of despotic rulers, such as the world has never before seen, all indicate that the great and dreadful day of the Lord is very near, even at our doors. We have been warned by the prophets from the beginning of time.

They have declared by revelation from the Lord, that in this present day, confusion, bloodshed, misery, plague, famine, earthquake and other calamities, would cover the face of the earth. The Lord told his disciples of these dreadful scenes and said men's hearts would fail them because of these things coming upon the earth:

> Ye look and behold the fig trees, and ye see them with your eyes, and ye say when they begin to shoot forth, and their leaves are yet tender, that summer is now nigh at hand.
>
> Even so it shall be in that day when they shall see all these things, then shall they know that the hour is nigh.
>
> And it shall come to pass that he that feareth me shall be looking forth for the great day of the Lord to come, even for the sign of the coming of the Son of Man.
>
> And they shall see signs and wonders, for they shall be shown forth in the heavens above, and in the earth beneath;
>
> And they shall behold blood, and fire, and vapors of smoke.
>
> And before the day of the Lord shall come, the sun shall be darkened, and the moon be turned into blood, and the stars fall from heaven.[1]

We Were Warned

It is very evident from what we see daily in the papers that we are living in perilous times. The present condition of the world should not, however, cause us any great surprise, for we have been amply informed that these days are at hand. Only the unbelieving and rebellious against the teachings of our Lord and his prophets, have failed to comprehend these momentous events. Enoch saw our day, in fact, the Lord revealed to him the history of mankind from the beginning to the end of time. He was anxious to know when the day would come wherein this earth should be cleansed from all the iniquity upon its face and have rest. The Lord answered him:

> . . . as I live, even so will I come in the last days, in the days of wickedness and vengeance, to fulfil the oath which I have made unto you concerning the children of Noah;

> And the day shall come that the earth shall rest, but before that day the heavens shall be darkened, and a veil of darkness shall cover the earth; and the heavens shall shake, and also the earth; and great tribulation shall be among the children of men, but my people will I preserve.[2]

Our Savior promised that the days preceding his second coming will be typical of the days of the flood. A glance at the sixth chapter of Genesis will reveal the conditions of the world in the days of Noah and the flood and the reason for the cleansing by water. This comparison is not to be taken figuratively, but literally as it is given. The world today is corrupt and filled with violence as it was at that earlier day, for now as then, "All flesh has corrupted his way upon the earth."[3] The Lord promised that he would never again destroy the entire world with a flood of water, but he did promise to cleanse it the second time with sword and with fire.

Remembers Promise

We may safely say that today the anger of the Lord is kindled against this generation for its wickedness and the earth again groans under the weight of iniquity which is practiced upon its face. The Almighty has not forgotten his promise made to Enoch, and the day is soon at hand when the earth again will be cleansed of all iniquity and shall rest for a thousand years.

It is very displeasing to some self-righteous souls to have any one speak of these things and say that punishment, by war, pestilence, famine and the disturbance of the elements, is coming upon mankind by decree of a just God, because of the transgressions of his holy laws. Nevertheless this happens to be the case, for the Lord has declared it. His anger is kindled against the abominations and sins of the world. Let us consider some of these predictions and warnings given to an unbelieving and rebellious generation.

Before doing so, however, it is in order to call attention to the fact that the Lord restored the fulness of the gospel for the salvation of mankind, if men would only hearken and obey his voice and the voice of his servants. His Church has again been established in the world, and the Master sent forth his servants to all parts of the earth proclaiming the day of repentance and salvation. These servants have gone forth crying as did the great prophet and forerunner of our Lord in his former coming, "Repent ye, for the kingdom of heaven is at hand."[4] They were promised that they should go forth with power and authority, "and the voice of warning shall be unto all people, by the mouths of my disciples, whom I have chosen in these last days, and they shall go forth and none shall stay them, for I the Lord have commanded them. . . . Wherefore, fear and tremble, O ye people, for what I the Lord have decreed in them shall be fulfilled." With this commission the servants of the Lord have gone forth with the message of salvation, and where they could not go they have sent the word, so that it has been proclaimed virtually in all parts of the earth. Moreover, the Lord clothed these servants of his with authority and sent them "unto the inhabitants of the earth, to . . . seal both on earth and in heaven the unbelieving and rebellious."[5]

Sword Shall Fall

Yea, verily, to seal them up unto the day when the wrath of God shall be poured out upon the wicked without measure—

Unto the day when the Lord shall come to recompense unto every man according to his work, and measure to every man according to the measure which he has measured to his fellow man.

Wherefore the voice of the Lord is unto the ends of the earth, that all that will hear may hear;

Prepare ye, prepare ye for that which is to come, for the Lord is nigh;

And the anger of the Lord is kindled, and his sword is bathed in heaven, and it shall fall upon the inhabitants of the earth.

And the arm of the Lord shall be revealed; and the day cometh that they who will not hear the voice of the Lord, neither the voice of his servants, neither give heed to the words of the prophets and apostles, shall be cut off from among the people.[6]

On another occasion the Lord said to these servants:

Behold, I sent you out to testify and warn the people and it becometh every man who hath been warned to warn his neighbor.

Therefore, they are left without excuse, and their sins are upon their own heads.[7]

And yet again, this warning has been given:

Hearken ye, for behold, the great day of the Lord is nigh at hand,

For the day cometh that the Lord shall utter his voice out of heaven; the heavens shall shake and the earth shall tremble, and the trump of God shall sound both long and loud, and shall say to the sleeping nations: Ye saints arise and live; ye sinners stay and sleep until I shall call again.

Wherefore gird up your loins lest ye be found among the wicked.

Lift up your voices and spare not. Call upon the nations to repent, both old and young, both bond and free, saying: Prepare yourselves for that great day of the Lord;

For if I, who am a man, do lift up my voice and call upon you to repent, and ye hate me, what will ye say when the day cometh when the thunders shall utter their voices from the ends of the earth, speaking to the ears of all that live, saying—Repent, and prepare for the great day of the Lord?

Yea, and again, when the lightnings shall streak forth from the east unto the west, and shall utter forth their voices unto all that live, and make the ears of all tingle that hear, saying these words—Repent ye, for the great day of the Lord is come?

Hearken to Words

And again, the Lord shall utter his voice out of heaven saying: Hearken, O ye nations of the earth, and hear the words of that God who made you.

O ye nations of the earth, how often would I have gathered you together as a hen gathereth her chickens under her wings, but ye would not!

How oft have I called upon you by the mouth of my servants, and by the ministering of angels, and by mine own voice, and by the voice of thunderings, and the voice of lightnings, and by the voice of tempests, and by the voice of earthquakes, and great hailstorms, and by the voice of famines and pestilences of every kind, and by the great sound of a trump, and by the voice of judgment, and by the voice of mercy all the day long, and by the voice of glory and honor and the riches of eternal life, and would have saved you with an everlasting salvation, but ye would not!

Behold the day has come, when the cup of the wrath of mine indignation is full.

Behold, verily I say unto you, that these are the words of the Lord your God.[8]

With these instructions, commandments and warnings, these missionaries of the Lord went forth humbly proclaiming this message of everlasting life unto the world. Many of the righteous, those of the scattered sheep of the house of Israel, were gathered out from the nations and have come to Zion with songs of everlasting joy, while the great majority of mankind have rejected these counsels and warnings, refusing to heed the revealed word of the Lord which was declared to them.

Testimony of Earthquakes

Once more the Lord issued a warning saying that after the testimony of his servants to the world—

. . . cometh the testimony of earthquakes, that shall cause groanings in the midst of her, and men shall fall upon the ground and shall not be able to stand.

And also cometh the testimony of the voice of thunderings, and the voice of tempests, and the voice of the waves of the sea heaving themselves beyond their bounds.

And all things shall be in commotion; and surely, men's hearts shall fail them; for fear shall come upon all people.[9]

At the very beginning of this dispensation the Lord said he would have all men know, "that the day speedily cometh . . . when peace shall be taken from the earth, and the devil shall have power over his own dominion."[10] Recent events indicate that the devil now has power over his dominion. In another warning the Lord adds this:

For behold, and lo, vengeance cometh speedily upon the ungodly as the whirlwind; and who shall escape it?

The Lord's scourge shall pass over by night and by day, and the report thereof shall vex all people; yea, it shall not be stayed until the Lord come.

For the indignation of the Lord is kindled against their abominations and all their wicked works.[11]

After saying this he pointed out to his people how they may escape in the following words:

Way to Escape

Nevertheless, Zion shall escape if she observe to do all things whatsoever I have commanded her.

But if she observe not to do whatsoever I have commanded her, I will visit her according to all her works, with sore affliction, with pestilence, with plague, with sword, with vengeance, with devouring fire.

Nevertheless, let it be read this once to her ears, that I, the Lord, have accepted of her offering; and if she sin no more none of these things shall come upon her.[12]

This way of escape, insuring the protection of the Lord, is a very simple one. Unfortunately, many of the people of Zion have refused to take advantage of this promise. What a pity it is that people will pay little heed to sacred counsels, and in their madness and love of the things of the world take the hard road and have to receive punishment when there is a means of escape. When these calamities come, what right have the people of Zion to expect protection? And, if the righteous among them are called upon to suffer, the sin will be at the door of the rebellious who have not hearkened to this counsel.

We were informed that when the testimony of the missionaries should be withdrawn from the world, *then* should come the testimony of the voice of calamity. The missionaries have been withdrawn from the greater part of the world in fulfilment of the Lord's prediction. Referring to this eventful day, President Brigham Young once said:

Scarcely a Prelude

Do you think there is a calamity abroad now among the people? . . . All we have heard and all we have experienced is scarcely a preface to the sermon that is going to be preached. *When the testimony of the Elders ceases to be given,* and the Lord says to them, "Come home; I will now preach my own sermons to the nations of the earth," all you now know can scarcely be called a preface to the sermon that will be preached with fire and sword, tempest, earthquake, hail, rain, thunders and lightnings, and fearful destruction. What matters the destruction of a few railway cars? You will hear of magnificent cities, now idolized by the people, sinking in the earth, entombing the inhabitants. The sea will heave itself beyond its bounds, engulfing mighty cities. Famine will spread over the nations, and nation will rise against nation, kingdom against kingdom, and states against states in our own country and in foreign lands; and they will destroy each other, caring not for the blood and lives of their neighbors, of their families, or for their own lives.

They will be like the Jaredites who preceded the Nephites upon this continent and will destroy each other to the last man, through the anger that the devil will place in their hearts, because they have rejected the words of life and are given over to Satan to do whatever he listeth to do with them. You may think that the little you hear of now is grievous; yet the faithful of God's people will see days that will cause them to close their eyes because of the sorrow that will come upon the wicked nations. The hearts of the faithful will be filled with pain and anguish for them.[13]

The parable the Lord taught of the *Wheat and the Tares* had reference to the last days. According to the story a sower planted good seed in his field, but while he slept the enemy came and sowed tares in the field. When the blades began to show, the servants desired to go and pluck up the tares but the Lord commanded them to let both the wheat and the tares grow up together until the harvest was ripe, lest they root up the tender wheat while destroying the tares. Then at the end of the harvest, they were to go forth and gather the wheat and bind the tares to be burned. In the explanation of this parable, the Lord said to his disciples that "the harvest is the *end of the world;* and the reapers are the angels."[14]

Cloud of Darkness

President Wilford Woodruff declared in 1896:

> I want to bear testimony to this congregation, and to the heavens and the earth, that the day is come when those angels are privileged to go forth and commence their work. They are laboring in the United States of America; they are laboring among the nations of the earth; and they will continue. We need not marvel or wonder at anything that is transpiring in the earth. The people of the world do not comprehend the revelations of God. They did not in the days of the Jews; yet all that the prophets had spoken concerning them came to pass. So in our day these things will come to pass. . . . We cannot draw a veil over the events that await this generation. *No man that is inspired by the Spirit and power of God can close his ears, his eyes or his lips to these things.*[15]

Two years earlier he said:

> Over the millions of people on this earth, there hangs a cloud of darkness almost entirely upon their shoulders. Can you tell me where the people are who will be shielded and protected from these great calamities and judgments which are even now at our doors? I will tell you. The *priesthood of God,* who honor their priesthood, and who are worthy of their blessings, are the only ones who shall have their safety and protection. They are the only mortal beings. No other people have a right to be shielded from these judgments. They are at our very doors; not even this people will escape them entirely. They will come down like the judgments of Sodom and Gomorrah, and none but the priesthood will be safe from their fury.
>
> God has held the angels of destruction for many years lest they should reap down the wheat with the tares; but I want to tell you now these angels have left the portals of heaven, and they stand over this people and this nation now, and are hovering over the earth, waiting to pour out the judgments. And *from this very day* they will be poured out. Calamities and troubles are increasing in the earth, and there is a meaning to these things.[16]

Hour is Nigh

It is plain to our vision, if we have the spirit of discernment, that the time spoken of is at hand and the anger of the Lord is now kindled and what he has said is being fulfilled:

> Behold the day has come, when the cup of the wrath of mine indignation is full.[17]
>
> I, the Lord am angry with the wicked; I am holding my Spirit from the inhabitants of the earth.
>
> I have sworn in my wrath, and decreed wars upon the face of the earth, and the wicked shall slay the wicked, and fear shall come upon every man.[18]

Again the Lord said:

> For the hour is nigh and the day soon at hand when the earth is ripe; and all the proud and they that do wickedly shall be as stubble; and I will burn them up, saith the Lord of Hosts; that wickedness shall not be upon the earth.
>
> For the hour is nigh, and that which was spoken by mine apostles must be fulfilled; for as they spoke so shall it come to pass;
>
> For I will reveal myself from heaven with power and great glory, with all the hosts thereof, and dwell in righteousness with men on the earth a thousand years, and the wicked shall not stand.[19]

In regard to the wars now raging on the earth, I am sure the prophets have spoken of them. The Lord told Joseph Smith that the war between the states commencing with the rebellion of South Carolina, was the beginning of the end. At that time peace was taken from the earth, and the prediction was made that *beginning* at that place, eventually war would be "poured out" upon all nations, bringing misery, death, mourning, famine, plague, earthquake, vivid lightnings, etc., causing the "inhabitants of the earth to be made to feel the wrath, and indignation, and chastening hand of an Almighty God, until the consumption decreed hath made a full end of all nations."[20] It appears that now this is in course of fulfilment.

Prophets Tell of Wars

Ezekiel has given us in the 38th and 39th chapters much in detail in relation to the great battle which shall precede the coming of the Son of Man to reign. Daniel also prophesied of these great events, which may even now be on the way to complete consummation. One thing we are given by these prophets definitely to understand is that the great last conflict before Christ shall come, will end at the siege of Jerusalem. So said Ezekiel and Daniel, and the Lord declared to Joel:

> For behold, in those days, and in that time, when I shall bring the captivity of Judah and Jerusalem. (i.e. the return from captivity.)
> I will also gather all nations, and will bring them down into the valley of Jehosaphat, and will plead with them there for my people and for my heritage Israel, whom they have scattered among the nations and parted my land.[21]

At this time, prophesied Joel, will the Lord judge the heathen:

> Put ye in the sickle, for the harvest is ripe; come, get you down; for the press is full, the fats overflow; for their wickedness is great.
> Multitudes, multitudes, in the valley of decision: for the day of the Lord is near in the valley of decision.[22]

So we are given to understand that when the armies gather in Palestine will be the time when the Lord shall come in judgment, and to make the eventful decision which will confound the enemies of his people and establish them in their ancient land forever.

Zechariah is another prophet who has plainly spoken of these great events. According to his predictions the nations will gather and lay siege to Jerusalem. Part of the city will fall with dire consequences to its inhabitants, when a great earthquake will come, the Mount of Olives will cleave in twain and the persecuted people will flee into this valley for safety. At that particular time will the Savior come as their deliverer and show them his hands and his feet. They will look upon him and ask him where he received his wounds, and he will tell them they were received in the house of his friends, he is Jesus Christ, their Redeemer. Then will they fall to the ground and mourn, every family apart, because their ancestors persecuted their King and the children have followed in the footsteps of the fathers.

At that time shall come the redemption of the Jews. Jerusalem shall then be rebuilt and the promises that it shall become a holy city will be fulfilled. The punishment which shall come upon those who lay siege to this land, will be their destruction. The prophets have portrayed this in much detail with all its horrors. These events are confirmed in the revelations to the Prophet Joseph Smith, as found in the Doctrine and Covenants, particularly Sections 29, 45 and 133.[23]

Much could be written in detail regarding these conflicts, but what is written will suffice. It is, of course, a gloomy picture; but is it not the duty of the elders of Israel to speak of these things with warning voice? Shall we close our eyes and our ears and seal our understandings simply because some things are unpleasant to the ear and to the eye? Shall we refuse to raise a warning voice when danger approaches? When trouble is near? When destruction is at our door? Such a course would be cowardly if we know the truth. We cannot cry "all is well" when danger lurks on every side. We must not lull the people to sleep in a false security. President Woodruff declared that "no man that is inspired by the Spirit and power of God can close his ears, his eyes, or his lips to these things!"

The cup of indignation is full and the Lord's wrath is being poured out upon the wicked as he said it would be. Yet we are seeing only the beginnings of sorrow. The whole world needs repentance—repentance and the humble acceptance of the gospel as it has been revealed. This is all that will, or can, save the world from the destruction which awaits it.

Time to Repent

It is time for all those who belong to the Church who have been careless, thoughtless, indifferent, to humble themselves and set their houses in order. It is time for all who have broken sacred covenants to turn from their evil ways. Judgments and punishments are promised for the Sabbath-breakers, the immoral, the unclean, those who lie and cheat and are dishonest with their fellow men. It is time for the backbiters and all who bear false witness, to humble themselves in sackcloth and ashes. It is time for all who have not been honest with the Lord with their tithes to repent and seek forgiveness before it is too late. The day is near at hand when the judgments will be executed upon all those who have been gathered into the kingdom of God who have been rebellious, ungodly, unclean and who have practiced deception and fraud, for the word of the Lord will be fulfilled:

> For the Son of Man shall send forth his angels, and they shall gather out of his kingdom all things that offend, and them which do iniquity.[24]

It is time also for the Gentiles and the Jews in our midst, who have not embraced the gospel and who have not received the testimony of the elders of Israel and the revelations of the Lord, to repent and seek forgiveness and remission of sins in the waters of baptism. The heavens have been opened. The light of truth has been revealed for the *last time,* and it is vital that men do not procrastinate the day of their repentance to the end. These are the last days, and men will be judged according to their works, and that day of judgment is near at hand.

Pluck Out Wicked

> And until that hour there will be foolish virgins among the wise; and at that hour cometh an entire separation of the righteous and the wicked; and in that day will I send mine angels to pluck out the wicked and cast them into unquenchable fire.[25]
>
> Watch therefore: for ye know not what hour your Lord doth come.

But know this, that if the goodman of the house had known in what watch the thief would come, he would have watched, and would not have suffered his house to be broken up.

Therefore be ye also ready; for in such an hour as ye think not the Son of Man cometh.[26]—(Church Section, *The Deseret News,* Aug. 2, 1941.)

---

[1]D&C 45:37-42.
[2]Moses 7:60-61.
[3]Gen. 6:12.
[4]Matt. 3:2.
[5]D&C 1:4-8.
[6]*Ibid.,* 1:8-14.
[7]*Ibid.,* 88:81.
[8]*Ibid.,* 43:17-27.
[9]*Ibid.,* 88:89-91.
[10]*Ibid.,* 1:35.
[11]*Ibid.,* 97:22-24.
[12]*Ibid.,* 97:25-27.
[13]Brigham Young, *J. of D.,* 8:123.
[14]Matt. 13:24-30, 37-40.
[15]Wilford Woodruff, *Millennial Star,* 58:738.
[16]Wilford Woodruff, *Young Woman's Journal,* p. 512.
[17]D&C 43:26.
[18]*Ibid.,* 63:32-33.
[19]*Ibid.,* 29:9-11.
[20]See D&C, Section 87.
[21]Joel 3:1-2.
[22]*Ibid.,* 3:13-14.
[23]Read Zechariah, chapter 14.
[24]Matt. 13:41.
[25]D&C 63:54.
[26]Matt. 24:42-44.

That which we learn in all the experiences of life should be with the ultimate aim of eternity in view. The man who has the correct understanding of things, if he studies anything, it is with the idea that it will be useful to him not merely in this life but through eternity. We, at least, as members of the Church, should conclude that all we learn has a bearing upon the spiritual welfare of man.

"And the Truth Shall Make You Free"

As you have been listening each day since Monday to discourses on the subject "And the Truth Shall Make You Free," I trust that you will pardon me this afternoon if there shall be some criss-crossing and repetition in what I have to say. President Grant, when he was here, stated, if the report in the paper is correct, that this institution was established for the purpose of teaching eternal truth and of making Latter-day Saints. It seems to me that every institution of learning, no matter where it is or what it is, should be teaching eternal truth, and whatever is taught that does not conform to truth must eventually perish. Further, that which we learn in all the experiences of life, should be with the ultimate aim of eternity in view. The man who has the correct understanding of things, if he studies anything it is with the idea that it will be useful to him not merely in this life but through eternity. We, at least, as members of the Church, should conclude that all we learn has a bearing upon the spiritual and eternal welfare of man.

This thought will be the foundation of my remarks this afternoon. The Lord, in one of the revelations to the Church, said that at no time had he ever given a temporal commandment, and yet he had given commandments to the people on various things that we might call temporal.[1] The building of houses, printing presses, tanneries and many other things which were for the benefit and upbuilding of the Church, and yet the Lord declares that these, from his point of view, at least, were not temporal but spiritual commandments.

I will read to you a statement by President Brigham Young:

> All truth is for the salvation of the children of men, for their benefit and learning, for their furtherance in the principles of divine knowledge, and divine knowledge is any matter of fact—truth; and all truth pertains to divinity.[2]

Now, I am sure that when President Young uttered that remarkable thought that he was inspired, and I think that is the view we should take of truth whether it is taught in mathematics or in physics or in history or in any department of education. Whatever we learn should have a bearing upon the eternities and not merely upon this mortal life.

In the early days of the Church, the Lord sent the elders out to preach the gospel. Of course, we understand that these brethren who came into the Church in the year 1830 and 1831 had come out of the sectarian world. They had been trained in the traditions of that world, and they had to eliminate much of the teaching that they had received through their traditions and training before they were properly prepared to teach the gospel. And yet, in their enthusiasm, they went out with a testimony of the truth without a doubt, but they had failed to eliminate or to rid themselves of some of the traditions that they had absorbed before they became members of the Church and which had really become part of them. And the Lord had to call them in question.

The Lord's Counsel to Missionaries

I am going to read to you a few verses from this revelation where the Lord very gently but firmly rebukes these missionaries and tries to put them in order so far as the principles of the gospel are concerned:

> Let us reason even as a man reasoneth one with another, face to face.
>
> Now, when a man reasoneth he is understood of man, because he reasoneth as a man; even so will I, the Lord, reason with you, that you may understand.
>
> Wherefore I the Lord, ask you this question—unto what were ye ordained?
>
> To preach my gospel by the Spirit, even the Comforter, which was sent forth to teach the truth.[3]

And to that they were ordained. Unto that we have been ordained, each one of us. And I am taking this word "ordained" in a broader sense than we usually give to it, for I think that every sister in the Church, every member of the Church—male and female—has been ordained by the power of God—in other words, has been called by commandment—to teach divine truth. I do not mean ordained by the laying on of hands as we ordain elders in the Church. Perhaps that is what the Lord meant in this revelation, but I am using the word in the broader sense, I mean that which has been required of us, which is expected of us as members of this Church by commandment to teach the truth as it has been revealed.

Ordained to Teach Truth

Now, these men were ordained to teach the truth by the Spirit of truth or the Comforter, which is the Holy Ghost. And so, the Lord asked them this question, and said:

> And then received ye spirits which ye could not understand, and received them to be of God; and in this are ye justified?

Behold, ye shall answer this question yourselves; nevertheless, I will be merciful unto you; he that is weak among you hereafter shall be made strong.

Verily, I say unto you, he that is ordained of me and sent forth to preach the word of truth by the Comforter, in the Spirit of truth, doth he preach it by the Spirit of truth, or some other way?

And if it be some other way, it is not of God.

And again, he that receiveth the word of truth, doth he receive it by the Spirit of truth, or some other way?

If it be some other way, it is not of God.

Therefore, why is it that ye cannot understand and know that he that receiveth the word by the Spirit of truth receiveth it as preached by the Spirit of truth?

Wherefore, he that preacheth and he that receiveth understand one another, and both are edified and rejoice together.[4]

We who are called and ordained to the ministry or to teach in The Church of Jesus Christ of Latter-day Saints carry a very grave responsibility. Every man that teaches holds a great responsibility. And he that teaches error and leads men from the path of truth is committing one of the greatest crimes that it is possible for man to commit. If he, through his teachings, is presenting false doctrine, and leading men astray from that which is eternal truth, away from the kingdom of God, he is taking upon himself a grave responsibility for which he will have to answer at the judgment seat of God.

The Lord said in one of the early revelations before the organization of the Church that the worth of souls is great in the sight of God. Then he said if a man should labor all his days and convert but one soul, he should have great joy in the kingdom of our Father, and if he should convert many souls, then much greater would be that joy.[5] Reversing the picture, he who blinds one soul, he who spreads error, he who destroys, through his teachings, divine truth, truth that would lead a man to the kingdom of God and to its fulness, how great shall be his condemnation and his punishment in eternity. For the destruction of a soul is the destruction of the greatest thing that has ever been created.

The Lord's Instructions Continued

Now, to continue the instructions the Lord gave to these elders. What I am going to read now I consider to be one of the greatest truths that was ever revealed to man. I have marveled to think that a boy, unlearned as the Prophet was in as early a period as 1831 could give the world such a thought as this. It seems to me any rational man must reach the conclusion, that Joseph Smith never could have said this of himself, and he could only say it through the inspiration of the spirit of the Lord.

> Wherefore, he that preacheth and he that receiveth, understand one another and both are edified and rejoice together. That is, if the truth is taught.
>
> And that which does not edify is not of God and is darkness.
>
> That which is of God is light; and he that receiveth light, and continueth in God, receiveth more light; and that light groweth brighter and brighter until the perfect day.[6]

What a wonderful saying! That is one of the great gems, a diamond truth, that the Lord has given to us and to the world, if they would receive it, through the Prophet Joseph Smith. No matter what you teach, if it is not of God, it is darkness. And eventually, no matter how well it may be received, it must come to an end.

"That which is of God is light, and he that receiveth light and continueth in God . . ." That is the key to the situation. . . . "receiveth more light, and that light groweth brighter and brighter until the perfect day."

So we understand from this that the man who seeks God and in the Spirit of truth, guided by the Spirit of truth, or the Comforter, and continues in God, will grow in knowledge, in light, in truth, until eventually there will come to him the perfect day of light and truth.

Now, we will not get all that in this life. It is impossible for a man to reach that goal in the few years of mortal existence. But what we learn here, that which is eternal, that which is inspired by the Spirit of truth, will continue with us beyond the grave and then we shall go on, if still continuing in God, to receive light and truth until eventually we shall come to that perfect day.

Now again, in another revelation given to the Church, the Lord adds something to this thought.

> For if you keep my commandments you shall receive of his fulness, and be glorified in me as I am in the Father; therefore, I say unto you, you shall receive grace for grace.
>
> And now, verily I say unto you, I was in the beginning with the Father, and am the Firstborn;
>
> And all those who are begotten through me are partakers of the glory of the same, and are the Church of the Firstborn.
>
> Ye were also in the beginning with the Father; that which is Spirit, even the Spirit of truth;
>
> And truth is knowledge of things as they are, and as they were, and as they are to come:
>
> And whatsoever is more or less than this is the spirit of that wicked one who was a liar from the beginning.
>
> The Spirit of truth is of God. I am the Spirit of truth, and John bore record of me, saying: He receiveth the fulness of truth, yea, even of all truth;
>
> And no man receiveth a fulness unless he keepeth his commandments.
>
> He that keepeth his commandments receiveth truth and light, until he is glorified in truth and knoweth all things.[7]

Fulness of Truth

From these passages of scripture which I have read and which we have accepted as the word of the Lord, coming by revelation from him, teach us that a man cannot receive the fulness of truth except in the kingdom of God.—In other words, if you please, The Church of Jesus Christ of Latter-day Saints. No man, no matter how great his education, no matter how much he studies in the things of the world, no matter what he does in the eternities to come, will ever reach the goal of perfection in truth or the fulness of light and understanding outside of the kingdom of God. And when I say the kingdom of God I have reference to the celestial kingdom.

Let me read this verse again: "And no man receiveth the fulness unless he keepeth his commandments. He that keepeth his commandments receiveth truth and light, until he is glorified in truth and knoweth all things." And that is the promise that is made to us as members of the Church if we will walk in the light of the Spirit of truth, or the Comforter, and in the fulness of the gospel of Jesus Christ, keeping the commandments of God. You can't get a fulness anywhere else. Men may search, they may study, they may learn, of course, a great many things; they may lay up a great fund of information, but they will never be able to come to the fulness of truth and the brightness spoken of in this revelation unless they are guided by the Spirit of truth, the Holy Ghost, and keep the commandments of God.

Here is another thought we hear a great deal about. "The elements are the tabernacle of God; yea, man is the tabernacle of God, even temples; and whatsoever temple is defiled, God shall destroy that temple."[8] Now, destruction does not mean annihilation. We know that because we are taught in the revelations of the Lord that a soul cannot be destroyed. Every soul born into this world shall receive the resurrection and immortality and shall endure forever. Destruction does not mean, then, annihilation. When the Lord says, "They shall be destroyed . . ." he means that they shall be banished from his presence, that they shall be cut off from the presence of light and truth and shall not have the privilege of gaining this exaltation; and that is destruction.

"The glory of God is intelligence." How many times we have heard that. And how many of us think that this is the complete thought, but that is only half of the sentence. And I have often marveled that we have paid so much attention to this expression just that far and have not continued farther.

"The glory of God is intelligence, or in other words, light and truth." The light and truth which leads us to a full understanding of all things and by which we are glorified in the presence of God the Father. "The glory of God is light and truth." And light and truth are intelligence.[9]

Intelligence and Knowledge

There is a vast difference between intelligence and knowledge. Men may have a great fund of knowledge and have no intelligence. We have men of that kind in the world, very well educated, with a wonderful knowledge, but lacking absolutely in the intelligence to use that knowledge; as you will see as I further read. "Light and truth (which is the same as intelligence, the Lord declares here), forsake that evil one." Light and truth; the intelligent man, the man who is possessed with intelligence or light and truth, forsakes the evil one.

> Every spirit of man was innocent in the beginning, and God having redeemed man from the fall, men became again, in their infant state, innocent before God.
>
> And that wicked one cometh and taketh away light and truth through disobedience, from the children of men, and because of the traditions of their fathers.
>
> But I have commanded you to bring up your children in light and truth.[10]

We ought to be the most thankful people in the world, to think that the Lord has opened the heavens and made known to us such wonderful things as these that I have been reading to you. I wonder if we have appreciated them. I wonder if we have understood them. I wonder if we have thought that a man may reach the exaltations without the guidance of the Spirit of God. If any man has that idea, he should repent. We cannot reach the exaltations unless we are guided by the Spirit which possesses the truth of the eternal God. The Holy Ghost is given unto us for the very purpose of bringing us to a knowledge of truth. The Lord said it would quicken our understandings; it would show us things to come. He would *partake* of the things of the Father and reveal them unto us. And the man who is not in possession of the Spirit of truth, the guidance of the Holy Ghost, can never understand and comprehend the things of the kingdom of God. And hence he is barred, no matter what his knowledge may be, from receiving the fulness.

Power of the Priesthood

Here is another revelation I want to call to your attention. The Lord, speaking of the priesthood and the power of the priesthood, and the ordinances of the Church which we receive through the priesthood, had this to say:

> And this greater priesthood administereth the gospel and holdeth the key of the mysteries of the kingdom, even the key of the knowledge of God.[11]

So if there is no priesthood, there is no knowledge of God. And that is why the world is in darkness today, because they have no priesthood. They have lost the knowledge of God. And so they have been teaching all manner of tradition, all manner of false doctrine, all manner of man-made philosophy in relation to God and the principles of truth pertaining to the salvation of men, and that can only be received, if you please, through the power of the priesthood, for it is by that power that the keys of the knowledge of God are obtained. Let me read that again:

> And this greater priesthood administereth the gospel and holdeth the key of the mysteries, of the kingdom, even, the key of the knowledge of God.
>
> Therefore, in the ordinances thereof, the power of Godliness is manifest.

And without the ordinances thereof and the authority of the priesthood, the power of Godliness is not manifest unto men in the flesh;

For without this, no man can see the face of God, even the Father and live.[12]

When we read things of this nature, it ought to make every man among us who holds the priesthood rejoice to think that we have that great authority by which we may know God. Not only the men holding the priesthood know that great truth, but because of that priesthood and the ordinances thereof, every member of the Church, men and women alike, may know God. And when we study these things, then we can comprehend the words of the Savior, which is the slogan for this Leadership Week.

The destiny of the faithful man in this Church and the faithful woman is to become a son and daughter of God. That is the great gift that the Lord holds out to the members of the Church, that through our obedience and our faithfulness to the principles of truth, we shall become the sons and daughters of God. We must enter into the covenants; we must receive the obligations; we must take upon us those necessary requirements which the gospel gives to us. If we will do that and continue in God, we shall rise until we shall know all things and we shall become the sons and daughters of God, even gods ourselves. And that is not blasphemy; this truth has been taught down the ages when the truth has been upon the face of the earth.

Another Statement from the Lord

Now, may I call attention to another statement that comes from the Lord.

Whatever principle of intelligence we attain unto in this life, it will rise with us in the resurrection.

And if a person gains more knowledge and intelligence in this life through his diligence and obedience than another, he will have so much the advantage in the world to come.[13]

We are not going to lose in the grave the knowledge we gain in this life. We came here to receive knowledge of things we could not get anywhere else, to get experiences here that we could not get anywhere else. The errors that we may have gained through ignorance or whatever cause while sojourning in this life we must discard, for only the truth will remain.

"It is impossible for a man to be saved in ignorance."[14] We have heard this so many times; I wonder if we have not, very frequently, misapplied this expression, that a man cannot be saved in ignorance. In ignorance of what? Does that mean that a man must come to school and learn everything that can be known in regard to science in all its branches? That he must learn everything that is taught in regard to social matters, in relation to history, to all these teachings that can be obtained in the public schools and universities? No, it does not mean that. It means that he cannot be saved in ignorance of the saving principles of the gospel, things pertaining to the kingdom of God.

I want to read to you a few statements from the discourses of the Prophet Joseph Smith.

> We consider that God has created man with a mind capable of instruction, and a faculty which may be enlarged in proportion to the heed and diligence given to the light communicated from heaven to the intellect; and that the nearer man approaches perfection, the clearer are his views, and the greater his enjoyment till he has overcome the evils of his life and lost every desire for sin, and like the ancients, arrives at the point of faith where he is wrapped in the power and glory of his Maker and is caught up to dwell with him. But we consider that this is a station to which no man ever arriveth in a *moment*: He must have been instructed in the government and laws of that kingdom by proper degrees until his mind is capable in some measure of comprehending the propriety, justice, equality, and consistence of the same.[15]

Every man who has natural faculties has been created with a mind capable of instruction, the faculty which may be enlarged in proportion to the heed and diligence given to the light and communication from heaven to his intellect. And I maintain, based upon that which is written in these revelations and these statements coming from the Prophet, which I receive without any reservation, that the man who is guided by the Holy Spirit and who keeps the commandments of God, who abides in God, will have the clearest understanding and the better judgment always, because he is directed by the Spirit of truth. And the man who relies upon himself or the knowledge of other men will not have as clear a vision as will the man who abides in the truth and is directed by the Holy Spirit. I think that is self-evident.

A Statement from the Prophet

Here is another statement from the Prophet:

> As far as we degenerate from God, we descend to the Devil and lose knowledge, and without knowledge we cannot be saved. And while our hearts are filled with evil, and we are studying evil, there is no room in our hearts for good, or studying good. Is not God good? Then you be good: if he is faithful, then you be faithful: Add to your faith virtue, to virtue knowledge, and seek for every good thing. The Church must be cleansed, and I proclaim against all iniquity. A man is saved no faster than he gets knowledge, for if he does not get knowledge, he will be brought into captivity by some evil power in the other world as evil spirits will have more knowledge, and consequently more power than many men who are on earth. Hence, it needs revelation to assist us, and give knowledge of the things of God.[16]

That is what the Prophet means when he says a man is saved no faster than he gets knowledge. And man cannot be saved in ignorance. The man who does not gain the knowledge which comes through the Spirit of God and the keeping of the commandments of the Lord may be led astray by some evil spirits for the very good reason that he will not have the opportunity of entering into the kingdom of God where evil spirits cannot go.

One more statement from the Prophet:

> There are a great many wise men and women too in our midst who are too wise to be taught; therefore, they must die in their ignorance, and in the resurrection they will find their mistake. Many seal up the door of heaven by saying, so far God may reveal and I will believe.
>
> All men who become heirs of God, and joint heirs with Jesus Christ, will have to receive the fulness of the ordinances of his kingdom, and those who would not receive all the ordinances will come short of the fulness of that glory if they do not lose the whole.[17]

These are the teachings of the Prophet Joseph Smith; I shall not take time to read more concerning them.

There is one other statement that has greatly impressed me all my days; it has been an anchor to my soul. I have reference to the words of Alma to Zeezrom when the latter began to seek for knowledge concerning salvation and knowledge of the kingdom of heaven. Alma explained to him these truths and said:

> . . . It is given unto many to know the mysteries of God; nevertheless they are laid under a strict command that they shall not impart only according to the portion of his word which he doth grant unto the children of men, according to the heed and diligence which they give unto him.
>
> And therefore, he that will harden his heart, the same receiveth the lesser portion of the word; and he that will not harden his heart, to him is given the greater portion of the word, until it is given unto him to know the mysteries of God until he know them in full.
>
> And they that will harden their hearts, to them is given the lesser portion of the word until they know nothing concerning his mysteries; and then they are taken captive by the devil, and led by his will down to destruction. Now this is what is meant by the chains of hell.[18]

Darkness Replaces Truth

The man who receives the light of truth and then turns away loses the light which he had and if he continue in that course eventually he will be bound by the chains of spiritual darkness. Darkness will take the place of truth as the truth becomes gradually dimmed until he has lost knowledge of spiritual things. He who walks in the light of truth receives more truth until he is glorified in divine truth—the truth that saves. I also call your attention to the first sixteen verses of Section 76 of the Doctrine and Covenants, and humbly ask that the Spirit of the Lord may rest upon you to lead you in divine truth.

I repeat, in all of our teachings, whether in this school or elsewhere, we should teach in the spirit of prayer, of faith in the gospel of Jesus Christ. The successful teacher, as Elder Karl G. Maeser taught, will even teach the arithmetic tables in the spirit of prayer. The successful teacher will weave into his story, whatever he teaches, the fundamental doctrines of the gospel. If we understand the truth, we will make everything conform to that which God has revealed, and therein is the path of safety.—(Address delivered at BYU Leadership Week assembly, Jan. 26, 1940.)

---

[1]D&C 29:34.
[2]*Discourses of Brigham Young*, p. 17.
[3]D&C 50:11-14.
[4]*Ibid.*, 50:15-22.
[5]*Ibid.*, 18:10-16.
[6]*Ibid.*, 50:22-24.
[7]*Ibid.*, 93:20-28.
[8]*Ibid.*, 93:35.
[9]*Ibid.*, 93:36.
[10]*Ibid.*, 93:38-40.
[11]*Ibid.*, 84:19.
[12]*Ibid.*, 84:19-22.
[13]*Ibid.*, 130:18-19.
[14]*Ibid.*, 131:6.
[15]*Teachings of the Prophet Joseph Smith*, p. 51.
[16]*Ibid.*, p. 217.
[17]*Ibid.*, p. 309.
[18]Alma 12:9-11.

The Lord has placed upon us the responsibility to preach the gospel, but there is another great responsibility. . . . It is just as necessary that we warn the world as it is to declare the way of eternal life. Every missionary who goes out should see to it that he leaves his testimony so that he will be free, . . . and every man should be warned and left without excuse, and thus the blood of every man may be upon his own head.

"The Field Is White Already to Harvest"

We have heard a great deal about the preaching of the gospel and the burden which is upon us to carry this message to the world. I would like to add a few words in regard to this responsibility and something in regard to the condition of the world into which we are sent.

Adam was commanded by our Father in heaven to teach his children the everlasting truth. We read in the scriptures the following:

> And Adam and Eve blessed the name of God, and they made all things known unto their sons and their daughters. And Satan came among them, saying: I am also a son of God; and he commanded them, saying: Believe it not; and they believed it not, and they loved Satan more than God. And men began from that time forth to be carnal, sensual, and devilish.[1]

So they turned away from the truth unto the worship of all manner of false doctrines and gods, refusing to hearken to the prophets that were sent among them, and it became necessary for the Lord to bring in the flood upon them and cleanse the earth of its iniquity. Once again the world started out with just one family, and as men began to spread upon the face of the earth, they were taught by the prophets and were given revelation from the Almighty; but they, too, in course of time rebelled and set up their own churches and worshiped their own gods and graven images. Under these conditions the Lord called a man out of the land of the Chaldees and sent him into the land of Canaan, promising him great blessings and his posterity after him, through obedience to the Lord's commandments. Today we call that people Israel. But in course of time Israel also rebelled. They would not listen to their prophets, so they were scattered over all the face of the earth for their rebellion. This has been the history all through the ages, because men became carnal, sensual, and devilish.

One of the ancient prophets on this continent, speaking of our day, said:

Warning from an Ancient Prophet

> But, behold, in the last days, or in the days of the Gentiles—yea, behold all the nations of the Gentiles and also the Jews, both those who shall come upon this land and those who shall be upon other lands, yea, even upon all the lands of the earth, behold, they will be drunken with iniquity and all manner of abominations—
>
> And when that day shall come they shall be visited of the Lord of Hosts, with thunder and with earthquake, and with a great noise, and with storm, and with tempest, and with the flame of devouring fire.[2]

The Lord saw fit to restore, after a great apostasy, the truth of the gospel through the Prophet Joseph Smith. He sent angels from his presence. In fact, this great prophet was visited by both the Father and the Son and was given authority to commence this great dispensation of the fulness of times and to teach the truth of the everlasting gospel, because again men had turned away from the truth to the worship of their idols and the practice of false doctrines. They have set up churches of their own where the Spirit of the Lord is not found. The Lord sent out his missionaries in the beginning of this dispensation to preach the restored gospel, and he said to them that he was sending them with this message of truth among the "congregations of the wicked"; and this he repeated many times. In a revelation given in October 1830, when the Church had been restored but six months, the Lord said this:

> For verily, verily, I say unto you that ye are called to lift up your voices as with the sound of a trump, to declare my gospel unto a crooked and perverse generation.
>
> For behold, the field is white already to harvest; and it is the eleventh hour, and the last time that I shall call laborers into my vineyard.[3]

Meaning of "Last Time"

By the "last time" the Lord meant the dispensation of the fulness of times.

The Prophet Joseph Smith instructed his brethren and informed them of the calamities that were to come. He warned the world of its wickedness, and he told these good men of the Council of the Twelve, who were associated with him, that because of the wickedness of the world and its corruption, destruction would come upon it. Some of these brethren say that as he told them of these things he wept as our Savior wept when he looked upon Jerusalem. President Wilford Woodruff, speaking of this testimony and this warning to the world which the Prophet had seen in vision of things which were coming upon the earth, said: "I heard the Prophet Joseph Smith bear his testimony to these events that would transpire in the earth," and after predicting that they were now at our doors, he said also: "We cannot draw a veil over the events that await this generation. No man that is inspired by the Spirit and power of God can close his ears, his eyes, or his lips, to these things." I think we have no right to close our ears, and we have no right to be silent and shut our eyes against the warnings that the Lord has given and placed before us which we are commanded to declare to the nations of the earth.

Again the Lord says:

> For all flesh is corrupted before me; and the powers of darkness prevail upon the earth, among the children of men, in the presence of all the hosts of heaven—
>
> Which causeth silence to reign, and all eternity is pained, and the angels are waiting the great command to reap down the earth, to gather the tares that they may be burned; and, behold, the enemy is combined.[4]

I heard President Wilford Woodruff, in this stand, this same place where I stand, bear witness as he had done in other places, in 1893, and up to the time of his death, that the angels who had been waiting to go forth to reap down the earth had now been sent upon that mission and they were in the earth. Therefore, he said, we may look for calamities, for destruction, for plague and bloodshed.

Warning Given by the Prophet Nephi

Now let me read a little to you by way of warning, something given by prophecy to Nephi concerning our own day. Speaking to the people who are living now, he said:

> O the wise, and the learned, and the rich, that are puffed up in the pride of their hearts, and all those who preach false doctrines, and all those who commit whoredoms, and pervert the right way of the Lord, wo, wo, wo be unto them, saith the Lord God Almighty, for they shall be thrust down to hell!
>
> Wo unto them that turn aside the just for a thing of naught and revile against that which is good, and say that it is of no worth! For the day shall come that the Lord God will speedily visit the inhabitants of the earth; and in that day that they are fully ripe in iniquity they shall perish.
>
> But behold, if the inhabitants of the earth shall repent of their wickedness and abominations they shall not be destroyed, saith the Lord of Hosts.

But behold, that great and abominable church, the whore of all the earth, must tumble to the earth, and great must be the fall thereof.

For the kingdom of the devil must shake, and they which belong to it must needs be stirred up unto repentance, or the devil will grasp them with his everlasting chains, and they be stirred up to anger, and perish;

For behold, at that day shall he rage in the hearts of the children of men, and stir them up to anger against that which is good.

And others will he pacify, and lull them away into carnal security, that they will say: All is well in Zion; yea, Zion prospereth, all is well—and thus the devil cheateth their souls, and leadeth them away carefully down to hell.

This has reference, if you please, largely to those who are in Zion.

And behold, others he flattereth away, and telleth them there is no hell; and he saith unto them: I am no devil, for there is none—and thus he whispereth in their ears, until he grasps them with his awful chains, from whence there is no deliverance.

Yea, they are grasped with death, and hell; and death, and hell, and the devil, and all that have been seized therewith must stand before the throne of God, and be judged according to their works, from whence they must go into the place prepared for them, even a lake of fire and brimstone, which is endless torment.[5]

There is much more that I would like to present if time would permit. Let me call your attention to the fact that this world is not growing better. If I may be pardoned for the expression: We need not "kid" ourselves into thinking that this world is growing better. If so, then the prophecies have failed. This world today is full of wickedness. That wickedness is increasing. True, there are many righteous people scattered throughout the earth, and it is our duty to search them out and give unto them the gospel of Jesus Christ and bring them out of Babylon. The Lord has said to them: "Go ye out of Babylon," which is the world.

Now the Lord has said this is the last time the gospel should be given to men and his servants should cry nothing but repentance, and he has further said:

For behold, the field is white already to harvest; and it is the eleventh hour, and the last time that I shall call laborers into my vineyard.

And my vineyard has become corrupted every whit; and there is none which doeth good save it be a few; and they err in many instances because of priestcrafts, all having corrupt minds.

And verily, verily, I say unto you, that this church have I established and called forth out of the wilderness.[6]

And for what purpose is the gospel preached? To bring the people to a knowledge of the truth and as a witness before the end of the world shall come or the end of wickedness. Even before the organization of the Church, back in 1829, the Lord drew attention by revelation to the preaching of his servants, and he said:

And their testimony shall also go forth unto the condemnation of this generation if they harden their hearts against them.[7]

This was said more particularly in reference to the testimonies of these men who are witnesses of the Book of Mormon, and their testimony has gone forth through all the world. But this is also true of the testimonies of all others who have gone forth to preach the gospel. Then the Lord adds:

For a desolating scourge shall go forth among the inhabitants of the earth, and shall continue to be poured out from time to time, if they repent not, until the earth is empty, and the inhabitants thereof are consumed away and utterly destroyed by the brightness of my coming.

Behold, I tell you these things, even as I also told the people of the destruction of Jerusalem; and my word shall be verified at this time as it hath hitherto been verified.[8]

The Lord has placed upon us the responsibility to preach the gospel, but there is another great responsibility. I think some of our missionaries have had an idea that all we had to do was to make friends, and if they wanted to come in the Church, well and good, and the missionaries have not realized that they were under the obligation to leave a warning, and it is just as necessary that we warn the world as it is to declare the way of eternal life. The Lord said to the missionaries who went out in the early days:

> That ye may be prepared in all things when I shall send you again to magnify the calling whereunto I have called you, and the mission with which I have commissioned you. Behold, I sent you out to testify and warn the people, and it becometh every man who hath been warned to warn his neighbor. Therefore, they are left without excuse, and their sins are upon their own heads.[9]

Every Missionary Should Leave His Testimony

Every missionary who goes out should see to it that he leaves his testimony, so that he will be free as the Lord has declared he should be in Section 4 of the Doctrine and Covenants; and so that every man with whom he comes in contact should be warned and left without excuse, and thus the blood of every man may be upon his own head.

If you think the world is getting better, just observe and witness the vulgarity and the near-approach to indecency that we find published in some pictorial magazines, and so frequently on the screen. Think of the corruption and the debasing conditions due to the indulgence in liquor and tobacco and other narcotics and drugs. Think of the immorality which is so prevalent throughout the country. We are made aware of the evils which existed in our army camps by the reports in the papers, the magazines, and from the lips of our own boys who have returned. Now pressure is brought upon us to bring to pass the compulsion of our youth at the tender years when they are most impressionable, and force them into military camps where they will have no protection, or very little, from the vices which are so prevalent in army camps. I want to say to you, my brethren and sisters, for one, I am opposed to it!

Now let us go forth and preach this gospel with the understanding that we have the dual responsibility of bearing witness and leading the righteous, the honest, to a knowledge of the truth, and then leaving all others without excuse, by the witness which we bear to them.—(*Conference Report*, April, 1946.)

---

[1]Moses 5:12-13.
[2]2 Nephi 27:1-2.
[3]D&C 33:2-3.
[4]*Ibid.*, 38:11-12.
[5]2 Nephi 28:15-23.
[6]D&C 33:3-5.
[7]*Ibid.*, 5:18.
[8]*Ibid.*, 5:19-20.
[9]*Ibid.*, 88:80-82.

There is a great responsibility resting upon the members of the Church, both men and women, to proclaim the words of eternal life, but more especially upon these men who have accepted the priesthood with a promise that they would be true and faithful and would magnify their callings.

Proclaim the Words of Eternal Life

I have always taken a great interest in Section 4 of the Doctrine and Covenants, one reason being that it was given directly to my great-grandfather, who made inquiry to know what the Lord would have him do. Second, because I have always considered that this revelation was written to me, not only to me, but also to every man in the Church holding the Holy Priesthood.

It was not intended as a personal revelation.

I do not wish to detract from anything that has been said by President McKay, but I would like to make this comment in relation to verse 4: "For behold the field is white already to harvest; and lo, he that thrusteth in his sickle with his might, the same layeth up in store that he perisheth not, but bringeth salvation to his soul."

There is a great responsibility resting upon the members of the Church, both men and women, to proclaim the words of eternal life, but more especially upon these men who have accepted the priesthood with a promise that they would be true and faithful and would magnify their callings, and in the verse that I have read the Lord proclaims this fact: that if we fail in the duties that are assigned to us and refuse to accept the responsibilities which come from that priesthood, that we ourselves are in danger of losing our own salvation. It is a great responsibility resting upon each of us to proclaim this truth to a benighted world. I say benighted because for hundreds of years they have been without the guidance of the Spirit of the Lord and the proper understanding of the things which are written in the scriptures. They have not had a correct understanding of the nature of God, not until the Prophet Joseph Smith came to reveal it.

Plainness of Revealed Doctrine

Strange as that may be, considering the plainness with which the doctrine is taught throughout the scriptures, and so plainly presented this morning by President Clark in his radio talk, that Jesus Christ is the Son of God, that they are separate individuals or personages, one the Father and one the Son, but the world did not understand. They do not understand it today notwithstanding the fact that the Lord has made it so plain through the revelations that came through the Prophet Joseph Smith.

It is rather remarkable, is it not, that all the great religious teachers of the world, since the time of the passing of the Apostles to the time that this youth went out into the woods to pray, had no clear understanding of the nature of God.

The men of the Protestant Reformation did not understand it, and in their endeavors to correct the evils that they saw then existing, it never entered into their minds that the doctrine that had been proclaimed since the third century or the fourth century of the Christian era was not in accord with the revelations given by the Apostles of God as they are recorded in the New Testament. That never entered their minds, but they continued that same doctrine of the mysterious nature of God, that Jesus Christ lost his body after the resurrection and was swallowed up in some mysterious way into the great body of God, ethereal in its nature.

Great Truths Restored by Joseph Smith

Now, when Joseph Smith went out into the woods to pray, he had no understanding that the Father and the Son were separate Personages. I am sure of that. How could he know it after listening to the teachings of the ministers of his day? But he came back after the manifestation was given to him, having been instructed by the Son of God with that knowledge clearly in his mind, and proclaimed it to the world—that Jesus Christ is literally the only begotten Son of God in the flesh, and that he is in the image of his Father.

He gave that great truth back again to the world, and unfortunately many of them, even to this day, are not ready nor willing to receive it.

Now, in the preface to the book of Doctrine and Covenants, the Lord's preface, the first section in the book, we have some proclamations given for the benefit of the world which I would like to read to you.

> Wherefore, I the Lord, knowing the calamity which should come upon the inhabitants of the earth, called upon my servant Joseph Smith, Jun., and spake unto him from heaven, and gave him commandments;
>
> And also gave commandments to others, that they should proclaim these things unto the world; and all this that it might be fulfilled, which was written by the prophets—
>
> The weak things of the world shall come forth and break down the mighty and strong ones, that man should not counsel his fellow man, neither trust in the arm of flesh—
>
> But that every man might speak in the name of God the Lord, even the Savior of the world;
>
> That faith also might increase in the earth;
>
> That mine everlasting covenant might be established;
>
> That the fulness of my gospel might be proclaimed by the weak and the simple unto the ends of the world, and before kings and rulers.

Behold, I am God and have spoken it; these commandments are of me, and were given unto my servants in their weakness, after the manner of their language, that they might come to understanding.

And inasmuch as they erred it might be made known;

And inasmuch as they sought wisdom they might be instructed;

And inasmuch as they sinned they might be chastened, that they might repent;

And inasmuch as they were humble they might be made strong, and blessed from on high, and receive knowledge from time to time.

And after having received the record of the Nephites, yea, even my servant Joseph Smith, Jun., might have power to translate through the mercy of God, by the power of God, the Book of Mormon.

And also those to whom these commandments were given, might have power to lay the foundation of this church, and to bring it forth out of obscurity and out of darkness, the only true and living church upon the face of the whole earth, with which I, the Lord, am well pleased, speaking unto the church collectively and not individually—

For I the Lord cannot look upon sin with the least degree of allowance.[1]

I wish the Lord could have said, and I wish he could say it today, that this is the only Church upon the face of the earth with which he is well pleased considering this Church individually. That he cannot say, but if we would humble ourselves, if those who are wayward and indifferent, who have received the testimony of the truth would repent, and if every man and every woman and child who is old enough to understand would turn unto the Lord with full purpose of heart and honor and serve him as we are commanded to do, the Lord would be able to say it.

The day is promised when righteousness shall prevail, and when it shall cover the face of the earth as the waters do the sea, and I am sure that many of us will have to humble ourselves if we live to see that day, and if we do not humble ourselves, and should that day come, we will have to be removed.

Brethren and sisters, let us keep the commandments of God as they have been revealed. Let us set the example before the people of the earth, that they, seeing our good works, may feel to repent and receive the truth and accept the plan of salvation, that they may receive salvation in the celestial kingdom of God.—(*Conference Report,* April, 1954.)

---

[1]D&C 1:17-31.

The first duty pertaining to the children of the Church belongs in the home. It is the responsibility of the parents to bring up their children in light and truth, and the Lord has declared that wherein they fail to do it, they will stand before the judgment seat to give answer.

First Duty of Parents Belongs in the Home

The first duty pertaining to the training of the children of the Church belongs in the home. It is the responsibility of the parents to bring up their children in light and truth, and the Lord has declared that wherein they fail to do it, they will stand before the judgment seat to give answer. Nevertheless, we are all grateful for the auxiliary organizations, the Sunday School, the Primary, the Mutual Improvement organizations, for they have a place in the Church given to them by revelation, and their duty is to assist the parents in the home and the priesthood, too, to train our children to walk in the light and understanding of the gospel of Jesus Christ.

They are doing an excellent job. The Lord is blessing them for it.

I have been asked to make some remarks and I pray that I may have the guidance of the spirit of the Lord that I may say those things which will be edifying, which would tend to build up and strengthen you teachers and you officers who belong to the Mutual Improvement organization and the members of the organization throughout the Church.

Your Work Is Important

We cannot get along without you. Your work is extremely important. It must be continued and must have the support of all of the Authorities of the Church.

If this life were all and death the end, then injustice would rule, justice would be defeated, righteousness would be overcome, mercy would have failed, and wickedness would triumph. But that was never intended.

There are crimes, many of them, committed in this world, unjust acts committed that go unpunished, so far as this world is concerned. But this is not the end. Retributive justice demands reparation for every wrong and every misdeed, and, if not remedied in this life, they will be remedied in the life to come.

Now, I, in keeping with your program, wish to refer to one or two things.

First, the statement from the Prophet Joseph Smith:

> If you wish to go where God is, you must be like God, or possess the principles which God possesses, for if we are not drawing towards God in principle, we are going from him and drawing towards the devil. Yes, I am standing in the midst of all kinds of people.
>
> Search your hearts, and see if you are like God. I have searched mine, and feel to repent of all my sins. . . .
>
> As far as we degenerate from God, we descend to the devil and lose knowledge, and without knowledge we cannot be saved, and while our hearts are filled with evil, and we are studying evil, there is no room in our hearts for good, or studying good. Is not God good? Then you be good; if He is faithful, then you be faithful. Add to your faith virtue, to virtue knowledge, and seek for every good thing.[1]

Prophet's Declaration

Again, this is from the Prophet:

> A man is saved no faster than he gets knowledge, for if he does not get knowledge, he will be brought into captivity by some evil power in the other world, as evil spirits will have more knowledge, and consequently more power than many men who are on the earth.

Hence it needs revelation to assist us, and give us knowledge of the things of God.

Here are one or two other quotations; this one from Emerson, from his essay on *Compensation*:

> The world looks like a multiplication-table or a mathematical equation, which, turn it how you will, balances itself. Take what figure you will, its exact value, nor more nor less, still returns to you. Every secret is told, every crime is punished, every virtue rewarded, every wrong redressed, in silence and certainty. What we call retribution is the universal necessity by which the whole appears wherever a part appears.

One more quotation, that I have taken from the writings of Frederick Paulsen, written nearly a century ago, he being the teacher of philosophy at the University of Berlin at the beginning of this century:

> Whoever disregards the laws of medicinal dietetics will pay the penalty with indisposition and disease, whether he believes in the validity of these laws or not. Similarly, whoever violates the laws of morality will pay for it with his own life's happiness, regardless of what he may think of them. Whoever disregards the duties which he owes himself, whoever abandons himself to intemperance and dissipation, destroys the fundamental conditions of his own welfare.

Law of Human Nature

> Whoever surrenders himself to idleness and love of pleasure, expecting in this way to find his happiness, will ultimately perish in satiety and disgust; that is a biological law of human nature as well as the other law that successful activity is followed by pleasure, and that capacities grow through exercise. Finally, whoever disobeys the commands of social morality disturbs the life of others, and suffers for it himself as a social being. Whoever treats his surroundings inconsiderately, haughtily, and meanly, arouses aversion and hatred and the behavior corresponding to those feelings, his views concerning the nature of moral laws to the contrary notwithstanding.
>
> No one exists, however, to whom these things are altogether indifferent. There is not a man in the world who can do without the love and confidence of his fellows, to whom distrust and hatred

are not painful in themselves and destructive in their consequences. And even if any one should succeed in perpetrating wrong and baseness undiscovered and with impunity, he could not escape the reaction.

The fear of discovery would remain, for it is a strange fact that the man who has something to conceal always believes himself to be watched and seen by others. Consciousness of guilt makes a man lonely and should anyone succeed in shaking off all relations with others, he would not be secure against one—the judge in his own heart. Blinded by passion, he may momentarily delude himself into the belief that he has torn out his conscience by the roots; but it will come again someday and audibly speak to him.

"Be not deceived," said Paul. "God is not mocked; for whatsoever a man soweth, that shall he also reap."[2]

Now, Professor Paulsen was speaking from the human standpoint. We speak from the standpoint of our Eternal Father. Justice must and will triumph. Truth is eternal. Falsehood must eventually come to an end.

The Lord has said in one of the revelations, that which remains is of him. All other things will perish.

Retributive Justice Sure

Retributive justice is just as sure as life. It cannot be avoided. What an awful world it would be if there were in it no hope of justice. All down through the ages, in lands of tyranny people have suffered unrighteously even to the death, but the time will come when there will be recompense, justice meted out, and everything levelled.

Alma, in speaking to his son Corianton, has given us some wonderful advice, and that by the inspiration of the Almighty, in regard to this principle of eternal justice, and the restoration of that which is right:

I say unto thee, my son, that the plan of restoration is requisite with the justice of God; for it is requisite that all things should be restored to their proper order. Behold, it is requisite and just, according to the power and resurrection of Christ, that the soul of man should be restored to its body, and that every part of the body should be restored to itself.

> And it is requisite with the justice of God that men should be judged according to their works; and if their works were good in this life, and the desires of their hearts were good, that they should also, at the last day, be restored unto that which is good.
>
> And if their works are evil they shall be restored unto them for evil. Therefore, all things shall be restored to their proper order, everything to its natural frame—mortality raised to immortality, corruption to incorruption—raised to endless happiness to inherit the kingdom of God, or to endless misery to inherit the kingdom of the devil, the one on one hand, the other on the other. . . .
>
> Now the decrees of God are unalterable; therefore, the way is prepared that whosoever will may walk therein and be saved.[3]

He was talking to his son who had been somewhat wayward and who had wondered about the justice of the Almighty. And when his father was talking to him about restoration, he wondered about it, and the father said to him:

> And now behold, is the meaning of the word restoration to take a thing of a natural state and place it in an unnatural state, or to place it in a state opposite to its nature?
>
> O, my son, this is not the case; but the meaning of the word restoration is to bring back again evil for evil, or carnal for carnal, or devilish for devilish—good for that which is good; righteous for that which is righteous; just for that which is just; merciful for that which is merciful.
>
> Therefore, my son, see that you are merciful unto your brethren; deal justly, judge righteously, and do good continually; and if ye do all these things then shall ye receive your reward; yea, ye shall have mercy restored unto you again; ye shall have justice restored unto you again; and ye shall have a righteous judgment restored unto you again; and ye shall have good rewarded unto you again.
>
> For that which ye do send out shall return unto you again, and be restored; therefore, the word restoration more fully condemneth the sinner, and justifieth him not at all.[4]

From my early youth I have remembered one statement in the discourse that Alma gave to his son Corianton. It has stayed with me all through the years, and it has been an anchor to my soul. I think of it frequently. And it is just four little words. I would like to impress it upon your hearts, and I think it would be a protection against all manner of sins. These four little words are just simply these: "Wickedness never was happiness."

Wickedness Never Happiness

That is the tenth verse of the forty-first chapter of Alma. . . . "Wickedness never was happiness."

How many there are in the world who try to find happiness in wickedness, in the violation of the commandments of God. We have all had temptations, haven't we? I should more properly say, each of us. And sometimes we think that it is just a little sin, it will not matter very much if we do this or that.

The Lord will forgive us, and besides it is so small that we will not be punished very severely, and so we step aside and we do something that we know we ought not to do. Oh, not too serious, no, but still contrary to the commandments that the Lord has given. We have turned aside and how we felt later when we took time to think and realize in our hearts that the pleasure we got out of it was not worth the price, and then we were troubled.

One little thing wherein we step aside and do something that is contrary to the commandments of the Lord, and we do not repent, how much easier it is to repeat it, and every time we repeat it, what are we doing? We are drawing farther away from God, nearer to the devil. And every little act, no matter how insignificant we may consider it to be, that is contrary to that which we have been taught, is just one step in the wrong direction and makes it easier to make the second step and then the third, until we find ourselves in dire difficulty and beyond the power of the guidance of the Holy Ghost.

Every member of this Church has been baptized for the remission of his sins. I wonder if we realize fully what that means? It means that we come into the Church and kingdom of God free from sin. Then we have hands laid upon our heads by someone who has the authority and receive the gift of the Holy Ghost. What does that mean? It means that if we will walk in the light of truth, if we will observe the commandments the Lord has given us, remembering all things that he has commanded, that we will have the guidance of his Holy Spirit to direct us. And goodness knows, we cannot do without that guidance.

Time for Reflection

Are there any who have not felt the influence of the Spirit of the Lord? Who have not had the whisperings come to him or to her in regard to the principles of the gospel of Jesus Christ? In regard to the truth of the gospel or the organization of the Church? Have we lived without receiving that manifestation coming from the Spirit of the Lord bearing witness to our souls that these things are true? If so, then we should take inventory. We would do some reflecting.

We should find out what is the matter with us, that we have not had the assurance which we were entitled through our righteousness to receive, that this work is true, that Joseph Smith was really called to be a Prophet of God, that the Father and the Son really appeared to him, not in a dream, not in any imaginary thinking, but in the light of the day, when his eyes were open and when he knelt in earnest prayer to know the truth, when he asked for light earnestly and humbly and it was given to him.

Do we remember our prayers? Do we go to the Lord? Do we thank him for these blessings that we have received, and we have received so many of them? Or do we forget? Are we grateful to him for the many blessings that we have received?

Now, all good things come from him. Nothing comes from him that is not good. He sends his Spirit to those who are just and true and directs them, and each member of this Church is entitled to have that revelation given to him by which he may know that Jesus Christ is the Son of God; and that Joseph Smith was a Prophet of God; that the Father and the Son actually, in person, appeared to him; that Moroni came and revealed the Book of Mormon; that John the Baptist came and restored the Aaronic Priesthood; Peter, James and John came and restored the Melchizedek Priesthood, because it was not here, and by that restoration the Church of Jesus Christ was restored.

This Church is not a new Church. Many people think it is. It did not have its beginning on the 6th day of April, 1830. It was organized in the days of Adam, and it has been on the earth every time the Lord has had servants who would do his will, and there have been occasions when there have been apostasies, when men have turned away from the truth and ways of righteousness.

When even those who were chosen to bear his name and hold the priesthood in the authority of the living God have turned away into paths of darkness there has come an apostasy. That has occurred more than once, and it was because of that condition prevailing in the year 1830 that the Lord sent his messengers to restore again to the earth his gospel and establish his truth and send forth his word into all parts of the earth that all who will might repent and come into the Church and receive salvation in the kingdom of God.—(MIA Conference, June, 1957.)

---

[1]*Teachings of the Prophet Joseph Smith,* pp. 216-217.

[2]Frederick Paulsen, *Introduction to Philosophy,* pages 72-73. See also Galatians 6:7.

[3]Alma 41:2-4, 8.

[4]*Ibid.,* 41:12-15.

The tendency of the times is towards evil. I deplore, and I know my brethren do, the tendency in the world which Latter-day Saints imitate and copy. . . . We are the people of the Lord. Why should we follow the world, why can we not be modest, why can't we do the things the Lord would have us do?

Teach Virtue and Modesty

This is certainly a wonderful sight to think that you good sisters have come from all parts of the world to attend this conference. I congratulate you for your faith and your integrity and I want to say to you, we pray for you constantly. You are doing a wonderful work, and the Prophet certainly was inspired by the Spirit of the Lord to have such an organization as the Relief Society given to the Church. You have a great work to perform. We remember you in our prayers, we want you to know that the work that you are performing is fully appreciated by the brethren of the Authorities of the Church.

Now, there are a great many good, honest people in the world, but that does not change the fact that we are living in a wicked world, a fallen world. In fact, it has always been fallen since Adam and Eve were driven out of the Garden of Eden. But that does not mean that there have not been good people down through the ages, at least most of the time. Your work is just as important as any other work in the Church. I want you to know that your brethren appreciate it.

Our Day Was Seen by Isaiah

I want to say a few words, too, along the line that was mentioned by Elder Petersen. Our day was seen in the days of Isaiah. The Lord opened the eyes of Isaiah. He saw the gathering of the Latter-day Saints to these valleys of the mountains and spoke about it and about the blessings of the Lord that would attend them. But he also saw in that great vision some of the pitfalls and the difficulties and the transgressions that would befall the Latter-day Saints, along with other people, and he has spoken of it. When Isaiah spoke of Zion, he did not mean the world, and when he spoke of the daughters of Zion, he meant the daughters of The Church of Jesus Christ of Latter-day Saints.

I am going to read you a few verses.

> As for my people, children are their oppressors, and women rule over them. O my people, they which lead thee cause thee to err, and destroy the way of thy paths.
>
> The Lord standeth up to plead, and standeth to judge the people.
>
> The Lord will enter into judgment with the ancients of his people, and the princes thereof: for ye have eaten up the vineyard; the spoil of the poor is in your houses.[1]

Then he goes on to talk about Zion. Who is Zion? We, the Latter-day Saints.

> Moreover the Lord saith, Because the daughters of Zion are haughty, and walk with stretched forth necks and wanton eyes, walking and mincing as they go, and making a tinkling with their feet:
>
> Therefore the Lord will smite with a scab the crown of the head of the daughters of Zion, and the Lord will discover their secret parts.
>
> In that day the Lord will take away the bravery of their tinkling ornaments about their feet, and their cauls, and their round tires like the moon.
>
> The chains, and the bracelets, and the mufflers,

The bonnets, and the ornaments of the legs, and the headbands, and the tablets, and the earrings.

The rings, and nose jewels . . .[2]

We haven't quite reached that point yet, have we?

The changeable suits of apparel, and the mantles, and the wimples, and the crisping pins,

The glasses, and the fine linen, and the hoods, and the veils.

And it shall come to pass, that instead of sweet smell there shall be stink; and instead of a girdle a rent; and instead of well set hair baldness; and instead of a stomacher a girding of sackcloth; and burning instead of beauty.[3]

Teach Your Children

That is as far as I need to read.

Now, you good mothers, you should teach your children virtue, chastity, and they should be taught from their early childhood. And they should be made aware of the pitfalls and the dangers that are so prevalent throughout the world. We are living in a wicked day. When you read your newspapers you can discover that, and they give us but a small fraction of what goes on. Wickedness prevails. One of my good brethren who had the right to speak some years ago said, "Chastity is dead." I hope that isn't true of virtue.

The tendency of the times is towards evil. I deplore, and I know my brethren do, the tendency in the world which Latter-day Saints imitate and copy, as far as the women are concerned, at least in their dress. When I was a young man going to school the girls wore dresses that came down to their ankles. They were modest. They don't do that now. I went out occasionally in my youth to Saltair to bathe, when the water was up under the pavilion. I had a bathing suit that covered my body to my ankles, so did the men, and so the women. I remember when a young lady came in to go bathing. She passed one of the men in charge, and he stopped her. He said, "You can't go in dressed like that." Well, she had a dress on that covered her body down below her knees, but he said, "You have to get stockings on."

A woman came into my office one day, she might be here in this group for all I know, and showed me a picture that she had taken, somewhere near the beginning of the century, of a group bathing at Saltair. I tried to get it from her and she would not let me have it. "No," she said, "I am going to keep this, I am in this picture." But every bather was covered—men and women alike. That's why I wanted to get it, to see it, to show it.

Now they go in bathing together, men and women at the resorts, with very scanty clothing on. Some of our good, clean, virtuous daughters vie to become Miss America or Miss Utah or California or some other state, and they have to be put on exhibition like prize cattle and go through all kinds of stunts and dress so they have to show their bodies. Pardon me for talking plainly. I think it is disgraceful that we have reached that point in our lives where, as one of my good brethren said several years ago, "Virtue, modesty are dead." Now we need reformation.

Keep Children Properly Clothed

You mothers in your homes, are you in the habit of letting your little children run around scantily clothed because it is warm weather, practically naked or nearly so? And they grow up that way, that is, thinking that there is nothing wrong in exposing their bodies. What did the Lord give Adam and Eve garments for? To clothe themselves, and the Lord does not like nakedness. And I think the Latter-day Saints should not follow the fashions and the immodesty of the world. We are the people of the Lord. He expects us to live clean, virtuous lives, to keep our thoughts clean and minds pure and faithful in the observance of all his other commandments. Why should we follow the world, why can we not be modest, why can't we do the things the Lord would have us do? (Relief Society Annual General Conference, October, 1962.)

---

[1]Isa. 3:12-14.
[2]*Ibid.*, 3:16-21.
[3]*Ibid.*, 3:22-24.

There is not anybody in the Church who could not have in printed form the revelations of the Lord, the history of Israel, the words of our Redeemer as recorded in the four gospels, the writings of the apostles of old, as far as they have come to us. They are accessible and they ought to be available where we can find them.

Search for Knowledge and Understanding

Contrary to what I usually do, I have chosen a text that I am going to read to you. It is from the 19th Psalm:

> The law of the Lord is perfect, converting the soul: the testimony of the Lord is sure, making wise the simple.
>
> The statutes of the Lord are right, rejoicing the heart: the commandment of the Lord is pure, enlightening the eyes.
>
> The fear of the Lord is clean, enduring for ever: the judgments of the Lord are true and righteous altogether.
>
> More to be desired are they than gold, yea, than much fine gold: sweeter also than honey and the honeycomb.
>
> Moreover by them is thy servant warned: and in keeping of them there is great reward.
>
> Who can understand his errors? cleanse thou me from secret faults.
>
> Keep back thy servant also from presumptuous sins; let them not have dominion over me: then shall I be upright, and I shall be innocent from the great transgression.
>
> Let the words of my mouth, and the meditation of my heart, be acceptable in thy sight, O Lord, my strength, and my redeemer.[1]

That is one of the most beautiful psalms in all the psalms that have been written, that have come down to us. The people today, I think many of them at least, have varied, incorrect ideas about these old prophets. They were poets and they had inspiration, and how the spirit of the Lord had touched their souls has come down to us in these words that have been preserved. How grateful we ought to be that some of these very choice instructions, prayers uttered from the sincerity of the hearts of men who believed in God, have come down to us. I wonder how much we appreciate them.

Now these men that wrote were prophets. Many of the psalms were written by David. David was a good man at heart. He made one very serious error that will stand against him even unto the judgment day. But in deep humility, he sorely repented, so in sincerity of his humility and when I read these words, I can't help but feel the greatest sympathy for this great man.

But what I want to talk to you about is not the fact that these ancient prophets had the inspiration and poured out their souls in prayer, but I want to call attention to the counsels that they gave to us.

When this psalm was written, there was no Bible. The Israelites had copies of the Five Books of Moses, and they had a few other writings, but they were not distributed generally. They were in manuscript form and mostly in the hands of the priests.

Members Did Not Have Copies of the Scriptures

The members of the Church were not fortunate enough to have copies of the scriptures in their possession. They listened to the instructions that were given to them. They were taught to be humble and faithful before the Lord, to pray, to worship properly, but they did not have the opportunity to sit down at their tent doors or their porches and pick up the scriptures and read them. Those privileges were denied them because they were not to be had.

There came a time when there was a period that no

scripture was had among them. The scriptures had become lost, and then one day in the cleaning of the temple, the scriptures were found and were brought to the king. They had a righteous king on the throne at that time, and he rejoiced and called his people together and reiterated to them the commandments that the Lord had given him, because they were forgetting them, and so they made new covenants.

When I read these beautiful sayings that have come down to us and think of the circumstances under which they were written, and the scarcity of copies and the need of the people at large to depend upon the teachings that came to them through their scribes and teachers, I can understand how they so frequently became careless and indifferent and forgot the commandments of the Lord. And so the Lord had to send his prophets among them every little while to stir them up to remembrance of the covenants they had made.

You know when they had come out of Egypt and had crossed the Jordan, Joshua had them build the monument of stone in memory of their deliverance and their coming into the promised land—the land that had been given to Abraham as an eternal possession—and so to build the monument to keep the people reminded of their great blessings and of their deliverance, they all took a covenant that they would teach the words of the Lord. They would be true to his covenants and remember them, but it was not long after this that they began to forget. I can see a little more occasion for their forgetting than there is for us in our day. In fact, I see no occasion for us to forget. How greatly blessed we are!

Now, it isn't necessary for us to go to meeting to hear the word of the Lord, to hear somebody read from the scriptures. We are not depending upon the elders and the priests of the Church to instruct us. The Israelites were, more or less, more than less, because they did not have these meetings at hand, and when I think of their turning away and forgetting, then, there comes into my mind a little feeling of sympathy for those poor people. Our memories are more or less short, if we do not keep everything in mind at all times. And when they only heard the word of the Lord occasionally, they could not sit down in their homes and open the scriptures and read the commandments of the Lord. Maybe I ought to be a little more charitable to them for their disobedience.

We Have the Scriptures

It is different with us. There is not a home in any part of the world where the Bible should not be found. There is not a home where the Book of Mormon should not be found. I am speaking of the Latter-day Saint families. There is no home where the Doctrine and Covenants and the Pearl of Great Price should not be. Not necessarily on the shelves or in the cupboard, but opened where they can be easily reached, and the members of the family might find access to them and sit down and read and study the principles of the gospel for themselves. Now it is possible with us anywhere, in any stake or ward or branch of this Church, and yet, my good brothers and sisters, I am indeed sorrowful in my thinking because of the lack on the part of the members of this Church to search for knowledge and understanding. While all these things are before us, we can have them.

There is not anybody in the Church who could not have in printed form the revelations of the Lord, the history of Israel, the words of our Redeemer as recorded in the four gospels, the writings of the apostles of old, as far as they have come to us. They are accessible and they ought to be in every home, and they ought to be available where we can find them, where we could sit down when we have a few minutes to spare and read a chapter and a few verses and keep ourselves posted.

Now, why am I talking like this? I am going to tell you why. Foolishly, maybe, I accepted a responsibility of answering questions and having them published, many of them. Well, I don't publish all that I get by any means. In fact, I don't answer them all because I can't, there are too many of them. But what is astonishing to me is the nature of some of the questions that some of the members of the Church write to me about, which, if they would turn to their Standard Works and spend just a little time studying them, they would not have to ask the questions, because they are all answered, and the Lord has given them to us. Yet, I will have the same question coming to me over and over again, even after it has been published as an answer to a question.

I feel that the Latter-day Saints—our sisters as well as our brethren, many of them, are under condemnation before the Lord because he has given us so much pertaining to our present needs and our salvation, and yet the great majority of us, if I have the right understanding of us, we don't study, and we don't hunt for these things and we don't know about them, and so we are in danger—danger of being led astray.

Above all else, we ought to live the truth. That is, the truth of the gospel of Jesus Christ. That ought to be the choicest thing in all of the world, and why not? These words are so beautiful here:

> More to be desired are they than gold, yea, than much fine gold: sweeter also than honey and the honeycomb.[2]

How many of us feel that way? Are they sweet to us like that? Well, sisters, if they are not, we have nobody to blame but ourselves. In the Lord's preface to the Doctrine and Covenants—his own preface, one that he dictated, speaking of those revelations—he says:

> Search these commandments, for they are true and faithful, and the prophecies and promises which are in them shall be fulfilled.[3]

Well, I get so many questions sent to me that are simple and that are answered completely in those revelations which we are commanded to search, and as I say, I answer them and they are published and here within a week, a month, after they are published, this question comes back again. Now, you think I am complaining don't you? I am not complaining. I am only calling attention to one of our responsibilities as mothers and fathers and as children.

I will ask you this question, and you can answer it to yourself. Who should have a better understanding of the fundamental principles of the gospel than the mother in the home? Well, I don't know of anybody. Why? Because she is with those little children of hers more than the father, if she is doing her duty she is, and they come to her with their questions. They come to her knee, and that is why she ought to instruct them. She could make a far better job of it than the father can, and I am not excusing the father. It is as much his responsibility to see that the children are raised in light and truth as the Lord has said. The Lord has placed that responsibility upon us. He has made it so definite, and he also gave us a warning that it is the fathers and mothers of children who will have to answer if their children go wrong, if they have neglected those responsibilities.

Not Fault-finding

I am not finding fault with any of you good sisters here, and what I am saying maybe doesn't apply to a single one of you, because you are the women who are active. You are the women who are teaching and directing. I am not talking to you particularly, but to the sisters of all of the Church and to the fathers of all of the Church, for that matter. When you go into the homes to visit, can't you do something to encourage the mothers to teach their children, to read the scriptures to them, and bring them up as the Lord has said in light and truth?

I am going to read another passage to you. The Lord said in the last days he was going to make a covenant with Israel. He has made it, but I want to read these verses to you:

Behold, the days come, saith the Lord, that I will make a new covenant with the house of Israel, and with the house of Judah:

Not according to the covenant that I made with their fathers in the day that I took them by the hand to bring them out of the land of Egypt; which my covenant they brake, although I was an husband unto them saith the Lord:

But this shall be the covenant that I will make with the house of Israel; After those days, saith the Lord, I will put my law in their inward parts, and write it in their hearts; and will be their God, and they shall be my people.

And they shall teach no more every man his neighbour, and every man his brother saying, Know the Lord: for they shall all know me, from the least of them unto the greatest of them, saith the Lord: for I will forgive their iniquity and I will remember thy sin no more.[4]

I am just foolish enough, maybe, to believe the Lord has given us the covenant that he promised. Where do we get it? In the house of the Lord, but we don't want you going into the house of the Lord, or anybody going there to receive a covenant, unless he intends to keep it. Now, I don't believe I quite finished that, did I? Well, that is enough anyway. The Lord has given us the covenant and we are not to break it. We are to keep the covenants, so the time will come when it will not be necessary for anyone to teach his neighbor. For as the Lord says, ". . . they shall all know me, from the least of them to the greatest of them. . . ." Oh, if we could just get to that place!

Sister Smith went with me to a stake conference. The president of that stake put his people under a covenant that they would read the Book of Mormon. They are going to do it piecemeal. That is—so many chapters a quarter, and then during that quarter they were to write to him and tell him that they had finished the assignment, and then he would give them another one until they had finished the Book of Mormon through the year. Sister Smith took that covenant, along with the others, not because she had to read the Book of Mormon, because I happen to know that she has read it and had been reading it constantly, but she took that covenant, and she is carrying it through and reporting to that stake president, and she is right up on her lessons, going through the Book of Mormon again.

Now, you sisters, when you go home, teach your good sisters in the stakes to have a little more interest in revelations the Lord has given us pertaining to our exaltation. —(Relief Society Annual General Conference, October, 1960.)

---

[1]Psalm 19:7-14
[2]*Ibid.*, 19:10.
[3]D&C 1:37.
[4]Jer. 31:31-34.

We have security, the security of the protection of our Father in heaven and his Son Jesus Christ, but that protection is based on our faithfulness in the keeping of his commandments. There is no other security. In fact, there never was security in any other way, only in obedience to the commandments of the Lord.

Keep the Commandments

It is a wonderful sight to look into the faces of you good sisters and see this tabernacle filled. It is a wonderful work that you are doing, and I commend you, I pray for you, and I add a blessing for you in the work which you are called upon to do. We could not get along without you.

Frequently, almost daily, I get a letter from someone who is troubled in spirit because of the conditions which prevail in the world today. These conditions have been predicted. They were spoken of by our Lord and Savior, Jesus Christ. The Lord has called our attention to them in his teachings to his disciples when he was on the earth, and in the revelations of the Lord. We are living in critical days, but days that have been spoken of by the prophets since almost the beginning of time.

You sisters have a glorious work to do laboring with the sisters of the Church and teaching them to keep the commandments of our Eternal Father. The Savior said "If ye love me, keep my commandments."[1] Never in the history of the world has the need of keeping the commandments of the Lord been made manifest more than today. I get letters almost weekly from people asking questions about conditions, the conditions prevailing in the world, the distress and the trouble, and the fears in the hearts of people, wondering what in the world we can do. There is one answer to that. They want to know if they should build bomb shelters and take other methods of protection. I am not prepared to talk about matters of that kind, but I am prepared to talk about one kind of protection, and that is keeping the commandments of the Lord. I have opened my Book of Mormon to the fifth chapter of Helaman. In this chapter I discover counsel that was given by Helaman to his sons. He had some very good, faithful sons. When Helaman began to get old, like his father did before him, he gave counsel to his sons. I want to read you a paragraph.

> And now, my sons, remember, remember that it is upon the rock of our Redeemer, who is Christ, the Son of God, that ye must build your foundation; that when the devil shall send forth his mighty winds, yea, his shafts in the whirlwind, yea, when all his hail and his mighty storm shall beat upon you, it shall have no power over you to drag you down to the gulf of misery and endless wo, because of the rock upon which ye are built, which is a sure foundation, a foundation whereon if men build they cannot fall.[2]

Counsel Good for Everyone

Now that counsel is just as good to sisters and daughters as it is to sons. We belong to the kingdom of God, the kingdom that has been set up according to the revelations the Lord has given to his prophets of old, never to be thrown down or given to another people, the kingdom that is to grow and spread until it eventually will fill the earth. Now you good sisters are playing your part in this great undertaking of bringing to pass righteousness and truth and a love of God in the hearts of the members of the Church. We ought to be grateful that we live in this day, notwithstanding all the fears and the troubles and the anxiety which come upon us because of conditions that prevail in the world.

We have security, the security of the protection of our Father in heaven and his Son Jesus Christ, but that protection is based on our faithfulness in the keeping of his commandments. There is no other security. In fact, there never was security in any other way, only in obedience to the commandments of the Lord. Now, as you travel and as you hold your meetings with our good sisters scattered throughout the Church, tell them there is a protection far greater than the building of places of protection in the earth. The Lord has promised to guide his people and bless them on one condition, that we keep the commandments of the Lord, that they are true and faithful before him. There is no security in any other course.

Our Duty to Search the Scriptures

It is the duty of our sisters, as well as it is of our brethren, to search the scriptures, to become familiar with the things the Lord has revealed. The promises he has made, the covenants he has offered to us, and to walk with understanding and in faith. In the revelation given to John, he saw Satan in all his power, laboring among the children of men in the day in which we live, more determined, more energetic perhaps than ever before in the history of mankind on this earth, and John records he was industrious, energetic, because he knows he has but a short time.

We are living in the days of fulfilment of prophecy. We are living in the days spoken of by our Lord and Savior Jesus Christ, that were to precede his second coming. The signs, many of them, that he enumerated are here, we can see them. Signs in the heaven, signs in the earth, the perplexity, the distress of nations, men's hearts failing them for fear.

We are living in that day when the Lord said these things would take place here. We have all the evidence that anybody could need to know that the signs the Lord predicted were to come upon the face of the earth, before his coming, are here. Now I don't mean to say that every sign has been given; there are other things yet to come, but the distress in the world, the wickedness, and men's hearts failing them, everyone fearful for fear destruction will overtake them, all of this was told and recorded by prophets of old and our Savior when he stood with his disciples in his ministry before his departure from them.

I want to read you another scripture from the Doctrine and Covenants on this same point:

> And, now, behold, if Zion do these things she shall prosper, and spread herself and become very glorious, very great, and very terrible.[3]

Do what things? Just keep the commandments of our Lord and Savior Jesus Christ.

> And the nations of the earth shall honor her, and shall say: Surely Zion is the city of our God, and surely Zion cannot fall, neither be moved out of her place, for God is there, and the hand of the Lord is there;
>
> And he hath sworn by the power of his might to be her salvation and her high tower.
>
> Therefore, verily, thus saith the Lord, let Zion rejoice, for this is Zion—THE PURE IN HEART; therefore, let Zion rejoice, while all the wicked shall mourn.[4]

Now there is a great blessing and promise the Lord makes to the members of the Church, protection, guidance, to give unto them his laws and direct them in righteousness and truth, and they will be called Zion, which is the pure in heart. I cannot stop the reading of this at this point because the Lord says something more, what he adds to what I have read is the part that troubles me and I want to do my part, as far as I can, to keep our people in the paths of righteousness and truth that they may be the pure in heart and have the protecting care of our Father in heaven and his Son Jesus Christ.

Some Have Hardened Their Hearts

Oh, I wish we could make all of the members of the Church understand this. We have those among us who have hardened their hearts, who are dull of hearing, and as the prophets have said, even in Zion, who love the things of this world more than they love the things of the kingdom of God, and whose ambitions are centered upon worldly things, the things that perish, and so the Lord is under the necessity of adding something:

> For behold, and lo, vengeance cometh speedily upon the ungodly as the whirlwind; and who shall escape it?
>
> The Lord's scourge shall pass over by night and by day, and the report thereof shall vex all people; yea, it shall not be stayed until the Lord come.
>
> For the indignation of the Lord is kindled against their abominations and all their wicked works.
>
> Nevertheless, Zion shall escape if she observe to do all things whatsoever I have commanded her.
>
> But if she observe not to do whatsoever I have commanded her, I will visit her according to all her works, with sore affliction, with pestilence, with plague, with sword, with vengeance, with devouring fire.
>
> Nevertheless, let it be read this once to her ears, that I, the Lord, have accepted of her offering; and if she sin no more none of these things shall come upon her;
>
> And I will bless her with blessings, and multiply a multiplicity of blessings upon her, and upon her generations forever and ever, saith the Lord your God. Amen.[5]

Now, it is my duty to cry repentance, to teach our people, to try to get them to walk in ways of righteousness and truth. It is your duty as sisters to teach your sisters that they may do likewise, just as it is the duty of all those who hold the priesthood to cry repentance and teach our people to prepare themselves for the coming of the Son of God. The Lord is not going to tell anybody when he will come. He is not going to tell me or anybody else, but he will come when least expected; when people are full of this world and its affairs rather than the things that pertain to the kingdom of God. So I plead with you sisters in your labors to keep yourselves humble, that you may go forth and teach in your various organizations, build up and strengthen the sisters, and counsel them to teach their husbands and members of their families that they, too, may realize the importance of obedience to every command the Lord has given us.

Not a Day of Many Words

The Lord said "This is not a day of many words," but I feel to talk to you in this manner at this particular time, due to the fact that the hearts of our people, many of them, are failing them. They don't know what to do, where to run, where to hide, fearing dreadful destruction may overtake them. We have one way of escape and that is the best, and that is the protection of our Lord and Savior, Jesus Christ, providing we will keep his commandments.

The Lord bless you good sisters. I am grateful for you and for the work you are doing and for your loyalty, and for the integrity and loyalty of these good sisters who preside and who direct you in your labors. The Church of Jesus Christ is not a Church governed by one minister. The Lord has spread the work so that every member of it may have some important duty to perform. The Lord has called this organization and the other organizations of our sisters into existence for the building up and strengthening of his kingdom. I am sure your good brethren, I being among them, love you for the great work you are doing and the integrity of your hearts. We pray for you, we uphold you, we want you to walk in the light and the understanding of the gospel of Jesus Christ.—(General Relief Society Conference, September 27, 1961.)

---

[1]John 14:15.
[2]Hela. 5:12.
[3]D&C 97:18.
[4]*Ibid.*, 97:19-21.
[5]*Ibid.*, 97:22-28.

We, the Latter-day Saints, should keep ourselves in order, humble, sincere, obeying the commandments of the Lord. Otherwise those who rebel shall be removed out of their place—the Lord said it.

Obedience to the Truth

As I have been sitting here, I have been thinking of the ages past and how the women, members of the Church, were invited always to take back seats and keep silent in the churches. Paul, himself, gave counsel to that effect, that the women should be silent, and if they wanted to know anything about the gospel they were to ask their husbands at home. Well, I am grateful that that day is not now. I am grateful that the Lord revealed to the Prophet Joseph Smith that there is a work for the sisters in the Church to perform, and there are responsibilities which rest upon them just as well as there are responsibilities resting on the shoulders of the brethren.

Salvation is not something that is confined solely to the men. The women have to be saved also, and they are saved by the same principles and ordinances. It is just as important that a woman repent of her sins, believe the truth, accept it, and be baptized for the remission of her sins and to receive the gift of the Holy Ghost, as it is for a man. The same principles that save the men will save the women. There is one glorious thought that has been given to us through the revelations to the Prophet Joseph Smith and that is that the men cannot be saved alone, neither can the women.

Man Cannot Receive Fulness of Blessings Alone

In order to fulfill the purposes of our Eternal Father, there must be a union, husbands and wives receiving the blessings that are promised to those who are faithful and true that will exalt them to Godhood. A man cannot receive the fulness of the blessings of the kingdom of God alone, nor can the woman, but the two together can receive all the blessings and privileges that pertain to the fulness of the Father's kingdom. The women will become queens, priestesses, in the eternal order that the Lord has given for the fulness of his kingdom. The gospel means just as much to our sisters as it does to the brethren. They are just as much concerned in it as are the brethren. And when the Lord said to the Prophet Joseph Smith, "Search these commandments, for they are true and faithful, and the prophecies and promises which are in them shall all be fulfilled," he did not limit that commandment to the male members of the Church. This revelation from which I have quoted begins as follows:

> Hearken, O ye people of my church, saith the voice of him who dwells on high, and whose eyes are upon all men; yea, verily I say: Hearken ye people from afar; and ye that are upon the islands of the sea, listen together.[1]

Now, people include both men and women. When we say this people or that people, we don't just single out the men. It means everybody. Therefore, it is just as important that our sisters understand the plan of salvation as it is for the men. It is just as essential that they keep the commandments. No woman is going to be saved in the kingdom of God without baptism for the remission of sins and the laying on of hands for the gift of the Holy Ghost. Now someone might read what's in our scriptures and conclude to the contrary.

Inspiration Is for Men and Women

Our sisters are entitled just as much to the inspiration for their needs of the Holy Spirit as are the men. They are entitled to the gift of prophecy concerning matters that would be essential for them to know as it is for the men. When they pray they should pray earnestly, expecting to have an answer to their prayers. The Lord will hear them, if they are earnest, true, just as well as he will the brethren.

I can remember the struggle that the women of this country went through in order to get the franchise. I am sorry to say that after they got it, many of them have failed to know just how to use it. They haven't been any worse than the men, but, nevertheless, they had to struggle in order to obtain that great gift or blessing and have a voice in the government. The women have a voice in the government of the Church. When someone is appointed to an office, we do not ask the men only to vote, but we ask the whole congregation. The women have a right to raise their hands. They have a right to speak. And it was by the inspiration of the Almighty that the Relief Society came into existence. The Young Women's Mutual Improvement Association, and the Primary, give our sisters opportunity to teach, to give instruction, as well as to learn. When the Lord said that no person could be saved in ignorance, I think he meant women as well as he did men, and I think the women of the Church are under the obligation of studying the scriptures just as well as for the men.

We are living in a day of turmoil, strife, and contention, I think nearly as bad as the world has ever seen. There may have been times worse, but I don't know of any other or reading of anything worse than what we are getting today—the violation of law, the selfishness of men, the greed, the ambitions, the turning away from faith in God. I think we are getting today, speaking of the world, in a very serious condition in relation to matters of that kind.

Even the so-called Christian churches are moderating the doctrines, changing them. Many of them today are beginning—if they have not already reached the point—of denying the divinity of Jesus Christ. I think as far as the women are concerned, if they believe that sort of thing they learned it from the men.

The Gospel Still True Today

The gospel is just as true today as it was in the days of the Lord, Jesus Christ, when he came to restore it. The mission of the Prophet Joseph Smith is just as necessary today as it was in the beginning. The need of mankind to know that God lives and Jesus Christ is his Son, the Redeemer of the world, the Savior of men, is just as vital today as it has ever been. It is just as true as it was when Peter, James, and John, and Paul were teaching. The world needs repentance today just as much as it ever did.

Now it is my opinion, and I have a very strong opinion to that effect, that this world is rapidly reaching the point when the cup of iniquity will be full, and we send our missionaries out to warn the people. Among those missionaries now, for many, many years, we have been sending our sisters. They have been doing a good work. The Lord says:

> Verily I say unto you, that they who go forth bearing these tidings unto the inhabitants of the earth, to them is power given to seal both on earth and in heaven, the unbelieving and rebellious;
>
> Yea, verily, to seal them up unto the day when the wrath of God shall be poured out upon the wicked without measure.[2]

I think that day of wickedness is rapidly drawing upon us. We need the help of our sisters, you good sisters of the Relief Society, to help us teach the principles of eternal truth just as well as we do the elders of the Church. You can teach it in your organizations. Our sisters need to be taught, many of them, just as well as do our brethren. We have sisters in the Church who are losing their faith. We have sisters who love the world more than they do the kingdom of God. There is plenty of work to do for the sisters of the Relief Society and of the Mutual Improvement Association.

We, the Latter-day Saints, should keep ourselves in order, humble, sincere, obeying the commandments of the Lord. Otherwise, those who rebel shall be removed out of their place, the Lord said it.

Today there is a condition existing in this country among our youth. When I read the papers, our own local papers here, it seems to me that those same conditions are creeping into our communities. Our young people are becoming rebellious, filled with the spirit of wickedness, and something ought to be done as far as we are concerned to see if we can't correct it. I hope that our good sisters will join, if they have not joined, the Relief Society, instead of going out to join clubs to play cards and waste their time while their children, perhaps, roam the streets.

"Light and Truth Forsake That Evil One"

Our Mutual Improvement Association has a slogan which is only half of the sentence, "The glory of God is intelligence, or, in other words, light and truth." Now we have cut that off right in the middle. I have no objection to it. It is all right, but that is what the Lord said, "the glory of God is intelligence, or, in other words, light and truth." Then he said, "Light and truth forsake that evil one." Well, we want to live so that the evil power will have no influence with us, and we want to exercise our responsibilities in the Relief Society and in the other organizations to keep this commandment. "Light and truth forsake that evil one," says the Lord.

Every spirit of man was innocent in the beginning. God having redeemed man from the Fall, men became again in their infant state, innocent before God. Every child born into this world is innocent. No matter what he did before he came here, he comes here innocent, as far as this life is concerned. Every spirit of man was innocent in the beginning, and God having redeemed man from the Fall, men became again in their infant state, innocent before God. We should remember that. But here's our trouble,

> . . . that wicked one cometh and taketh away light and truth, through disobedience, from the children of men, and because of the tradition of their fathers.
>
> But I have commanded you to bring up your children in light and truth.[3]

A Commandment to the Church

That is the commandment to the members of the Church. Now our sisters of the Relief Society can help in this matter, as can the other organizations, to see that the children of the Latter-day Saints obey counsel, understand the truth, walk in its light, are taught to pray, and have a love for their fellow men.

We don't want our sisters, because of responsibilities given to them in the organizations of the Church, to have to neglect their families. We don't want any sister in the Relief Society to have to attend her meetings and at the same time leave her children to run the streets. If her Church duties require her attention, then she should see to it that some provision is made to care for her children, if she has children, that they might be protected and taught to pray and to be faithful and true, and brought up in light and truth. That is our responsibility. No, we do not want any sister to neglect her responsibility, but we do not want her to have to do it at the sacrifice of children by neglect, leaving them to find bad company or to be idle. Let us see to it that our children, if we are called into the work of the ministry in this regard, are provided for, that they have protection.

We are in a wicked world. I know there are good people in the world, yes. But the Lord says it is wicked, and if he says it is wicked, I think maybe I can, too, and I think it is getting more so every day. We have many responsibilities, but none of them to cause us to neglect our homes. —(General Relief Society Conference, October 7, 1959.)

[1]D&C 1:1.
[2]*Ibid.*, 1:8-9.
[3]*Ibid.*, 93:39-40.

Brethren and sisters, teach your children from their infancy to believe in Jesus Christ as our Redeemer, in Joseph Smith as a Prophet of God, and in his successors in this kingdom, and let them grow up with a knowledge of this truth in their hearts built upon faith and obedience to the commandments the Lord has given to us through the guidance of that Holy Spirit which will not dwell in unclean tabernacles.

An Anchor to Our Souls

My beloved brethren and sisters, I have a testimony of this truth. I am grateful for it. I do not remember the time when I did not believe in the mission of our Lord and Savior Jesus Christ nor in the mission of the Prophet Joseph Smith, and I hope you will forgive me if I get a little personal.

I was trained at my mother's knee to love the Prophet Joseph Smith and to love my Redeemer. I never knew my Grandmother Smith. I have always regretted that, because she was one of the most noble women who ever lived, but I did know her good sister, my Aunt Mercy Thompson, and as a boy I used to go and visit her in her home and sit at her knee, where she told me stories about the Prophet Joseph Smith, and, oh, how grateful I am for that experience.

I know that The Church of Jesus Christ of Latter-day Saints is in very deed the kingdom of God, the same kingdom that was seen by a great king long before the birth of Christ in a dream or a vision that he received that had to be interpreted by a prophet of the Lord. The Lord made known to that king, not for his benefit, but to the benefit of the nations of the earth and the peoples who should follow after and more particularly I think for the Latter-day Saints of this dispensation, that the Lord set up a kingdom, or would, for this king was seeing into the future to a time when the Lord would set up a kingdom that would endure forever, would never be destroyed or given to another people.

I have always been very grateful for the testimony coming to me through the Spirit of the Lord that Joseph Smith, the Prophet of God, was called to stand at the head of the dispensation of the fulness of times when this kingdom would be set up, never to be destroyed or given to another people. That ought to be an anchor to our souls.

False Organizations

We have people who go out of the Church from time to time and set up organizations of their own, claiming that the kingdom of God has failed, that they have something better. I am sorry for these people. I cannot believe that any of them are sincere. If they are, then they are to be pitied, but I think that they are malicious deceivers, trying to destroy the kingdom of God.

Every person coming into this Church through the waters of baptism has hands laid upon his or her head by which they are to receive the gift of the Holy Ghost to be a guide to them through time and all eternity. I wonder how many of those who have been baptized and confirmed members of this Church have so lived that they have had that guidance and have had the testimony come to them through the Holy Ghost that Joseph Smith was a Prophet of God, that Brigham Young was a successor in the Presidency of the Church, and so have each of the other brethren who have been called to that high and holy calling down through the years to President David O. McKay?

The Church has not gone astray. The kingdom of God that was set up never to be destroyed or given to another people is The Church of Jesus Christ of Latter-day Saints, and it is not going to be destroyed, and is not going to be given to any other people. There will be members of this Church because of their lack of faith and obedience to the commandments of the Lord who will go astray, for the Spirit of the Lord will not dwell in unclean tabernacles, and when a person turns from the truth through wickedness, that Spirit does not follow him and departs, and in the stead thereof comes the spirit of error, the spirit of disobedience, the spirit of wickedness, the spirit of eternal destruction.

Brethren and sisters, teach your children from their infancy to believe in Jesus Christ as our Redeemer, in Joseph Smith as a Prophet of God, and in his successors in this kingdom, and let them grow up with a knowledge of this truth in their hearts built upon faith and obedience to the commandments the Lord has given to us and through the guidance of that Holy Spirit which will not dwell in unclean tabernacles.

The Lord bless you, my good brethren and my good sisters here; do not let anything interfere with your faith, and if you will keep the commandments of the Lord and be faithful and do not forget your prayers in humility, you will not go astray.—(*Conference Report*, April, 1962.)

It is just your privilege, the privilege the Lord has given you to act for yourself. You are agents with the power within you to obey or to disobey. If it were not so, no one could be tried for disobedience. We read in the scriptures that every man will be tried according to his works.

"He That Loveth Me Shall Be Loved of My Father"

For a theme I thought I would take the text of your sacrament gem, the words of Jesus:

> He that hath my commandments and keepeth them, he it is that loveth me; and he that loveth me shall be loved of my Father.[1]

Two more days and we will be celebrating the day quite universally accepted as the birthday of our Savior Jesus Christ. Therefore, throughout the entire country today I think people are listening to discourses, or have listened to them, in regard to our Lord and Savior Jesus Christ. But many of those discourses will be by men who don't know him, by some who do not receive him as the Son of God. But throughout The Church of Jesus Christ of Latter-day Saints, in all the discourses that have and will be delivered, mention will be made of the fact that he is in very deed our Redeemer, the literal begotten Son of God, our Eternal Father. Of course I would be entirely out of place if I do not speak of him and of his mission.

Moreover, since this is the anniversary of the birth of the Prophet Joseph Smith, I feel inclined to say a word about him, about his mission. As one of the greatest of all the prophets, he presides over the last dispensation and no prophet has been given a greater mission, save perhaps it could have been Adam; and no prophet in the past has done more for the salvation of the human family, in my judgment, than did Joseph Smith the Prophet. As the Lord revealed to Lehi, in the record that was kept by Joseph who was sold into Egypt, the Prophet Joseph Smith was named, his mission was pointed out by that great ancestor of most of us, who became the ruler in Egypt and one of the great prophets, too, of God. Joseph Smith came into this world to perform a work in the greatest of all the dispensations since the world began, to bring salvation again to a fallen world, a world that had gone astray, a world that in large measure professed to worship the Son of God but that knew not how to worship him—because they had been taught so many traditions, had received so many terms regarding the Christ and regarding the gospel which he brought to mankind—that the world has been in constant error throughout the ages of time.

Joseph Smith Sent to Restore

Joseph Smith was sent to the world to restore what had been taken away, that which men had rejected because, as our Savior says, we loved darkness rather than light. So I had to mention the Prophet tonight. Much can be said about him and his mission that would be very profitable, but I must forego that and speak of the mission of our Savior Jesus Christ.

I am going to read to you a few words of Paul the Apostle, who spoke to the Corinthian Saints. Now, the people out in the world have a strange idea about these epistles of Paul and of the men who have written the epistles we have and the Bible. They read these epistles and apply them unto themselves and they look upon them as being declared as messages to all the world. But that isn't so. Definitely, each of these epistles were written to members of the Church—not to denominations—but to those who heard the words of the apostles of old, had received them and had been baptized and confirmed members of the Church of Jesus Christ in that dispensation.

Therefore, we should have the understanding when we read these scriptures that the things said by the apostles are not things that apply to those who have not made covenants through the gospel of Jesus Christ and did not in that day. I am going to read a most definite statement, an emphatic statement to members of the Church, some of them who had been drifting a little—like we do today—some who are not fully converted, some who had forgotten the messages that the brethren taught to them and which they received when they came into the Church—just like members of the Church are today.

So Paul instructing these members of the Church calls attention to certain conditions which are peculiar to those who have made covenants with Jesus Christ. And Paul is not speaking to this generation. He is speaking of the generation in which he lived. And so to these Corinthian members he said,

> Now if any man build upon this foundation gold, silver, precious stones, wood, hay, stubble;
>
> Every man's work shall be made manifest: for the day shall declare it, because it shall be revealed by fire; and the fire shall try every man's work of what sort it is.
>
> If any man's work abide which he hath built thereupon, he shall receive a reward.
>
> If any man's work shall be burned, he shall suffer loss: but he himself shall be saved; yet so as by fire.
>
> Know ye not that ye are the temple of God, and that the Spirit of God dwelleth in you?[2]

Paul couldn't say that to those who hadn't been baptized and confirmed, for the Lord has said definitely that those who are not members of the Church can't receive the Holy Ghost, and so Paul has said,

> If any man defile the temple of God, him shall God destroy; for the temple of God is holy, which temple ye are.
>
> Let no man deceive himself. If any man among you seemeth to be wise in this world, let him become a fool, that he may be wise.
>
> For the wisdom of this world is foolishness with God. For it is written, He taketh the wise in their own craftiness.[3]

We Can Not Build on Any Other Foundation

So we should take notice of this. We can not build on any other foundation. I think that there are members of the Church who have pride, who have placed gold, silver, precious things—because the world considers these—as their great goal. And they have neglected their duties and responsibilities which their membership in the Church requires of them.

Now, let me read another passage spoken to these same members of the Church, many of whom had sadly departed from the true teachings that they had received from Paul and others who had been sent to teach them:

> What? Know ye not that your body is the temple of the Holy Ghost which is in you, which ye have of God, and yet are not your own?
>
> For ye are bought with a price: therefore glorify God in your body, and in your spirit, which are God's.[4]

Paul couldn't say that to those who had not made covenants. He could have told anybody anywhere that he was bought with a price, but he could not tell them that the Holy Ghost had been given to them, because it was not given except to members of the Church. But the fact remains that every soul upon the face of the earth was bought with a price—Jew and Gentile, the heathen, the atheist. No matter where a man lives or what he believes or the circumstances under which he lives, he was bought and paid for with a price, a price that was paid by our Lord and

Savior Jesus Christ, and he was the only one who could pay it. No one else was ever born into this world who could pay this price.

And from what were we bought? Before I answer that question, I want to say something else. I have heard people say, and members of the Church, "I have a right to do as I please." No, you don't. You haven't any right at all to do as you please. There is only one right that you have, and that is to do just what I read to you. Keep the commandments of Jesus Christ. He has a perfect right to tell us so. We have no right to refuse. I don't care who the man is. I don't care where he lives, don't care what he is; when the gospel of Jesus Christ is presented to him, he has no right to refuse to receive it. He has the privilege. He wasn't compelled to receive it, because our Father in heaven has given to everyone of us in the Church and out, the gift of free agency. That free agency gives us the privilege to accept and be loyal to our Lord's commandments, but it has never given us the right to reject them. Every man who rejects the commandments of our Father in heaven is rebellious.

Thousands Have Never Heard the Gospel

Of course I realize, that there are thousands of people who have never heard the gospel. They are not going to be punished for that. We can't expect a person to observe a commandment he never heard. But all those who never had the privilege of hearing it, at some time will have that privilege. If it isn't in this life, it will be in the spirit world. And every soul will have the opportunity to accept the mission of our Savior Jesus Christ or to reject it. When the Lord commands us, if we love him we will keep the commandments. This is the law to members of the Church, this little paragraph: "He that hath my commandments and keepeth them, he it is that loveth me." Again, the Savior said, "If ye love me, keep my commandments."

There are a lot of rebellious people in the world. We have rebellious people in the Church. We have members of the Church who set aside the commandments the Lord has given us, who fail to strictly observe them. That isn't your right. It is just your privilege, the privilege the Lord has given you to act for yourself. You are agents with the power within you to obey or to disobey. If it were not so, no one could be tried for disobedience. We read in the scriptures that every man will be tried according to his works. Well, if we are not under obligation, who can try us? Did you ever think of that? If there was no obligation for me to keep the commandments of the Lord, if I broke them, I couldn't be punished.

We don't punish men for doing something that is not contrary to the law, do we? But the Lord has given us these laws, the gospel of Jesus Christ not because it is pleasing to him, not because he is going to get anything out of it. He has given us these laws that we might get something out of them. And of course every person who keeps his commandments add that much to his glory. There is no question about that—because when we sustain him and are true and faithful to him, he is the benefactor. But are we not benefited and are not the benefits greater to us by far than they would be to him? Our Lord never gave a commandment in this world to any man or community that was not intended to be to his eternal benefit. I think sometimes we overlook that.

I get some letters from time to time. I get quite a number of letters from people who don't want to observe the Sabbath day, and they are trying to find excuses and loopholes so they won't have to keep the commandment. It isn't a grievous commandment to keep. The Lord never gave us a commandment which was hard to keep. I have heard people say it is hard to keep the commandments of the Lord. I don't want to confess a thing like that. I don't want to say his commandments are hard to keep. They are not hard for anyone to keep if they make up their minds to keep them. And in keeping them, they get great joy and satisfaction. And the pleasure and happiness that comes from the keeping of those commandments is far greater than the little pleasure they get out of breaking them. Breaking the commandments always results in remorse. It may not all come in this life, but if we go into the next life unrepentant and have not made right the violations of the law when we have broken it, we will have to pay the price.

A Misunderstanding

Let us not get the idea in our heads that we are masters of our souls. There is a little poem that some think very, very beautiful by Mr. Henley which says I am master of my soul. Many of you know it. We are only masters of our souls when we put them in perfect harmony and agreement with the commandments of God. When a man rises up and says, "I am the master. My head is bloody but unbowed," he needs repentance. No, I am ready to bow my head.

I hope the Lord will help me to keep his commandments. As I said, his commandments are not hard to keep. He said that himself. Some people say that his commandments are hard to keep. That's an admission, isn't it, that we are not keeping them?

I was talking to a man a few days ago who came into the Church not very long ago—just a short time. He said, "I never knew there was so much happiness in all this world as I get out of the gospel of Jesus Christ. Why didn't I discover these things earlier? Some of the members of the Church who have been baptized for the remission of their sins haven't discovered how wonderful the gospel is. If we had, we would study it. We would want to make ourselves familiar with it and know all about it. We would be seeking for knowledge. We would be praying for wisdom. If we spent more time doing that, we would spend less time going to picture shows and we wouldn't have time to violate the Sabbath day. Perhaps I have said enough along that line.

Now let us talk about the mission of Jesus Christ. He bought us. Let's go back to that now. He bought us with a price. No one else could pay the price. Let me read his own words to you:

> For behold, I God have suffered these things for all, that they might not suffer if they would repent;
>
> But if they would not repent they must suffer even as I;
>
> Which suffering caused myself, even God, the greatest of all, to tremble because of pain, and to bleed at every pore, and to suffer both body and spirit—and would that I might not drink the bitter cup and shrink—
>
> Nevertheless, glory be to the Father, and I partook and finished my preparations unto the children of men.
>
> Wherefore, I command you again to repent. . . .[5]

We don't fully realize the price. I don't. I am quite sure you don't. I don't think anybody does. I don't think it is within our power to comprehend the extent of the price of our redemption which caused the blood to ooze from every pore of his body before he went to the cross. Some people believe that the crucifiers drove nails in his hands and feet and left him there until he died. And goodness knows that would be terrific in and of itself. But others have suffered that. As terrible as that was, the Savior suffered far beyond that, and how it is done, I don't know. All I know is that it was done. I am fully convinced of that. His great suffering was done before he ever went to the cross.

All Have Committed Some Error

Let me ask you a question. Is there anybody here who hasn't committed some sin? If so, please raise your hand. I don't see any hands up. I can't raise mine. Well, you have done something wrong then. You admit it. Did you ever, after you had committed some wrong, feel sorry and get the spirit of repentance and wish you hadn't done it? If you haven't felt that way, you better see your bishop. I have done things I shouldn't have done and I have felt sorry. I know how I have felt. I want to tell you that being sorry after doing wrong is something that is awful. I never committed murder; I have kept my body clean; I haven't been stealing from people. When I was a kid I may have taken something that didn't belong to me like the neighbor's apples. But when I have done some wrong, I have been troubled. And I have had big, strong men, men who would face anything almost, not afraid of anything on the face of the earth, come trembling, weeping, and wondering what they could do to get cleansed from their sins.

I remember a man who was tormented almost beyond his endurance, trembling—a big, powerful fellow, who said, "Can you help me? I am afraid I have committed an unpardonable sin. I want relief. I want to know if I can get relief." And he wept and trembled. I felt sorry for him. That is just one instance.

The Savior never committed any sin nor carried any troubled conscience. He hadn't been under the necessity of repenting as you and I have; but in some way that I can not understand, he carried the weight of my transgressions and yours and the transgressions of every soul who comes into this Church from the days of Adam to our present time. He came and offered himself as a sacrifice to pay the debt for the things I have done that are wrong and that each of you individually have done that are wrong, and each other person who has been willing to repent of his sins and return to Jesus Christ and keep his commandments. He paid the price. Think of it if you can. Think of what one man can suffer for his wrongdoing. The Savior carried that burden in some way beyond our comprehension. But he carried it. I know that because I accept his word. And the great weight of the torment he went through to save us from the torment was so great that he plead with his Father that if it were possible he may not drink the bitter cup and shrink—"but nevertheless thy will be done." The answer he got from his Father was, "You have to drink it."

Can I help loving him? No, I can't. Do you love him? Then keep his commandments. If you don't, you will have to answer for them yourselves. "If ye love me, keep my commandments."

How often we think, "Oh, this is such a little thing. Surely the Lord will forgive us. We will only do it this once, just this once." When we do it once, it is rather easy to do it again. When we do it the second time, it is easy to do the third time, and so it goes.

Nephi Speaks of Our Day

I will turn to this passage:

> But, behold, in the last days, or in the days of the Gentiles [that is our day] behold all the nations of the Gentiles and also the Jews, both those who shall come upon this land and those who shall be upon other lands, yea, even upon all the lands of the earth, behold, they will be drunken with iniquity and all manner of abominations.
>
> And when that day shall come they shall be visited of the Lord of Hosts, with thunder and with earthquake, and with a great noise, and with storm, and with tempest, and with the flame of devouring fire.[6]

Now, remember Nephi is talking of us. When I read these words, he means us today, people living now:

> Behold, hearken ye unto my precept; if they shall say there is a miracle wrought by the hand of the Lord, believe it not; for this day he is not a God of miracles; he hath done his work.
>
> Yea, and there shall be many which shall say: Eat, drink, and be merry, for tomorrow we die; and it shall be well with us.
>
> And there shall also be many which shall say: Eat, drink, and be merry; nevertheless, fear God—he will justify in committing a little sin; yea, lie a little, take the advantage of one because of his

words, dig a pit for thy neighbor; there is no harm in this; and do all these things, for tomorrow we die; and if it so be that we are guilty, God will beat us with a few stripes, and at last we shall be saved in the kingdom of God.[7]

Do you think that isn't the philosophy today? I say it is. You hear this sort of philosophy right among members of the Church.

Yea, and there shall be many which shall teach after this manner, false and vain and foolish doctrines, and shall be puffed up in their hearts, and shall seek deep to hide their counsels from the Lord; and their works shall be in the dark.

And the blood of the saints shall cry from the ground against them.[8]

When Adam and Eve were placed in the Garden of Eden, they didn't have to die. They could be here today. They could have continued on for countless ages. There was no death then. But it would have been a terrific calamity if they hadn't broken the law under which they lived. If they had stayed in the Garden of Eden, we wouldn't be here; nobody would be here, only Adam and Eve. So the breaking of that commandment was not a sin. I don't like to hear it spoken of as a sin. It was part of the great plan, but it brought death upon Adam. Eating of that forbidden fruit subdued the power of the spirit and created blood in his body. No blood was in his body before the fall. The blood became the life thereof. And the blood was not only the life thereof, but it had in it the seeds of death. And so we grow old and we die. But that would have been a dreadful thing if Adam and his posterity had been forced because of the fall to die and remain dead; and there would have been no redemption.

That is what Satan wanted, so he worked on them. I think he had the idea: "Now, I have destroyed the Lord's plan. I have caused Adam and Eve to become mortal and they are going to die, and everyone will have to die, and they will become subject to me." And he laughed about it.

Only One Way of Redemption

There was only one way of redemption, one way in which reparation could be made and the body restored again to the spirit and that was by an infinite atonement, and it had to be made by an infinite Being—someone not subject to death and yet had the power to die. And so, our Father in heaven sent us his Son, Jesus Christ, into the world with life in himself. And yet, because he had a mother who had blood in her veins, he had the power to die. He could yield up his body to death and then take it again. Let me read his own words:

> Therefore doth my Father love me, because I lay down my life, that I might take it again.
>
> No man taketh it from me, but I lay it down of myself. I have power to lay it down, and I have power to take it again. This commandment have I received of my Father.[9]

So he had power to lay down his life, and on the cross he paid the price for our sins, and at the same time for Adam's transgression. So his infinite atonement resulted in two things, (1) restoration of the body to the spirit, and (2) the redemption of those who accept the gospel of Jesus Christ and who will be loyal in the keeping of his commandments—freedom from their own sins.

Now in conclusion, what are we going to do? Tuesday is the day we celebrate his birthday. Are we going to love him? Are we going to realize the great work he did for us and are we going to be grateful, or are we going to violate his commandments? I am thinking right now of what we are doing in the world. Sister Smith and I passed the liquor store. It was night. The lights were on inside and we could see through the windows, here in our community; and it was so crowded inside that it would be hard for someone else to get in. They were buying liquor so they could celebrate Christmas. What were they doing? They were showing their contempt for their Lord and Master whose day was to be celebrated. Is that a crime? Yes. Isn't it a crime to show contempt for the Son of God? And throughout the world today there will be millions of people carousing, drinking, doing all manner of evil, and to them it is not what it should be to us—a Holy Day.

When we go home tonight let's get on our knees and thank the Lord for his many blessings and our Lord Jesus Christ for his mercy and his greatness and goodness for making it possible for us through the keeping of his commandments to go back into the presence of God our Father and dwell with him.—(Christmas message, South Eighteenth Ward, December 23, 1956.)

---

[1]John 14:21.
[2]I Cor. 3:12-16.
[3]*Ibid.*, 3:17-19.
[4]*Ibid.*, 6:19-20.
[5]D&C 19:16-20.
[6]2 Nephi 27:1-2.
[7]*Ibid.*, 28:6-8.
[8]*Ibid.*, 28:9-10.
[9]John 10:17-18.

I tell you, my good brothers and sisters, it will not be every member of The Church of Jesus Christ of Latter-day Saints who gets into the celestial kingdom because many who have been baptized and become members of this Church will not prepare themselves to receive those blessings, and they have to come on merit just the same.

Whom Shall We Love and Obey?

It is good to look into the faces of you people. You have assembled here tonight to partake of the sacrament, to renew your covenants, take upon yourselves the name of Jesus Christ, by which we are known.

Throughout the Christian world at this time people are preparing to celebrate the birth of the Son of God, but they don't know him. He is a perfect stranger to most of the people who will celebrate. They don't understand his mission. They are getting farther and farther away from the fundamental truth that he is in very deed the Only Begotten Son of God in the flesh. During the past century the Christian world has departed farther and farther from the fundamental truth that he came into this world to be a sacrifice, to redeem man from the fall, and to restore them again to everlasting life.

Many of the teachers today in the Christian world are denying the resurrection of the dead. Had I thought of it when I was home I would have brought a little clipping from one of the largest magazines which shows that to be a fact, that they are now discarding the resurrection of the body and confining the resurrection merely to the continuation of the soul, as they call it, or the spirit of man. We, the members of The Church of Jesus Christ of Latter-day Saints ought to know fully why Jesus Christ came into the world, what his mission was while here, how he accomplished it, and what it means to us individually as well as collectively.

Now I know it is customary on occasions like this to talk about the birth of the Son of God, sing about his birth, to talk about the nativity; but how many of the people in the world are going to celebrate in that spirit of faith and love which we ought to give to the Redeemer of the world? Very few of them. With the great majority it has become—the Christmas day—a day of feasting and drunkenness, revelry and the committing of sin. It is a time when we ought to be humble and when our minds ought to be turned to contemplate the great mission which he came here to accomplish and which he fully accomplished for the benefit of mankind of the world.

Celebrate in a Spirit of Prayer

I hope that when we celebrate during this coming week we will do it in a spirit of prayer, humility, and thanksgiving and that we will remember he came here to fulfill a mission which he was given and voluntarily received, to redeem all mankind from death and restore their bodies to them again, whether they believe in him or whether they do not; and that he came also to redeem all who are willing to obey him and keep his commandments, from their sins. The world—that is, some of the Christians throughout the world—have a very strange idea why he came and they teach he came to save sinners and all the sinners had to do was confess the Son of God by their lips and they were saved.

No, he did not. He came to save the repentant and those who are willing to abide in his truth. His mission was to redeem every creature from death because one man was responsible for death and we inherited it. Now we didn't bring death into the world. We inherited it. Our fathers did before us and clear back to the beginning; and only one man was responsible for bringing death into the world. I can get on my knees and thank my Heavenly Father that he did it.

Now, I can open the Bible, almost any Bible—maybe I can this one—and find written here that Adam, not the words of the scriptures but man's interpretation, that he committed a dreadful sin. No, he didn't. Adam did not commit a sin. He came to do the thing that he was called upon to do, that he was assigned to do before he ever came here. He had to "transgress," in quotation marks, but he came and had to violate a law in order to keep another one which was far greater.

Necessary for Adam to Choose

We overlook, I think, the statement that occurs as we have it clearly stated in the version of Moses in the Pearl of Great Price when the Lord told Adam he could partake of all the fruit of the garden except one. He said to him in substance, "If you partake of that fruit, you will die and if you want to stay here then I forbid you to eat the fruit. Nevertheless you may choose for yourself." I could turn to that and read it to you: "Nevertheless you may choose for yourself. If you want to eat it, there it is." He had to.

I think I have said in this room before that I am very, very grateful for Mother Eve. If I ever get to see her, I want to thank her for what she did and she did the most wonderful thing that ever happened in this world and that was to place herself where Adam had to do the same thing that she did or they would have been separated forever. And I think of the words of Lehi, "Adam fell that man might be and men are that they might have joy."[1] The world has an idea that Adam just destroyed everything—he and Eve, because if he had kept the commandment the Lord gave him not to eat the fruit, this world would have gone on in peace and happiness, without sickness or death, no misery; and here they foolishly did this thing and brought death upon their posterity, disease, trouble of every kind.

Nothing could be more foolish than that. They had to partake of that fruit or you wouldn't be here. I wouldn't be here. No one would have been here except Adam and Eve; and they would have stayed there and been there today and been there forever. That is, they could have stayed there just as long as they wanted to in that condition if they had never partaken of that fruit; and they could have been there now and all along and would have had no children. We wouldn't be here.

So Father Lehi said, "Adam fell that man might be and men are that they might have joy." Adam and Eve did the very thing they had to. I tell you, I take my hat off to Mother Eve and I rejoice and I want to read what she said. When Eve learned what the full condition was, the result of that fall, she preached this discourse. It is the first discourse ever recorded—that is, that we have.

Our First Recorded Discourse

"And Eve, his wife, heard all these things," all the angel had revealed—"and was glad, saying: Were it not for our transgression we never should have had seed, and never should have known good and evil, and the joy of our redemption, and the eternal life which God giveth unto all the obedient."[2]

"Never would have known it." She learned what it meant. She was not sorry. Adam was not sorry and he did not commit a sin. Now transgression does not necessarily mean a sin. I have an explanation for that. I don't want any of you scientists to contradict me. I just want to present to you a scientific proposition. Now I have never performed this and I take the word of our good brethren who know. I take what they say, that water is composed of two elements, two parts hydrogen and one part oxygen—hydrogen and oxygen—and they make water when they are brought together and form water we drink, and our bodies have to have it. They might criticize, but I am sure they will agree that you transgress a law, just like Adam transgressed a law, if you take two elements and bring them together and make something else. In that combination then you have changed the nature of it. That is all they did, and they made it possible for children to come into the world. They made it possible to die.

Now Adam had no blood in his body before the fall. He could have lived forever, and there was no blood. But when they partook of that forbidden fruit, their bodies changed and blood became the life of the body, the life-giving fluid. It was not before and they had a spiritual life or activity in some way which I don't understand, but after the fall they became mortal and blood is the life of the mortal body.

They became mortal and subject to death and blood became the life of the body, but it made it possible for mankind to be born into this world and that is what we came here for. We read in the scriptures that we rejoiced over the council held in heaven and the privilege of coming here and partaking of bodies of flesh and bone and pass through all the vicissitudes of life and coming in contact with evil, with sin. It was necessary that all the conditions which we find should be here in this world, but it wasn't necessary that we should partake of evil.

This Life Is a Probationary State

Again I go back to Father Lehi. He called this life a probationary state. We are on probation. We are here to be proved. When we were in the presence of our Father, we walked by sight. In this life we have to walk by faith, and it was necessary that we be tempted, to be tried to see whether or not we will keep the commandments of God under all the vicissitudes of mortality. The Lord couldn't shut temptation out of our lives. It had to be here because we are here to be proved, to see whether or not we will keep the commandments of God. No, the Lord isn't going to save everybody in the celestial kingdom, and we are being tried, tested to see whether under all these conditions we can remain faithful and true. And if we can't, then we don't receive the rewards of faithfulness.

That is all preliminary to what I want to say about the mission of our Savior. This leads up to it. Adam brought death into the world. He brought a condition where if something hadn't been done, some infinite action hadn't been done, we would die because we would grow old. There is death in blood as well as life and we grow old and die, and without the atonement of Jesus Christ we would remain dead and our bodies would go back to the dust to remain. We would have been taken captive by Satan and subject to his will and that would have been our finish. That is what Satan hoped for.

But this was all prepared before we ever came here, before the earth was made and Jesus Christ was chosen and called the Lamb slain from the foundation of the world. The mission was given to him and he voluntarily received it, that he would come down here and through the shedding of his blood and death, he would make it possible for every soul to get his body back again. Everyone who believes on him and keeps his commandments will receive celestial exaltation. That was his mission.

It is nice for us to sing about the birth of the Son of God, the coming of the angels, the singing of the hosts of heaven, the new star appearing as a sign. Those are beautiful things. They stir your soul when you read them. But why did the heavens rejoice? Why was there all of this manifestation of happiness when the Savior came into the world and they knew that he came here to die the most terrible death that came upon any individual? They knew that. He knew it. And I want to tell you this—that nobody in this world ever suffered the excruciating punishment that came to Jesus Christ. No one else. No mortal man could do it.

The Savior's Great Suffering

And what was so terrible about it? Hanging on a cross with nails in his hands and feet and left to die must be something terrifically excruciating, but thousands died that way. Not only were some hung on the cross, nailed to them, but fire set under them, being scorched to death. That was terrible. But the punishment the Savior took upon himself was not only that torture, but one more terrific. It was the punishment of the spirit and soul. It was the carrying of a burden that is so great and so dreadful that I can not comprehend it.

What was that burden? The wrongs that I have done, that you have done and every other man and woman, every person who has repented of his sins and is willing now to keep the commandments of God and honor the Son of God. Jesus paid our debt. That punishment caused the blood to ooze from every pore. He had a terrific punishment, punishment of mind, of soul, before he ever got to the cross. And he was paying the debt that I owe and that you owe. Or I should put that in the past—the debt we owed because he paid it for us and he did that on one condition and that is that we keep his commandments. And, brothers and sisters, how many of us forget?

Now we have partaken of the sacrament tonight. Most of us have partaken of the sacrament time and time again. What did we do? We renewed again our covenants. What covenants? Three of them: That we take upon us the name of Jesus Christ, that we would always remember him, and that we would always keep his commandments. And each time we eat that bread and drink that water we covenant with our Father in the name of his Son that we will do these things, and then we go out and violate the Sabbath day and break the commandments in other ways and forget. Many of us do the things we promise we will not do because we don't comprehend the nature of the covenants which we take. But it is the most serious thing in all the world. And when we eat that bread and drink that water we covenant that we will take upon us the name of Jesus Christ—we are called by his name, that we will keep his commandments, that we remember what he did for us. And then we go out and don't do these things. We go out and violate immediately, sometimes, the Sabbath day and don't keep it holy. He has given us commandments and sometimes we set them aside because we have inclinations to do something else.

Whom Should We Love?

When we stop to think about it, who in this world should we love above everything else? Or who should we love above everything else in the world? Let me put it that way. The Lord and Savior Jesus Christ. Love him more than we do our own lives, or our own fathers and mothers or children; more than we love ourselves, because without his blessings we would have nothing. We owe all of that to him and he did that voluntarily. He wept over us when he was here. More particularly did he weep over those who did not keep any of his commandments and who were rebellious against him. We are not rebellious. We do these things thoughtlessly and without understanding and don't have in our minds the clear understanding of what it means to be true to him. Well, we ought to get it in our minds what being true to him and his Father means.

I read here in Section 76 of the Doctrine and Covenants that he is going to save somewhere, to some degree all of the children of men except those who have known the light, have had the knowledge and understanding of the knowledge and then turned away and become a son of perdition. All else he is going to do something for them, no matter how we transgress his commandments, but they have to pay the price of their own sinning and the Lord will then make them as happy as possible. He has made kingdoms for them. He can't bring all of them back into the celestial kingdom and the kingdom where his Father is. They have to be willing to keep the commandments to go there. And if they want exaltation, to become sons and daughters of God and receive the glory of godhood, then they have to keep every law and commandment and every covenant that has been offered to us and be true and faithful to them.

What Is the Reward?

And then what is the reward? We become joint heirs with Jesus Christ and the Father gives us the fulness of his kingdom. That is the reward of faithfulness and we shut all that out—or many of us—because we love this world more than we love him. We should love his Father, and that is the first great commandment. It has been given to us in our own day and repeated in our own day. It is our duty and responsibility to love him.

I tell you, my good brothers and sisters, it will not be every member of The Church of Jesus Christ of Latter-day Saints who gets into the celestial kingdom because many who have been baptized and become members of this Church will not prepare themselves to receive those blessings, and they have to come on merit just the same. They are based on our faithfulness and our integrity and our love of the truth, and if we don't keep them, we can't have them. We will go to one of the other kingdoms and the Lord will make us as happy as can be according to the law. And there are laws, eternal laws just as definite as the ones of nature, as of gravity. You suspend something and cut it loose and it will drop every time. You can't cut something loose and make it stay, because it will drop back to the earth. Well, if we are so attached to the earth, then we seal upon ourselves a place in one of the inferior kingdoms, not the kingdom of God, not the celestial kingdom. That requires our absolute faithfulness.—(Christmas message, Eighteenth Ward, December 20, 1959.)

[1]2 Nephi 2:25.
[2]Moses 5:11.

A wise man is the man who puts first things first. And what are the first things? To know why we are here, where we came from, and where we are going, and to discover the truths while we are here that will take us to the right place after we are gone. Anything short of that is folly.

"Seek Ye Earnestly the Best Gifts"

I have been thinking of quite a number of things while listening to the brethren and sister.

First of all, what is an education? I suppose it is going to school, taking several courses, being trained by men in all the philosophies of the world and getting a diploma, a degree. Then we are educated. I have been thinking of this great professor that Brother McConkie spoke about, a man who is renowned without question because of his great learning; but in my opinion, he will have to forget about everything he has learned and start over again. One simple truth pertaining to our salvation is worth all of the philosophies of men existing in the world without the knowledge of the gospel of Jesus Christ.

A wise man is the man who puts first things first. And what are the first things? To know why we are here, where we came from, and where we are going, and to discover the truths while we are here that will take us to the right place after we are gone. Anything short of that is folly.

Brethren and sisters, do you ever take time out from your busy days to reflect upon where you came from, why you are here, what you are expected to do while here, and what the end is going to be? If you don't, you are missing some great opportunities to help you to carry on correctly in your journey through this mortal life. I would rather know that Jesus Christ is the Son of God who came into this world to redeem us from death and give us life again, eternal life, immortality, and that he came to cleanse us from our sins upon conditions of our repentance and our obedience to his commandments, than to know all other things that the world can teach. For the one truth that Jesus Christ is the Son of God is worth more than all of the philosophies the world has produced.

All Knowledge and Wisdom Is Centered in God

The Lord has revealed to us from whence we came, and that was his presence. He has revealed to us why we are here—that is, all who are willing to be taught. He has pointed out to us the road we should travel and has pointed out clearly where we will end if we are faithful and true. These things are worth more than all the world can give you. Now, I don't want to leave the impression that the world can give us nothing that is worth having, but whatever they do give that is worth having does not come from them. It comes from God. It is knowledge that he has imparted, given to men, for all knowledge and wisdom are centered in God, and all that we receive comes from him, no matter from what source it comes.

It would be a wonderful thing to be a great scientist, a great mathematician, a great philosopher, a great poet—any one of these things—but what good would it be to you or to me to have given unto us all of the knowledge that the world can impart in any branch of science or all of the branches of science that the world can give, and yet we never learned the purpose of baptism is for the remission of sins; if we never discovered that it is essential to our exaltation to have faith in God; that we haven't learned the great principle of repentance? What good would all the other be to us?

I suppose this great teacher has a very vague idea of God or he has no idea at all, because I think he has never set before himself the task to find the way that leads to our Eternal Father. He has never learned the purpose of the mission of Christ in this world. If he had, he would have accepted Joseph Smith as a Prophet of God. So, as I say, putting first things first—a knowledge of God and the plan of salvation, and then to live in accordance with those principles of eternal truth is worth more than all the world can give without it.

Human Nature Hasn't Changed

You know, human nature hasn't changed in 6,000 years. We are not a bit different from what they were in the first century following the fall of Adam. Men have discovered a great many things. The Lord has revealed to them a great many things, but they have the same appetites, same desires, the same aspirations, the same greed, selfishness, seeking for advantages and power, the same as they had in the beginning.

In this book [Pearl of Great Price] I want to read this:

> And Adam and Eve blessed the name of God, and they made all things known unto their sons and unto their daughters.[1]

Now, the Lord commanded Adam to do that and to teach them the eternal truths that were revealed to him after he was driven out of the Garden of Eden. And in another place the Lord told Adam to teach these things to his children. Perhaps I ought to read that verse. After explaining to Adam the purpose of his fall, the results of it, how to come back into his presence, the Lord said,

> Therefore I give unto you a commandment, to teach these things freely unto your children, saying:
>
> That by reason of transgression cameth the fall which fall bringeth death, and inasmuch as ye were born into the world by water, and blood and by the spirit which I have made, and so

became of dust a living soul, even so must ye be born again into the kingdom of heaven, of water, and of the Spirit, and be cleansed by blood, even the blood of my Only Begotten; that ye might be sanctified from all sin and enjoy the words of eternal life in this world and eternal life in the world to come, even immortal glory.[2]

And so Adam told that to his children, and I will repeat,

> . . . Adam and Eve blessed the name of God and they made all things known to their sons and daughters.
>
> And Satan came among them, saying: I am also a son of God, and he commanded them saying: Believe it not, and they believed it not, and they loved Satan more than God. And men began from that time forth to be carnal, sensual, and devilish.[3]

Revelations Tell Much About History

We read in the revelations the Lord has given us many things about the history of this world and its inhabitants and what the end will be. The Lord gave a revelation to John on the Isle of Patmos and pointed out to him the conditions that prevailed and would prevail upon the face of the earth down through the ages, and how eventually would come the great last battle. The Lord has said much to us in the revelations to the Prophet Joseph Smith about these things and how Michael will fight our battle. And by the way, that is one war I want to get into—on the right side.

We [my good brethren] were discussing a few days ago the power of Satan. We were discussing about our Savior—and somebody asked the question: Does Satan really know that in the end he is going to lose? Then someone raised another question: Well, if he is sure he is going to lose, he would give up the struggle. We had quite a discussion. Then one of our brethren said, "He already has 90 per cent of the people who have lived on the face of the earth." We have all been on his side, or nearly, at times. You stood out and opposed him in the spirit world. He has captured most of the inhabitants of the world and perhaps he thinks that when the final war comes he will be strong enough to win the battle. I wonder if he does!

I think he is here this afternoon, so I am going to tell him that he is going to lose the battle. He is usually with us, he is right in the way. That's one thing we ought to learn—that his forces are organized and he would rather destroy a member of this Church than anyone else on the face of the earth, and he has a force big enough to send a legion after any one of us if he thought it took that many. Don't think he is sleeping and has lost any of his energy, whether he knows he is going to lose eventually or not. That matters little. But it does matter much whether we are going to be on his side or on the side of Jesus Christ.

You have read in the scriptures—I don't need to turn to them—where the Lord says, "Narrow is the way that leads to eternal life and few there are that enter in thereat, but broad is the way and wide is the gate that leads to destruction and many there are that go in thereat."[4] You have read it. It's been that way down through all the ages. And I have heard members of this Church say it is awful hard to keep the commandments of the Lord. Why? Are you listening to the whisperings of Satan? Do you follow the impressions that come from him? You get them. You don't realize it, but you get them. And is it difficult to follow the impressions that we are entitled to receive from the Holy Ghost?

Commandments Are Not Difficult

You know, I would be ashamed as a member of this Church to say that it is hard to keep the commandments of the Lord. I wouldn't want to confess it. I think I would keep it quiet even if I thought it true. It isn't hard if we would live as the Lord would have us live. If we have a contrite spirit, repentant, a pure heart of determination to keep his commandments, you are not going to find any commandment that the Lord has given that is going to be difficult. They won't be difficult. Satan will make you think they are, and don't think he hasn't power.

Does he have power to heal the sick? Yes. He also has power to make them sick. He has power over the elements and power to do great things. We read in Chapter 24 of Matthew—I am not going to read it to you but just for emphasis open the book. In Chapter 24 of Matthew the Lord tells us he will have power even to deceive the very elect. You people listening to the radio on Sundays—I mean TV—and that is left closed up on Sunday at my house. Nobody looks at it. You who do have seen this man who goes around healing people before the public. Do you think the Lord is with him? Do you think it is the Spirit of the Lord that is directing him? If you do, you have two more thinks coming. The Lord doesn't advertise his healings. He doesn't send men out with a blare of trumpets to invite people to come and get healed. And when someone comes in the name of the Lord to heal, he will also preach his gospel. These are to be keys to you so you can understand. Read what the Lord says in Section 46 of the Doctrine and Covenants. I am going to take just time to refer to a passage here that we all ought to be familiar with:

> But ye are commanded in all things to ask of God, who giveth liberally; and that which the Spirit testifies unto you even so I would that ye should do in all holiness of heart, walking uprightly before me, considering the end of your salvation, doing all things with prayer and thanksgiving, that ye may not be deceived by evil spirits, or doctrines of devils, or the commandments of men; for some are of men and others of devils.
>
> Wherefore, beware lest ye are deceived; and that ye may not be deceived seek ye earnestly the best gifts, always remembering for what they are given.[5]—(Ensign Stake Conference, July 1, 1956.)

---

[1]Moses 5:12.
[2]*Ibid.*, 6:58-59.
[3]*Ibid.*, 5:12-13.
[4]See Matt. 7:13-14.
[5]D&C 46:7-8.

The living of a clean life and faithful performance of duty in the building up and maintenance of the kingdom of God on the earth are essential to salvation. For the male members of the Church a faithful performance of duty in the priesthood and for women also to be true to every covenant pertaining to the exaltation. Without the sincere observance of all these laws and covenants, salvation cannot come in the celestial kingdom.

The Saving Ordinances of the Gospel

In a revelation given to the Church in 1843, the Lord made this emphatic declaration:

> Behold, mine house is a house of order, saith the Lord, and not a house of confusion.
>
> Will I accept of an offering, saith the Lord, that is not made in my name?
>
> Or will I receive at your hands that which I have not appointed?
>
> And will I appoint unto you, saith the Lord, except it be by law, even as I and my Father ordained unto you, before the world was?
>
> I am the Lord thy God; and I give unto you this commandment—that no man shall come unto the Father but by me or by my word, which is my law, saith the Lord.
>
> And everything that is in the world, whether it be ordained of man, by thrones, or principalities, or powers, or things of name, whatsoever they may be that are not by me or by my word, saith the Lord, shall be thrown down, and shall not remain after men are dead, neither in nor after the resurrection, saith the Lord your God.[1]

This statement should be beyond dispute on the part of every soul who truly believes in the authority of the Eternal Father and his Son Jesus Christ. In the kingdom of God there should be obedience to every law and deep gratitude for every blessing. We are instructed that the kingdom of God is a kingdom of order and obedience. Naturally we should accept the fact that in such a kingdom all things would be perfect. The kingdom must be one absolutely free from contention or variance of views. In this mortal world it is natural for men to have difference in their views on many things, but they should not be at variance in relation to any of the divine laws leading to eternal salvation. These eternal principles have, no doubt, been practiced and obeyed on millions of earths which have gone on to their glory according to the revelations given to Moses and others of the ancient prophets. So we reach the conclusion that the laws and ordinances which govern in the kingdom of God have reached the stage of eternal perfection. Therefore when Jesus said to his disciples, "Be ye therefore perfect, even as your Father which is in heaven is perfect,"[2] it has a very significant and definite meaning.

Important to Keep the Whole Law

James, in his epistle said: "For whosoever shall keep the whole law, and yet offend in one point, is guilty of all."[3] This statement has caused arguments and disputations; yet when it is understood it is plain to see that it is true. Surely no person could inherit eternal life who was not willing to abide in the whole law by which the kingdom is governed. Therefore if they kept all but one of the commandments on which salvation is based, and rebelled against that one, the blessing of salvation would be denied them. Yet the Savior has said:

> Take my yoke upon you, and learn of me; for I am meek and lowly of heart; and ye shall find rest unto your souls.
> For my yoke is easy, and my burden is light.[4]

Surely if we love the Lord we will not find any heavy burdens in observance of his divine laws.

Let us consider briefly what some of these essential

principles and ordinances are on which salvation and exaltation are based.

First we have the principle of faith, which we are informed is the foundation of revealed religion. Faith in God the Eternal Father and in his Son Jesus Christ, the Redeemer of the world, and in the Holy Ghost, who form the presiding authority in the universe.

Second: The principle of true repentance. On this subject the Savior has said:

> And it shall come to pass, that whoso repenteth and is baptized in my name shall be filled; and if he endureth to the end, behold, him will I hold guiltless before my Father at that day when I shall stand to judge the world.
>
> And he that endureth not unto the end, the same is he that is also hewn down and cast into the fire, from whence they can no more return, because of the justice of the Father.
>
> And this is the word which he hath given unto the children of men. And for this cause he fulfilleth the words which he hath given, and he lieth not, but fulfilleth all his words.
>
> And no unclean thing can enter into his kingdom; therefore nothing entereth into his rest save it be those who have washed their garments in my blood, because of their faith, and the repentance of all their sins, and their faithfulness unto the end.[5]

Third: Baptism for the remission of sins. This is by immersion in water by one who is duly commissioned to administer in this ordinance of the gospel. Paul has made this principle very plain in his epistle to the Roman members of the Church, wherein he said:

> What shall we say then? Shall we continue in sin, that grace may abound?
>
> God forbid. How shall we, that are dead to sin, live any longer therein?
>
> Know ye not, that so many of us as were baptized into Jesus Christ were baptized into his death?
>
> Therefore we are buried with him by baptism into death: that like as Christ was raised up from the dead by the glory of the Father, even so we also should walk in newness of life.

> For if we have been planted together in the likeness of his death, we shall be also in the likeness of his resurrection.
>
> Knowing this, that our old man is crucified with him, that the body of sin might be destroyed, that henceforth we should not serve sin.[6]

A Definite Statement

Here is a very definite statement that through baptism we have been transplanted from the life of sin to the life of faith and obedience to the kingdom of God. In other words obtained a spiritual resurrection, or transfer from the life of sin to the kingdom of God, where sin should no longer abound.

Fourth: The laying on of hands for the gift of the Holy Ghost. This is a great gift promised to every faithful member of the Church, by which they become, through their sincere faithfulness, a companion with the Holy Ghost, which the Savior said the "world cannot receive,"[7] and which gift is bestowed by the laying on of hands of one who holds divine authority.

Fifth: Obedience to all the other ordinances and covenants belonging to the kingdom of God. The living of a clean life and faithful performance of duty in the building up and maintenance of the kingdom of God on the earth are essential to salvation. For the male members of the Church a faithful performance of duty in the priesthood and for women also to be true to every covenant pertaining to the exaltation. Without the sincere observance of all these laws and covenants, salvation cannot come in the celestial kingdom.

Among these covenants which we are commanded to keep is that of marriage. Contrary to the prevailing doctrines in the world, marriage was decreed in the beginning to be an eternal union of husband and wife. The Lord never intended that marriage should be merely a civil or temporary contract between a man and a woman to endure only during their mortal lives, and then to come to an end. The first marriage ever performed was assuredly intended to be forever, for death had not come into the world. Nor is there any divine commandment which declares that when a marriage is performed according to the law of the Lord, it was to come to an end at death.

Perhaps the most misunderstood passage of scripture in the Bible is that recorded about the discussion which the Sadducees held with the Savior when they came to him and presented, evidently a fictitious story of the woman who had seven husbands. After telling their story they expected to trap the Savior and he would be unable to give them an answer, but he read their hearts and answered them according to their own folly. Be it remembered that these Sadducees did not believe in the resurrection of the dead, and this was but a catch question presented for the purpose of placing the Lord in an awkward situation, but he read their hearts and answered them according to their folly. He could not have given them any other answer than the one that he did, and that was to the effect, that this woman would have none of these husbands, but that those who held views like the Sadducees, if ever worthy to go to heaven would go there separately and singly, for *they* could have no marriage in eternity. The Lord has said the same thing by revelation to the Prophet Joseph Smith, of which I shall speak later.

Divorce and Marriage

When, however, the Pharisees came to the Savior in relation to divorce and marriage, the Lord gave them a very different answer. Let it be remembered that these Pharisees, although apostates at heart who had rejected the Savior, yet they believed in the resurrection of the dead, and while it is true that they also endeavored to trap the Lord into making some statement that could be criticized and perhaps confuse him, they did agree with him in the doctrine of the resurrection. To them the Savior gave the correct answer which I quote:

> And he answered them and said unto them, Have ye not read, that he which made them at the beginning made them male and female,
>
> And said, For this cause shall a man leave father and mother and shall cleave to his wife: and they twain shall be one flesh?
>
> Wherefore they are no more twain, but one flesh. What therefore God hath joined together, let no man put asunder.[8]

Here is a definite statement by our Savior that marriage was intended, when it was performed by the Lord's plan to endure forever. Now in the dispensation of the fulness of times, the Lord has revealed to Joseph and for the Church, the correct order of marriage which is to endure forever. The commandment given to the Church in relation to marriage is as follows:

> Therefore, if a man marry him a wife in the world, and he marry her not by me nor by my word, and he covenant with her so long as he is in the world and she with him, their covenant and marriage are not of force when they are dead, and when they are out of the world: therefore, they are not bound by any law when they are out of the world.
>
> Therefore, when they are out of the world they neither marry nor are given in marriage; but are appointed angels in heaven; which angels are ministering servants, to minister for those who are worthy of a far more, and an exceeding, and an eternal weight of glory.
>
> For these angels did not abide my law; therefore, they cannot be enlarged, but remain separately and singly, without exaltation, in their saved condition, to all eternity; and from henceforth are not gods, but are angels of God forever and ever.[9]

A Foolish Error

Now think of what these foolish young people do when they marry out of the Church or out of the temple and remain satisfied with such a union? They cut themselves off from the exaltation in the kingdom of God. They deny to themselves the glorious privilege of being members of the family of God which is spoken of by Paul. For said he the whole family of God are blessed by his name, and they deny to themselves the privilege of belonging to our Father's family.[10]

Moreover they place themselves where they cannot receive the blessings of eternal increase, but must remain forever alone, evidently miserable in the thought that they have willfully denied themselves the glorious privileges of eternal exaltation. If they accept the blessings coming from the eternal union granted to husbands and wives who accept the divine law the Lord has promised them the fulness of his kingdom, for the Lord has said:

> And he that receiveth me receiveth my Father;
> And he that receiveth my Father receiveth my Father's kingdom. Therefore all that my Father hath shall be given unto him.[11]

Paul taught this doctrine clearly to the Saints in his day, as this will indicate:

> For ye have not received the spirit of bondage again to fear; but ye have received the Spirit of adoption, whereby we cry, Abba, Father.
> The Spirit itself beareth witness with our spirit, that we are the children of God;
> And if children, then heirs; heirs of God, and joint-heirs with Christ; if so be that we suffer with him, that we may be also glorified together.[12]

Privileges and Blessings of Heirs

As heirs what will be our privileges and blessings in the kingdom of God? We shall be crowned with eternal *lives,* which means eternal increase forever, and we will be blessed with the inheritance of kingdoms, principalities and it is written:

> Then shall they be gods, because they have no end; therefore shall they be from everlasting to everlasting, because they continue;

then shall they be above all, because all things are subject to them. . . .[13]

Now the Lord has given us this caution:

Verily, verily I say unto you, except ye abide my law ye cannot attain to this glory.

For strait is the gate and narrow the way that leadeth unto the exaltation and continuation of the lives, and few there be that find it, because ye receive me not in the world neither do ye know me.

But if ye receive me in the world, then shall ye know me, and shall receive your exaltation; that where I am ye may be also.[14]—(Fireside talk, August, 1961.)

---

[1]D&C 132:8-14.
[2]Matt. 5:48.
[3]James 2:10.
[4]Matt. 11:29-30.
[5]3 Nephi 27:16-19.
[6]Rom. 6:1-5.
[7]John 14:17.
[8]Matt. 19:4-6.
[9]D&C 132:15-17.
[10]Eph. 3:14-15.
[11]D&C 84:37-38.
[12]Rom. 8:15-17.
[13]D&C 132:20.
[14]*Ibid.*, 132:21-23.

There is a blindness far more serious than to lose the sight of the eyes. It is not a blindness that comes without our help. It isn't forced upon us. You could call it a disease, but it is one that is acquired; and the majority of men upon the face of the earth are plagued with it.

Spiritual Blindness

There is a blindness far more serious than to lose the sight of the eyes. It is not a blindness that comes without our help. It isn't forced upon us. You could call it a disease, but it is one that is acquired; and the majority of men upon the face of the earth are plagued with it. In fact, a large percentage of the members of The Church of Jesus Christ of Latter-day Saints are troubled with it. I say it is acquired. It is easily obtained. It doesn't pain us now.

I am speaking of spiritual blindness. What I am going to say tonight has something to do with that. I am going to do something I have never done before that I recall. I am going to pay a little attention to the sermon that was preached by the man who is considered the wisest man in the world except the Son of God—the king of Israel—and that sermon is in the Bible. It is a discourse by Solomon. But I would like to say a few words about Solomon.

When he became king the Lord appeared to him. Therefore, Solomon without doubt had the priesthood. And he prayed to the Lord that he would receive blessings to guide him, that he would do the right things as king of Israel. He prayed as follows:

And thy servant is in the midst of thy people which thou hast chosen, a great people, that cannot be numbered nor counted for multitude.

Give therefore thy servant an understanding heart to judge thy people that I may discern between good and bad: for who is able to judge this thy so great a people?

And the speech pleased the Lord, that Solomon had asked this thing.

And God said unto him, because thou hast asked this thing, and hast not asked for thyself long life; neither hast asked riches for thyself, nor hast asked the life of thine enemies; but hast asked for thyself understanding to discern judgment;

Behold, I have done according to thy words; lo, I have given thee a wise and an understanding heart; so that there was none like thee before thee, neither after thee shall any arise like unto thee.

And I have also given thee that which thou hast not asked, both riches, and honour; so that there shall not be any among the kings like unto thee all thy days.[1]

Solomon Did Not Remain True

Now unfortunately Solomon didn't remain true. He served the Lord and had wisdom. But the time came when he fell into transgression and was led astray by the wives he had taken contrary to the commandments of the Lord. Therefore he lost his standing before the Lord. But nevertheless, before this he had shown his wisdom and had received the blessings the Lord had promised to him.

And it was while he was under the influence of the Spirit of the Lord that he, as the preacher in Israel, gave this discourse. Now I am only going to refer to certain things in it, but there are a few things in it of the words of the son of David, king of Israel. I say I am only going to refer to a few things in it, but I am going to refer to them with a plea to you, my good brothers and sisters, that you pay a little more attention to the things the Lord has written in his scriptures. I am not going to ask you if you have read the Book of Ecclesiastes, but if I do, I am sure I would not get too many hands. When Solomon wrote these things he was seeking for wisdom, and according to this story he tried to find it in many ways, to find peace and happiness, and he found it wasn't in sin. It wasn't found in the praise of men. It wasn't found in the pursuit of this world's goods.

This discourse is one that you may properly be inclined to say is a discourse on vanity. Solomon discovered that nearly everything in this life you can trace back to vanity and the desire for people to excel, to gain prominence or to seek for those things which bring recognition rather than happiness. If that can stimulate you enough to have you read the Book of Ecclesiastes, I will be doing something:

> Therefore I hated life; because the work that is wrought under the sun is grievous unto me: for all is vanity and vexation of spirit.
>
> Yea, I hated all my labour which I had taken under the sun: because I should leave it unto the man that shall be after me.
>
> And who knoweth whether he shall be a wise man or a fool? yet shall he have rule over all my labour wherein I have laboured, and wherein I have shewed myself wise under the sun. This is also vanity.
>
> Therefore I went about to cause my heart to despair of all the labour which I took under the sun.
>
> For there is a man whose labour is in wisdom, and in knowledge, and in equity; yet to a man that hath not laboured therein shall he leave it for his portion. This also is vanity and a great evil.
>
> For what hath man of all his labour, and of the vexation of his heart, wherein he hath laboured under the sun?
>
> For all his days are sorrows, and his travail grief; yea, his heart taketh not rest in the night. This is also vanity.[2]

Who Would Succeed?

Now he is talking about who would succeed, whether it be a wise man or a fool. When a child is born into this world, what do we know about what he is going to be? And as you look over the world and read the history of nations, you will discover that vanity has been the stimulating principle in the lives of most people. It has been the thing that has ruled kings and princes, men, rulers and magistrates; and it even gets into the hearts of the humblest of us. Therefore it would be well to see what Solomon has to say, to see if we could check ourselves from falling into the temptations that come through pride and through the feeling of desiring to be superior, to excel, instead of being humble and faithful before the Lord. I am going to read a few of these verses found in the third chapter:

> To every thing there is a season, and a time to every purpose under the heaven:
>
> A time to be born, and a time to die; a time to plant, and a time to pluck up that which is planted;
>
> A time to kill, and a time to heal; a time to break down and a time to build up;
>
> A time to weep and a time to laugh; a time to mourn, and a time to dance;
>
> A time to cast away stones, and a time to gather stones together; a time to embrace, and a time to refrain from embracing;
>
> A time to get, and a time to lose; and a time to keep, and a time to cast away;
>
> A time to rend, and a time to sew; a time to keep silence, and a time to speak.[3]

I wish I could learn to do that.

> A time to love, and a time to hate; a time of war, and a time of peace.
>
> What profit hath he that worketh in that wherein he laboureth?
>
> I have seen the travail which God hath given to the sons of men to be exercised in it.
>
> He hath made every thing beautiful in his time; also he hath set the world in their heart, so that no man can find out the work that God maketh from the beginning to the end.
>
> I know that there is no good in them, but for a man to rejoice, and to do good in his life.
>
> And also that every man should eat and drink, and enjoy the good of all his labour, it is the gift of God.
>
> I know that whatsoever God doeth, it shall be for ever; nothing can be put to it, nor any thing taken from it; and God doeth it, that men should fear before him.
>
> That which hath been is now; and that which is to be hath already been; and God requireth that which is past.
>
> And moreover I saw under the sun the place of judgment, that wickedness was there; and the place of righteousness, that iniquity was there.

> I said in mine heart, God shall judge the righteous and the wicked; for there is a time there for every purpose and for every work.[4]

Philosophy of Solomon

Occasionally a little of the philosophy of this great man —and he was a great man, and when he was writing this he had the inspiration of the Almighty. I think when you go home you should get your Bible and read it. It is not very long and you will study a little of the philosophy that is given by this king unto whom the Lord gave this wisdom and had to take it away again, before he fell into his own trap and violated the very things that he counseled others to do:

> I said in mine heart concerning the estate of the sons of men, that God might manifest them, and that they might see that they themselves are beasts.
>
> For that which befalleth the sons of men befalleth beasts; even one thing befalleth them; as the one dieth, so dieth the other; yea, they have all one breath; so that a man hath no preeminence above a beast; for all is vanity.
>
> All go unto one place; all are of the dust, and all turn to dust again.[5]

That reminds me of what the Lord has written in the revelation to the Prophet Joseph Smith, Section 93 of the Doctrine and Covenants. It is a great truth. Every soul born into this world came into it innocently, that is, so far as this life is concerned. There is no taint that can be laid to his charge. That is what Solomon is saying here. You know that the majority of men confessing to be Christians, don't believe it? That the Christian churches which call themselves orthodox in the Protestant world and the great church which the Lord has named and which I shall not name, has damned all little infants that come into the world, and the only way they can escape damnation is for someone to sprinkle them with a little water. And they say that every soul born into the world is tainted. How grateful we should be that the Lord has revealed to the Church of Jesus Christ the truth—that all children were innocent when they came into this world. There is no sin that can be laid to their charge and this is according to the decree of Almighty God before the foundation of this earth was laid. So, I will repeat the words of Solomon:

> Lo, this only have I found, that God hath made man upright; but they have sought out many inventions.[6]

The Lord didn't send wickedness into the world. It came from another source. Little children are born into this world just as innocent and as free from sin as is possible for anyone to be. They are not tainted. They don't have to be sprinkled with a little water to cleanse them from original sin because the Lord Jesus Christ came here and redeemed every soul in the world from original sin and I don't care who he is or what he believes. He paid the debt for original sin. Original sin is Adam's fall. Christ atoned for it by the shedding of his blood. It is the most wicked thing in all the world to teach that little children are damned and cannot go into the presence of God nor behold the face of Jesus Christ if someone has not been kind enough to dip his finger in water and touch them, the children, on the head.

I will read one more verse from the sayings of this once wise man:

> Let us hear the conclusion of the whole matter: Fear God and keep his commandments: for this is the whole duty of man.
>
> For God shall bring every work into judgment, with every secret thing, whether it be good, or whether it be evil.[7]—(Message, South Eighteenth Ward, July 13, 1958.)

---

[1] I Kings 3:8-13.
[2] Ecc. 2:17-23.
[3] *Ibid.*, 3:1-7.
[4] *Ibid.*, 3:8-17.
[5] *Ibid.*, 3:18-20.
[6] *Ibid.*, 7:29.
[7] *Ibid.*, 12:13-14.

We are here on probation, but we are not left to walk in darkness. We have been given divine assistance if we are willing to receive it, so that the judgments which shall be meted out will be just and every man judged according to his works.

The Purpose of Mortal Life

It is a fundamental doctrine of the Church that man is the offspring of God, that he is literally the Father of our spirits. Our Savior taught his disciples to pray, "Our Father which art in heaven, Hallowed be thy name."[1] Moreover he constantly taught them that his Father was their Father, and to Mary, after his resurrection he said: ". . . go to my brethren, and say unto them, I ascend unto my Father, and your Father; and to my God, and your God."[2]

In the Book of Hebrews it is written:

> Furthermore we have had fathers of our flesh which corrected us, and we gave them reverence: shall we not much rather be in subjection unto the Father of spirits, and live?[3]

Again of the vision given to Joseph Smith and Sidney Rigdon they have written:

> And now, after the many testimonies which have been given of him, this is the testimony last of all, which we give of him: That he lives!
>
> For we saw him, even on the right hand of God; and we heard the voice bearing record that he is the Only Begotten of the Father—
>
> That by him, and through him, and of him, the worlds are and were created, and the inhabitants thereof are begotten sons and daughters unto God.[4]

A Fundamental Doctrine of the Church

It is a fundamental doctrine of the Church, based on divine revelation, that we are dual personalities. That is to say we are combined spirits and bodies of flesh and bones, and as spirit children of God we dwelt in his presence before the foundation of the earth was laid. However, in the spirit existence it was impossible for us to receive a fulness of joy and obtain the ultimate destiny which our Father had prepared for us. To reach this goal it was necessary that we have bodies as tabernacles in which our spirit bodies could dwell, and thus we become perfect souls.[5] To bring to pass and give us needed experience that could not be obtained in the world of spirits, preparation was made for us to come to this earth where we obtain bodies of flesh and bones and pass through a short period of mortality where we are tried and proved to see if we will be true to all divine commandments in this mortal state; walking by faith and not by sight. In the spirit existence we walked by sight in the divine presence of our Eternal Father. In mortal life which was prepared for us, we are walking by faith through the guidance of divine revelation coming through chosen prophets who receive commandments from the Lord by which we are to be governed.

This mortal life is a probationary state where we are tested and tried under conditions of temptation from evil sources, and encouragement and guidance by divine assistance and revelation.

Lehi when instructing his son Jacob said:

> And after Adam and Eve had partaken of the forbidden fruit they were driven out of the garden of Eden, to till the earth.
>
> And they have brought forth children; yea, even the family of all the earth.
>
> And the days of the children of men were prolonged, according to the will of God, that they might repent while in the flesh; wherefore, their state became a state of probation, and their time was lengthened, according to the commandments which the Lord God

gave unto the children of men. For he gave commandment that all men must repent; for he showed unto all men that they were lost, because of the transgression of their parents.

And now, behold, if Adam had not transgressed he would not have fallen, but he would have remained in the garden of Eden. And all things which were created must have remained in the same state in which they were after they were created; and they must have remained forever, and had no end.[6]

Paul, also writing to the Corinthian Saints said:

For other foundation can no man lay than that is laid, which is Jesus Christ.

Now if any man build upon this foundation gold, silver, precious stones, wood, hay, stubble;

Every man's work shall be made manifest: for the day shall declare it, because it shall be revealed by fire; and the fire shall try every man's work of what sort it is.

If any man's work abide which he hath built thereupon, he shall receive a reward.

If any man's work shall be burned, he shall suffer loss: but he himself shall be saved; yet so as by fire.

Know ye not that ye are the temple of God, and that the Spirit of God dwelleth in you?

If any man defile the temple of God, him shall God destroy; for the temple of God is holy, which temple ye are.

Let no man deceive himself. If any man among you seemeth to be wise in this world, let him become a fool, that he may be wise.

For the wisdom of this world is foolishness with God. For it is written, He taketh the wise in their own craftiness.

And again, The Lord knoweth the thoughts of the wise, that they are vain.

Therefore let no man glory in man. For all things are yours.[7]

The Lord's Words to Joseph Smith

The Lord also taught us in this generation the nature of this probationary state, and that we are here to be tried and through obedience to the gospel we shall receive the eternal reward of exaltation in his presence. Speaking of Adam's transgression which brought death and banishment from the presence of the Father, the Lord said through the Prophet Joseph Smith, to the members of the Church:

> But, behold, I say unto you that I, the Lord God, gave unto Adam and unto his seed, that they should not die as to the temporal death, until I, the Lord God, should send forth angels to declare unto them repentance and redemption through faith on the name of mine Only Begotten Son.
>
> And thus did I, the Lord God, appoint unto man the days of his probation—that by his natural death he might be raised in immortality unto eternal life, even as many as would believe;
>
> And they that believe not unto eternal damnation; for they cannot be redeemed from their spiritual fall, because they repent not;
>
> For they love darkness rather than light, and their deeds are evil, and they receive their wages of whom they list to obey.[8]

From these passages we learn that we are here on probation, but we are not left to walk in darkness. We have been given divine assistance if we are willing to receive it, so that the judgments which shall be meted out will be just and every man judged according to his works.

One glorious doctrine of the gospel is that every soul shall have a chance. The thousands upon thousands who have died without any opportunity to hear the gospel and without the privilege of accepting its ordinances are not to be overlooked. Here is where the work of salvation of the dead comes in. In the justice of God every soul is to have the opportunity of repentance and acceptance of the gospel truth. Otherwise there could be no justice in the plan of salvation, and our Eternal Father would be unjust. But he is not unjust, and the mercies of the atonement of Jesus Christ reaches out to embrace all and restore them to immortal life and gives to all who will repent and receive the truth, the privileges of eternal life.

In a revelation to the Prophet Joseph the Lord said:

> All who have died without a knowledge of this gospel, who would have received it if they had been permitted to tarry, shall be heirs of the celestial kingdom of God; also all that shall die henceforth without a knowledge of it, who would have received it with

all their hearts, shall be heirs of that kingdom, for I, the Lord, will judge all men according to their works, according to the desire of their hearts.[9]

This Life Is a Proving Ground

We learn, then, that this life is a proving ground; and while its period is very short, it is the most vital one in our entire existence, pre-mortal, mortal, or the eternal life to come.

We see that those who will not repent and who reject the plan of salvation cannot be redeemed from their banishment, or "spiritual fall." In a moment of temptation or rebellion against divine commandments, one may lose all or a great part of divine approbation and righteous reward. A man may cut himself off from ever obtaining the blessing of eternal life. It should be remembered that those who enter the next life are divided into two classes (1) those who obtain immortality, which is the power to live forever, but banished from the presence of the Eternal Father, and (2) those who obtain eternal life, which will take them back into the presence of the Father and the Son to dwell in immortal glory.[10]

Every soul will receive a reward based on merit. All who obey the gospel, receiving all of its covenants will eventually receive the fulness of joy in the celestial kingdom. In mortal life, spirit and body are not inseparably connected, and there will come the separation in death, but in the resurrection they will be inseparable never to be divided, and the righteous will go on to become creators, for the Father has promised all who are faithful and true that they shall become his sons and his daughters receiving the fulness of glory in his kingdom.

Then shall they be gods, because they have no end; therefore shall they be from everlasting to everlasting, because they continue; then shall they be above all, because all things are subject unto them.

Then shall they be gods, because they have all power, and the angels are subject unto them.[11]

John the beloved apostle, writing to members of the Church in his day said:

Behold, what manner of love the Father hath bestowed upon us, that we should be called the sons of God: therefore the world knoweth us not, because it knew him not.

Beloved, now are we the sons of God, and it doth not yet appear what we shall be: but we know that, when he shall appear, we shall be like him; for we shall see him as he is.

And every man that hath this hope in him purifieth himself, even as he is pure.

Whosoever committeth sin transgresseth also the law: for sin is the transgression of the law.

And ye know that he was manifested to take away our sins; and in him is no sin.[12]—(Delivered May 1, 1956 at Brigham Young University.)

---

[1]Matt. 6:9.
[2]John 20:17.
[3]Heb. 12:9.
[4]D&C 76:22-24.
[5]*Ibid.*, 88:14-16.
[6]2 Nephi 2:19-22.
[7]1 Cor. 3:11-21.
[8]D&C 29:42-45.
[9]*DHC,* Vol. 3:380.
[10]Moses 6:43-60; 2 Nephi 2:15-21; Alma 24:33; D&C 29:42-44.
[11]D&C 132:20.
[12]I John 3:1-5.

Every baptized member of the Church receives the gift of the Holy Ghost by the laying on of hands. This, however, will not save them unless they continue in the spirit of light and truth. Therefore it is a commandment from the Lord that members of the Church should be diligent in their activities and study of the fundamental truths of the gospel as it has been revealed.

Study, Pray, Obey

The first time it was my privilege to speak to a congregation in this building it required an effort to have my voice carry to all parts of this tabernacle and be heard. Now when we are privileged to speak, we are conscious of the fact that our voices may go forth to various parts of this mortal world. This makes the speaker conscious of a grave responsibility which rests upon him and the need of weighing every word. I am grateful for the coming of the Prophet Joseph Smith and the restoration of the gospel of our Lord and Savior Jesus Christ in this the greatest of all dispensations—the greatest, because it is the last. I am also made aware of the responsibility which rests upon us, the elders of Israel, to proclaim the words of eternal life as they have been revealed from the heavens for the benefit of all the inhabitants of the world. We are sending missionaries to practically every country on the globe, except perhaps one where the lives of missionaries would be in grave danger and their message misunderstood. This obligation of declaring the words of eternal life devolves upon us by divine decree, given by the Lord to the Prophet Joseph Smith in November 1831 in the following words:

Hearken, O ye people of my church, saith the voice of him who dwells on high, and whose eyes are upon all men; yea, verily I say: Hearken ye people from afar; and ye that are upon the islands of the sea, listen together.

For verily the voice of the Lord is unto all men, and there is none to escape; and there is no eye that shall not see, neither ear that shall not hear, neither heart that shall not be penetrated.

And the rebellious shall be pierced with much sorrow; for their iniquities shall be spoken upon the housetops, and their secret acts shall be revealed.

And the voice of warning shall be unto all people, by the mouths of my disciples, whom I have chosen in these last days.

And they shall go forth and none shall stay them, for I the Lord have commanded them.[1]

We Are Fulfilling the Edict of the Son of God

It is because of this commandment which the Lord gave to the Church through the Prophet Joseph Smith that our missionaries are sent to all parts of the world. We are fulfilling the edict of the Son of God. Moreover, this is in fulfilment of the promise he made to his apostles just preceding his crucifixion, when he declared to them:

And again this Gospel of the Kingdom shall be preached in all the world, for a witness unto all nations, and then shall the end come, or the destruction of the wicked;

And immediately after the tribulation of those days, the sun shall be darkened, and the moon shall not give her light, and the stars shall fall from heaven, and the powers of heaven shall be shaken.

Verily, I say unto you, this generation, in which these things shall be shown forth, shall not pass away until all I have told you shall be fulfilled.[2]

The Lord has made great promises through his servants concerning these times. To Jeremiah the Lord said in speaking of this dispensation:

Behold, the days come, saith the Lord, that I will make a new covenant with the house of Israel, and with the house of Judah:

Not according to the covenant that I made with their fathers in the day that I took them by the hand to bring them out of the land of Egypt; which my covenant they brake, although I was an husband unto them, saith the Lord:

But this shall be the covenant that I will make with the house of Israel; After those days, saith the Lord, I will put my law in their inward parts, and write it in their hearts; and will be their God, and they shall be my people.

And they shall teach no more every man his neighbour, and every man his brother, saying, Know the Lord: for they shall all know me, from the least of them unto the greatest of them, saith the Lord: for I will forgive their iniquity, and I will remember their sin no more.[4]

Many Members Need to Repent

In order that this prophecy may be fulfilled, many members of the Church will need to repent and be more diligent in the study of the scriptures and in their prayers and obedience to the laws and commandments of the gospel. If they fail to do these things they will be cut off from the presence of the Lord in that great day when he shall descend as Lord of lords and King of kings to take his place and sit on his throne to rule and reign.

The Prophet Joseph Smith once said:

The great plan of salvation is a theme which ought to occupy our strict attention, and be regarded as one of heaven's best gifts to mankind. No consideration whatever ought to deter us from showing ourselves approved in the sight of God, according to his divine requirement. Men not unfrequently forget that they are dependent upon heaven for every blessing which they are permitted to enjoy, and that for every opportunity granted them they are to give an account. You know, brethren, that when the master in the Savior's parable of the stewards called his servants before him he gave them several talents to improve on while he should tarry abroad for a little season, and when he returned he called for an accounting. So it is now. Our Master is absent only for a little season, and at the end of it he will call each to render an account; and where five talents were bestowed, ten will be required; and he that has made no improvement will be cast out as an unprofitable servant, while the faithful will enjoy everlasting honors. Therefore, we earnestly implore the grace of our Father to rest upon you through Jesus Christ his Son that you may not faint in the hour of temptation, nor be overcome in the time of persecution.[4]

Words of the Prophet Joseph Smith

The Prophet Joseph Smith in one of his discourses said the following:

> . . . If God should speak from heaven, he would command you not to steal, not to commit adultery, not to covet, nor deceive, but be faithful over a few things. As far as we degenerate from God, we descend to the devil and lose knowledge, and without knowledge, we cannot be saved, and while our hearts are filled with evil, and we are studying evil, there is no room in our hearts for good, or studying good. Is not God good? Then you be good; if he is faithful, then you be faithful. Add to your faith virtue, to virtue knowledge, and seek for every good thing.
>
> ". . . A man is saved no faster than he gets knowledge, for if he does not get knowledge, he will be brought into captivity by some evil power in the other world, as evil spirits will have more knowledge, and consequently more power than many men who are on the earth. Hence it needs revelation to assist us, and give us knowledge of the things of God.[5]

We Are Troubled by Evil-designing Persons

How true this statement is. Today we are troubled by evil-designing persons who are endeavoring with all their power to destroy the testimonies of members of the Church, and many members of the Church are in danger because of lack of understanding and because they have not sought the guidance of the Spirit of the Lord. Every baptized member of the Church receives the gift of the Holy Ghost by the laying on of hands. This, however, will not save them unless they continue in the spirit of light and truth. Therefore it is a commandment from the Lord that members of the Church should be diligent in their activities and study of the fundamental truths of the gospel as it has been revealed. The Spirit of the Lord will not continue to strive with the indifferent, with the wayward and the rebellious who fail to live within the light of divine truth. It is the privilege of every baptized person to have an abiding testimony of the restoration of the gospel, but this testimony will grow dim and eventually disappear unless we are constantly receiving spiritual good through study, obedience, and diligent seeking to know and understand the truth.

May the Spirit of the Lord be our constant companion, and may we one and all be true to our covenants and obligations devolving upon us through our membership in the Church.—(*Conference Report,* October, 1963.)

---

[1]D&C 1:1-5.
[2]Joseph Smith 1:31, 33-34.
[3]Jeremiah 31:31-34.
[4]*DHC* 2:23-24.
[5]*Ibid.,* 4:588.

who fail to live within the light of their words. It is the privilege of every baptized [illegible] to [illegible] which testimony [illegible] [illegible] Simon [illegible] [illegible] [illegible] [illegible]

May the Spirit [illegible] hand by our constant companion, and [illegible] covenants and obligations [illegible] in the Church [illegible]

If you want to go into the presence of God and dwell in the celestial kingdom and see the glories of exaltation, then you must live by every word that proceeds from the mouth of God. . . . We must learn to be truthful, obedient, sincere, having the willingness to walk by every commandment the Lord has given.

Be True and Faithful to Every Covenant

It is a pleasure to me to have the opportunity of being here with you and meeting with you in this tabernacle. My first visit here was half a century ago. I have been here many times since, but I did not come to talk about how many times I have been here. I am glad to have the opportunity of meeting with you, and it has been very pleasing to me to have some of these simple truths of the gospel presented before us.

We, as Latter-day Saints, have a great many duties to perform. I wonder if we do not sometimes get a little careless, a little thoughtless, a little neglectful, and we do not pay as much attention to the simple things that belong to the gospel of Jesus Christ.

Theme Is in Relation to Prayer

The theme this morning has been in relation to prayer. I wonder if we ever stop to think why the Lord has asked us to pray? Did he ask us to pray because he wants us to bow down and worship him? Is that the main reason? I don't think it is. He is our Heavenly Father, and we have been commanded to worship him and pray to him in the name of his beloved Son Jesus Christ. But the Lord can get along without our prayers. His work will go on just the same whether we pray or whether we do not. He knows the end from the beginning. There are many worlds that have passed through the same experiences that we are going through. He has had sons and daughters on other earths where they have had the same privileges and the same opportunities to serve him and the same commandments that we have had given to us. Prayer is something that we need, not that the Lord needs it. He knows just how to conduct his affairs and how to take care of them without any help from us. Our prayers are not for the purpose of telling him how to run his business. If we have any such idea as that, then of course we have the wrong idea. Our prayers are uttered more for our sake, and to build us up and give us strength, and courage, to increase our faith in him.

Prayer Humbles the Soul

These principles of the gospel will bring us back again into his presence if we are true and faithful. Prayer is something that humbles the soul. It broadens our comprehension; it quickens the mind. It draws us nearer to our Father in heaven. And any way you look at it, it is a benefit to us, not to him. We need his help, there is no question about that. We need the guidance of his Holy Spirit. We need to know what principles have been given to us by which we may come back into his presence. We need to have our minds quickened by the inspiration that comes from him, and for these reasons we pray to him, that he may help us to live so that we will know his truth and be able to walk in its light, thus, keeping the many commandments that have been given unto us that we may, through our faithfulness and our obedience, come back again into his presence.

Our missionary brother, speaking of the words of the Lord to Job, drew attention to the fact that at one time we were in the presence of our Eternal Father. There is not a soul in this room, not one, that has not seen him. You do not remember it, I do not remember it, but nevertheless there was a time before we ever came into this world when we dwelt in his presence. We knew what kind of a being he is. One thing we saw was how glorious he is. Another thing, how great was his wisdom, his understanding, how wonderful was his power and his inspiration. And we wanted to be like him. And because we wanted to be like him, we are here. We could not be like him and stay in his presence, because we did not have glorious bodies of flesh and bones. We were just spirits, and the spirit does not have flesh and bones. But we saw him in his glory and it was made known to us that by keeping his commandments and observing every covenant that would be given to us on this earth, we could come back again into his presence, receiving our bodies in the resurrection from the dead—our spirits and bodies being united again, inseparably, never again to be divided.

Be True and Faithful to Every Covenant

If we will just be true and faithful to every covenant, to every principle of truth that he has given us, then after the resurrection we would come back into his presence and we would be just like he is. We would have the same kind of bodies—bodies that would shine like the sun. Moreover, if we are faithful and true while we are here, we would be his sons and his daughters.

We are all his children. All the people on the face of the earth are his children. And they will always be his children. But the Lord is going to make a great segregation after the resurrection of mankind, and many, in fact the greater part of the inhabitants of this earth, will no longer be called the sons and daughters of God, but they will go into the next world to be servants. You know the Lord said in that wonderful sermon we call the Sermon on the Mount:

> Enter ye in at the strait gate: for wide is the gate, and broad is the way, that leadeth to destruction, and many there be which go in thereat:
>
> Because strait is the gate, and narrow is the way, that leadeth unto life, and few there be that find it.[1]

Eternal life is the great gift held in reserve for all those who are willing to keep the commandments of the Lord here.

All Will Receive the Resurrection

All will receive the resurrection of the dead. Their spirits and bodies will be united again, never to die. Is not that eternal life? No, not in the words of our Father in heaven. It is true that all of the people upon the earth, all who have been on the face of the earth, all who will yet be, will get a resurrection. Their bodies and spirits will be united again after they have sojourned here upon the earth, and they will come forth from the grave never to die again. We call that immortality; the right to live forever. But the Lord has put his own interpretation upon eternal life. Eternal life is not only immortality, the right to live forever, but eternal life is to have the same kind of life that our Father in heaven has and to be crowned with the same blessings and glories and privileges that he possesses. In other words, that we might become on the other side of the veil sons and daughters of God, or as Paul states it, members of his household; members of the family of God. Now those who do not receive the gospel of Jesus Christ, no matter how good they may be when they return or come forth from the dead and receive immortality, will not be classed as members of the household of God because they have not kept the covenants that would make them sons and daughters of God. To become sons and daughters of

God we have to keep all of the covenants that belong to the gospel of Jesus Christ and be true in them to the end of our lives. Then we will inherit; we will be called heirs.

Paul speaks of our being joint heirs with Jesus Christ. And as heirs of God we will be entitled to inherit. To inherit what? Not that he is going to step down from his throne that we may ascend. Not that, but we will inherit the same blessings and privileges, opportunities of advancement that he possesses, so that in course, I was going to say of time, but I will say of eternity, we may become like him, having ourselves kingdoms and thrones. If any of you who are here present prefer, when you get on the other side, to be a servant and perhaps go into the terrestrial kingdom, you will have that privilege. You do not have to keep other commandments. You do not need to pay your tithing if you want to go into those other kingdoms. You do not need to pray to your Father in heaven, and you can go into one of those other kingdoms. You do not even have to be baptized for the remission of your sins to go into those other kingdoms. And as you have been baptized and are members of the Church, you do not have to keep all the commandments the Lord has given—you will have to keep some of them, but you will not have to keep them all—and you can go into the telestial kingdom or into the terrestrial kingdom. But if you want to go into the presence of God and dwell in the celestial kingdom and see the glories of exaltation, then you must live by every word that proceeds forth from the mouth of God. We must pray to keep us humble; to draw us out and nearer to our Father in heaven that we might be in closer communication with him. So we must learn to pray.

Learn to Be Truthful and Obedient

We must learn to be truthful, obedient, sincere, having the willingness to walk by every commandment the Lord has given. Now I have heard people say sometimes that it is awful hard to keep the commandments of the Lord. I am not going to make such a confession, and I do not believe it. I do not want it to be hard for me to keep the commandments of the Lord. I do not want it to be hard for you. I hope it is not. It ought to be an easy matter for the Lord says, "My yoke is easy and my burden is light," and when a man or a woman says, "Well, it's awful hard to keep the commandments of the Lord," then I wonder what ails them. Which one of the commandments is hard to keep? Which one are they breaking?

If we love the Lord as we should there is no commandment that he can give us that will be hard for us to keep. The paying of tithing seems to be a hard commandment for some people. Well, what ails them? Selfishness? Lack of the love of God? What is the first commandment given to us? To love the Lord our God with all our heart, might, mind, and strength, and in the name of Jesus Christ to serve him. That is the great commandment. If we do that we are keeping all of the commandments, every one of them. A man that cannot pay his tithing is not going to have the privilege of sitting down in the councils with the just. Why should he? He is not going to be classed among those who are entitled to be heirs in the kingdom of God. The man who never prays will not have the guidance of the Spirit of the Lord. He cannot. It is through prayer that the Spirit is drawn to us and we to that Spirit. And thus our hearts are made tender, our spirits become contrite, and through the keeping of this commandment we learn to love the Lord our God with all our heart and the Lord Jesus Christ. If we do not love our Savior with all our heart, then we do certainly need repentance. There is not time for me to tell you why. But we ought to love him above all things on the face of this earth, because he has done more for us than anyone else that ever lived in this world.—(Uintah Stake Conference, May 17, 1958.)

---

[1]Matt. 7:13-14.

I want the missionaries to remember their obligations in the priesthood quorums to which they belong, to their bishops, to the presidencies of stakes; and then when something is offered them to do in some Church capacity, to accept it—not find themselves so busy in the things that pertain to this world that they haven't time for the things of the kingdom of God.

Advice to Returned Missionaries

I have listened with a great deal of interest to the remarks of each of those who have spoken, and I want to give a little advice to these returned missionaries that will be profitable to them, I believe, if they will only hearken to it. For two years and perhaps more with some of them they have been off in the mission field among people who have no faith, or what faith they have is misplaced. They have been spending their time exclusively in the study and the preaching of the gospel. Now they have returned home.

I believe this is a critical period for them, because now they will be called upon to spend their time preparing for the needs of the mortal life. They will be perhaps building homes. If they are not married, and I suppose they are not, that will be one thing they will be expected to do and looking forward to. They are going to take upon themselves many responsibilities that mortal life will demand of them. They are going to come in contact with the world in a little different light from the one which they were in as missionaries for the Church. There, their whole time and attention was centered upon study and preaching and trying to convert people to a knowledge of the truth as has been revealed. And they testify that this has been a very profitable experience, which no doubt it is.

Matters Pertaining to Mortal Life

But now they are home. Some others perhaps will continue their courses in school, I suppose. There they will run into danger according to the times and the nature of education as I view it today—godless education for many. At any rate, their time is going to be very largely related to matters pertaining to the mortal life, and I do not want them to forget that they have been missionaries, nor lose the spirit of missionary labor, nor their integrity to the Church, and their necessity of obedience to the priesthood.

A great many of our missionaries that come home bear witness of the truth. They say they have a testimony. Then they go out into business, enter employment which requires a great part of their time. And so they come in contact with the world in a very different life from the one which they were in, in the mission field. I want to impress upon them the need of continuing in their exercises, and in their obedience to the duties and responsibilities which the Church places upon them. If they will do that, all will be well. Many of our missionaries return, and then their thoughts are centered upon the things of this life, the making of a living. They had certain ambitions and they find themselves perhaps forgetting the obligations which they owe to their priesthood and to their Church. As time goes on the danger is, as it has been proved by so many, that their ardor decreases and their thoughts and attentions are given more and more to the things of this life—perhaps the making of money which is one of the most dangerous things in all the world.

I want them to remember their prayers, and when I say that I just do not mean these returned missionaries. That is something we all should remember. I want them to remember their obligations in the priesthood quorums to which they belong, to their bishops, to the presidencies of stakes; and then when something is offered them to do in some Church capacity, to accept it—not find themselves so busy in the things that pertain to this world that they haven't time for the things of the kingdom of God.

Many Returned Missionaries Forget

A great many of our missionaries return, then they forget. I find them—missionaries who went into the field when I went into the field; many who have gone into the field since then—they come home, then they have been so busy and their minds have been centered so much on the things of this world that they have neglected their obligations in the Church and to their Heavenly Father. Under those conditions they find themselves drifting, getting farther and farther away from light and truth.

I want them to know and I want you all to know that Satan today is busier than he has ever been in the history of this world. He is filled with more hate and rage and determination, in my judgment, than ever before. Now John saw this and spoke of it. It is recorded in the Book of Revelation that this would be the case, and that he would put forth his efforts with greater vigor because he knows he has but a short time. What I say to these missionaries is just as true and needful to all members of the Church—those who have not been in the mission field and particularly to our young people.

We have reached a stage in our history, according to my understanding—and I have had some experience through the years—that the fashions of the world and the things and the pleasures of the world find more place in the hearts of members of the Church than ever before. I would like to have somebody point out to me that I was wrong, but I don't think they can. Many of our young people are growing up with the love of the world in their hearts, and the fashions of the world and following of the world.

Need for More Teaching in the Home

During this year we have been trying to impress upon parents the need of paying more attention to their children, having a little more of the spirit of the gospel in their homes, a little more unity and a little more faith; a little more responsibility religiously, spiritually on the part of the fathers; also, of the mothers; more of the teaching of the gospel in the home. The Lord had to condemn some of our brethren in the very early days, and he did it very severely because they were neglecting their children in the home.

From my observation I believe it is true the children of today in many of the homes of the Latter-day Saints are lacking in the discipline that ought to be given to them. They have too much freedom. I am not opposed to their having freedom. I do not want anybody to be slaves or unable to exercise their freedom and reason. But the children of the Latter-day Saints today are becoming rebellious and disobedient, and I think it is largely due to the fact that there is neglect of the responsibility the Lord has placed upon us to be exercised in the home.

We do not have family prayer as we ought to have it. I learned that some of these very missionaries—I do not mean those who have spoken here, but the young men and young women that I interview in the mission field—when I ask them if they have family prayer—not every time—they say, "No, we don't." That is a lost art. "Do you pray?" Then they hesitate, "Yes, occasionally." "Once in a while," they say, "when I feel the need." Are we only going to pray when we feel the need? The Lord said, "Seek me early that ye may find me." Are there times when we cannot find him? Yes, it is very possible.

So I call these things to your attention, you fathers and you mothers. In the early days of the Church here, President Brigham Young and others used to say, "It is the kingdom of God or nothing." We are not seeking the kingdom of God and nothing. There is no joy or peace nor salvation outside of it.—(Ensign Stake Conference, Sunday, August 14, 1960.)

The Prophet Joseph Smith stated that if we are not drawing nearer unto God, we are approaching nearer to the devil, a balanced education in which the truths of the gospel of Jesus Christ are emphasized is the only correct kind of education.

Fundamental Gospel Truths Balance Education

This is a wonderful sight. I doubt if it could be duplicated anywhere, in any school, in any country. But most, if not all, of you who are here assembled are here because you have advantages that you could not obtain in any other university—at least that I know of—on the face of the earth. You have the privilege here of receiving a balanced education. By that I mean an education where you obtain training and knowledge of the things pertaining to the kingdom of God—where the fundamental truths of the gospel are taught, and these are of more importance than any other subjects that may be presented to you here, no matter how important other subjects may be.

The Prophet Joseph Smith stated that if we are not drawing nearer unto God, we are approaching nearer to the devil. A balanced education in which the truths of the gospel of Jesus Christ are emphasized is the only correct kind of education. This great university was established for that purpose—that the students might come and be trained in the fundamental truths pertaining to their salvation and in the kingdom of God. That sort of an education is the most important; all other things are secondary. A school without the truths of the gospel of Jesus Christ is deficient. And that, of course, would apply to nearly every school everywhere, where they do not have the opportunities and the privileges which are given to you.

Fundamental Truths

In all your learning you should get understanding of the fundamental truths pertaining to your salvation and the kingdom of God. The Prophet Joseph Smith said a man could not be saved in ignorance. Ignorance of what? Of the saving principles of the gospel of Jesus Christ.

We came into this world having all former knowledge removed. There is not a soul in this building who has not been in the presence of God our Eternal Father. At one time we were acquainted with him. We came here into this world for two very important reasons that I would like to mention: First and foremost, to get tabernacles of flesh and bones for our eternal spirits, that we might go on to full perfection eventually in the kingdom of God. The other great purpose was to gain experience—to learn something that could be learned only through mortality. Now there were other important reasons. I could not name them all. Time would not permit it if I could. But we came here to be tried, tested, to see if we could walk in the light and understanding of eternal truth, shut out from the presence of God our Eternal Father.

We are in school. I do not mean in school in the Brigham Young University. We are in the school of mortal life, partaking of all the activities that come, which are given unto us—the trials, the temptations, the suffering; the physical suffering, the coming in contact with evil as well as with good. I have had the question come to me many times: Why, when Satan was cast out of heaven, was he privileged to come here to this world to tempt the sons and the daughters of God? He was permitted to come down here to tempt us, to try us. We are on probation to see whether, when we are shut out of the presence of our Eternal Father, we will be true and faithful to him. The Lord never left man helpless, to grope and find his way, without any guidance.

One Man's Opinion

I remember reading what one man, who was considered to be a very great character, said, speaking of this life, "The only guide we have is our reason." What a sad world this would be if the Lord had placed us here, had then withdrawn, left us alone to work out our temporal salvation without any guidance, any inspiration, any knowledge coming from the other side to help us, to direct us in the course we should take. What a dreadful world that would be, if men were groping in spiritual darkness, trying to find their way with nothing to guide them but what they, themselves, might figure to be right and wrong.

Mortality is just one step in our eternal advancement. It is a very short period. I do not know how long we lived in the spirit world. We may have been there a very long time, the way we would consider time. Considering eternity, we are here only for a moment. What is a hundred years, should a man live that long, in comparison to eternal life? And yet this life is the most important period, in my judgment, in our existence. It is the period of testing (on probation, as Father Lehi put it) to prove ourselves—guided of course, by the revelations of the Lord as he has sent his revelations to us by the presence of angels, the coming of is own Son, by the inspiration that he gives through his servants the prophets.

Reason for Mortality

The Lord has not left us just to grope, to find our way. After Adam's transgression an angel came to him and to

Eve and gave them instructions as to why they were here and what the Lord expected of them. I think that Mother Eve has given us one of the clearest statements in regard to the fall, our purpose for being here, and what it means. It is a very brief discourse, found in the Book of Moses in Chapter five:

> And in that day Adam blessed God and was filled, and began to prophesy concerning all the families of the earth, saying: Blessed be the name of God, for because of my transgression my eyes are opened, and in this life I shall have joy, and again in the flesh I shall see God.

But Eve added something that is very, very beautiful:

> And Eve, his wife, heard all these things and was glad, saying: Were it not for our transgression we never should have had seed, and never should have known good and evil, and the joy of our redemption, and the eternal life which God giveth unto all the obedient.[1]

Now she grasped this whole situation, the reason for mortality. We are here to be tried, tested, proved.

Lord Ready to Guide

The Lord did not leave Adam to grope and find his way, nor did he any of his descendants from that day until now. The Lord has always been ready to guide, to instruct, to bless. He started Adam and Eve out on the right track and told them to teach their children. The fulness of the gospel was presented to them and then, in obedience, they taught their children. But there is one statement that is very significant in this story:

> And Satan came among them, saying: I am also a son of God . . . Believe it not; and they believed it not (that is, the descendants of Adam believed it not) . . . And man began from that time forth to be carnal, sensual, and devilish.[2]

We are face to face with all these vicissitudes of life. Evil is here; righteousness is here. Any living soul can be directed in ways of truth and righteousness if he so desires, whether he is in the Church of Jesus Christ or whether he is not. There is one great gift that the Lord has given to every living soul—and that is the Light of Christ, which is given to every man who is born into the world—the Light of Christ. If they will hearken to the whisperings that come to them and the guidance that they may receive through the light, it will lead them to the truth.

Gift of Holy Ghost

There is a difference between the Light of Christ and the gift of the Holy Ghost. The gift of the Holy Ghost is only given to those who are baptized for the remission of their sins and have hands laid upon their heads for the gift of the Holy Ghost. That is a far greater blessing. But the Light of Christ will lead every soul to righteousness, to the keeping of the commandments of the Lord, if they will hearken to it. I think this light is many times spoken of as conscience.

What is it that speaks to you when you say your conscience troubles you or your conscience directs you to do this or that, maybe when you are tempted to do something that is contrary to that which is right? Well, I would interpret it as the Light of Christ that is in you, that gives you that spirit of discernment and understanding so that you can choose the right and avoid the evil, if you will just hearken to it. But how much greater is the light that comes through the gift of the Holy Ghost! And that is the privilege given to every member of this Church by the laying on of hands after baptism.

Now I am going to say something that maybe I could not prove, but I believe is true, that we have a great many members of this Church who have never received a manifestation through the Holy Ghost. Why? Because they have not made their lives conform to the truth. And the Holy Ghost will not dwell in unclean tabernacles where perhaps the Light of Christ remains. But the Holy Ghost will not dwell in unclean tabernacles or disobedient tabernacles. The Holy Ghost will not dwell with that person who is unwilling to obey and keep the commandments of God or who violates those commandments willfully. In such a soul the spirit of the Holy Ghost cannot enter.

That great gift comes to us only through humility and and faith and obedience. Therefore, a great many members of the Church do not have that guidance. Then some cunning, crafty individual will come along teaching that which is not true, and without the guidance which is promised to us through our faithfulness, people are unable to discern and are led astray. It depends on our faithfulness and our obedience to the commandments of the Lord if we have the teachings, the enlightening instruction, that comes from the Holy Ghost.

Manifestations Denied

When we are disobedient, when our minds are set upon the things of this world rather than on the things of the kingdom of God, we cannot have the manifestations of the Holy Ghost. Did you ever stop to think what a great privilege it is for us to have the companionship of one of the members of the Godhead? Have you thought of it that way? That is our privilege, if we keep the commandments the Lord has given us.

I have heard occasionally someone say, "It is hard to keep the commandments of the Lord." It is not hard if we love the Lord. We can keep his commandments if we have that love for him that he manifested for us. Then we could set aside temptation. It is not difficult to walk in the light and understanding of the gospel of Jesus Christ if our hearts are right, our spirits are contrite, and we are living in accord with the commandments that the Lord has given us in this, our mortal probation.

Now I say this is a probationary existence. We are placed here on probation. The people in our land, as well as in foreign lands, are all going crazy over getting to the moon, setting up headquarters there, and so forth. I think the Lord sits in the heavens and laughs at our foolishness. He does not have to do like he did in the days of the building of the Tower of Babel, come down to take a look. But I think he sits in the heavens and smiles at the foolishness of mortal men. I did not intend to say that, but I have something I am going to read. Then it is time to quit. I forgot the man's name who wrote this:

> Twinkle, twinkle, little star,
> I don't wonder what you are.
> I surmised your spot in space
> When you left your missile base.
> Any wondering I do
> Centers on the price of you.
> And I shudder when I think
> What you're costing us, each wink.

—(Address given before Brigham Young University Student Body, October 25, 1961.)

---

[1]Moses 5:10-11.
[2]*Ibid.,* 5:13.

The gospel of Jesus Christ is the most vital thing in the world to us. We should so live that we can accept every word that proceedeth forth from the mouth of God, and that is a commandment from him.

Obedience to Tenets

To stand before this great body, members of the Church, mostly priesthood, is something that creates in my soul a feeling of awe and of responsibility. I trust that I may have the guidance of the Spirit of the Lord in the words that I may utter. I am very grateful for what was said in our meeting this morning from our President and those who followed after him. I am sure that we have been edified in the remarks that have been made, and I feel my dependence upon the Spirit of the Lord to aid me in saying something that might be profitable on this occasion.

There may be some who wonder why we hold general conference twice a year, bring our people, particularly the presiding officers, together from all parts of the Church. But brethren, I do not know what we would do if this privilege should be withdrawn from us. I have wondered what, in the days of Peter, James, and John and following, the conditions might have been if they could have met quarterly and semi-annually in conferences. Perhaps the apostasy would have been postponed, if not altogether avoided. But those privileges were not theirs.

I think I feel the importance of these gatherings, and the bringing together the men who hold the priesthood particularly, to receive counsel, to be encouraged, and to return to their stakes renewed in their spirits. We can reach our people today better than they could anciently. We have many facilities that they did not have, and our people are naturally under present conditions, drawn closer together than they were in former days.

And now, my good brethren and sisters, what is our duty? To keep the commandments of God, and we are instructed to do that in our quarterly conferences, in our general conferences, and in all the meetings that are held in the various stakes and wards of Zion. Even as it is, there are conditions arising which should cause us to be alert, on our guard, diligent, persevering in the keeping of the commandments of the Lord, and in instructing the members of the Church. By all means, this is needed. Satan is not dead.

"Hath But a Short Time"

I think frequently of the words of the Lord to John when he said that Satan raged because "he knoweth that he hath but a short time." And he is more active today, perhaps, than ever before in the history of the world. His emissaries get among the Latter-day Saints. Some of them are very cunning and crafty. Some of them at one time had the light and understanding of the gospel, but have lost it. They come among our Latter-day Saints, and if we are not prepared by our faith, by our obedience and knowledge of the gospel, many of us stand in danger of being led astray.

The Prophet Joseph Smith made the statement that a man cannot be saved in ignorance. When he said man he meant mankind. Ignorance of what? Of the saving principles of the gospel of Jesus Christ. We are taught faith in God our Father and in his Son Jesus Christ. We are taught to study, make ourselves familiar with his life when he was upon the face of the earth, why he came, the nature of his work, how it concerns us, to prepare ourselves by our study and by our faith to stand worthy before him in the keeping of his commandments.

We read in the Doctrine and Covenants where the Lord says that all those who repent and are baptized are to receive the gift of the Holy Ghost by the laying on of hands. We baptize our children at the age of eight years—that is the age that the Lord has designated as the age of accountability. Little children before that age are redeemed, should they die, without any act upon their part. One of the most wicked doctrines ever taught in this world was that little children were born in sin, contaminated, and have to be cleansed from that sin of which they themselves were not responsible. Little children were innocent in the beginning, the Lord says, and by his decree until they reach the age of accountability they are free from sin, but from that age on they are under the necessity of baptism for the remission of sin, and entrance into the Church and kingdom of God.

When We Are Baptized

We are promised that when we are baptized, if we are true and faithful, we will have the guidance of the Holy Ghost. What is the purpose of it? To teach us, to direct us, to bear witness to us of the saving principles of the gospel of Jesus Christ. Every child old enough to be baptized and who is baptized is entitled to the guidance of the Holy Ghost. I have heard people say that a little child eight years of age could not understand. I know better than that. I had a testimony of this truth when I was eight years old, coming through the Holy Ghost. I have had it ever since.

We are commanded also to bring up our children in light and truth, to teach them the fundamental principles of the gospel, so that when they grow older they will understand, and have a knowledge of the gospel, a testimony of its truth, and be prepared to resist the persuasions and doctrines and teachings of those who would destroy that belief.

I am grateful for our Primary organizations and our Sunday Schools, and the other organizations of the Church, but brethren and sisters, the Lord has not placed all the responsibility upon our auxiliary organizations, nor upon the bishops of wards to teach the children of Zion the gospel of Jesus Christ. That should be taught them in their homes.

As we travel from stake to stake, we discover in many places that children who are eight years of age, nine years of age, and even older sometimes have not been baptized. Why? Who has neglected this? We cannot blame the child, but somebody is at fault. When a child gets to be nine or ten or eleven or more years of age and has not been baptized a member of this Church, then someone's at fault. Primarily, I would say that that fault is in the home. But the fault is not altogether in the home. The fault rests with those who have charge in the wards of looking after the interests of the young, and the bishops who are to look after all the members of the Church. No child should be permitted to go unbaptized after he or she reaches the eighth year, and when there is that kind of neglect someone is responsible.

Light and Truth

Bring up your children, my brethren and sisters, in light and truth. Teach them by example. Fathers and mothers have to set the example. They cannot say to their children, "You follow the teachings of the Church, but in our lives we are going to make exceptions." It cannot be done, not properly. You parents, set the example. There should be unity in the home, and if there is unity in the home, then there is likely to be unity in the Church. But we begin in the home.

The gospel of Jesus Christ is the means of our salvation. I have often wondered why some members of the Church were members of the Church because they do not live in accordance with the principles of eternal truth. There is only one reason for membership in this Church, as I understand it, and that is as a means of receiving salvation and exaltation in the celestial kingdom of God. If that is not our aim then why are we in the Church?

I know a man who went to school when I went to school, we played together, went to school together. When he grew to be a man he went east and became a scientist. He came back, and then he began to create a great deal of disturbance in the Sunday School classes, questioning the revelations that had been given through the Prophet Joseph Smith. This came to my attention when one of the members of that class came to me and said, "This brother comes to our class and he is a disturbance." As I was well acquainted with him, I made it my duty to get hold of him and asked him why he did those things and was disturbing members of the class.

"Well," he said, "I cannot accept all the revelations that were given to the Prophet Joseph Smith."

"Are there any of them that you can accept?"

"Yes," he said, "I can accept some of them," but he could not accept all of the doctrines that had come through the revelations of our Father in Heaven and his Son Jesus Christ to the Church.

After we got through with the conversation, and I had a long conversation with him, he said, "Now, I am going to ask you one favor. Please do not take any steps to have me excommunicated."

Raised in Church

I said, "Why do you want to stay in the Church when you are opposing its doctrines?"

He said, "I will tell you why. I was raised in the Church, and my friends are members of the Church. I have few associates outside of the Church. If I should be excommunicated that means that I should be cut off from all communication, all fellowship with the people with whom I am now associating, and I do not want that to happen. So please do not take any steps to have me excommunicated."

I thought there was some hope for him so I did not take any such step, but I did talk to him kindly and try to get him to see the folly of his ways, to repent, and when he went to the classes, and he should go to the classes, he should not go with that spirit of defiance or opposition to the doctrines which the others believed. I said, "If you don't believe them, then keep still and see if you cannot get the Spirit of the Lord so that you can accept them."

Well, he is dead now. I do not know whether he repented or not, but brethren, the gospel of Jesus Christ is the most vital thing in the world to us. We should so live that we can accept every word that proceedeth forth from the mouth of God, and that is a commandment from him.

If we have the right spirit that is what we are going to do. If there is any doctrine or principle connected with the teachings of the Church that we do not understand, then let us get on our knees. Let us go before the Lord in the spirit of prayer, of humility, and ask that our minds might be enlightened that we may understand.

This Church is not teaching false doctrine. All the revelations given to the Prophet Joseph Smith are absolutely true. They are given for our salvation, for our knowledge, for our understanding, that we may draw nearer and nearer to our Father in Heaven, and be found worthy before him and eventually have the privilege of coming into his presence, there to be crowned as sons and daughters of God, receiving the fulness of his kingdom.—(*Conference Report*, October, 1959.)

In his justice the Lord has revealed to The Church of Jesus Christ of Latter-day Saints, just as he revealed it in the days of the apostles, that there is a salvation even for the dead, and the time must come when every soul must have an opportunity to hear it.

Message of Salvation to Reach Every Soul

For the few minutes that I have I would like to take a text from the words of our Savior, "Except a man be born of water and the Spirit, he cannot enter into the kingdom of God."[1]

I am firmly convinced that nowhere else in the world, outside of The Church of Jesus Christ of Latter-day Saints, is there anyone who has the authority to perform the ordinances that would bring the birth of the water and of the Spirit to mankind. That would have to be from someone who has the authority of the priesthood of God, and that authority was revealed in these latter-days, the Aaronic Priesthood first by John the Baptist to the Prophet Joseph Smith and Oliver Cowdery, and then the Melchizedek Priesthood under the hands of Peter, James and John, also to the Prophet Joseph Smith and Oliver Cowdery.

Obtained Priesthood

And from that source we have obtained the priesthood of God by which we act and by which we go forth into the world to preach the gospel to those who sit in darkness. I know this statement is not pleasing to the great majority of people upon the face of the earth, but nevertheless it is true. And I realize that it is impossible for us—all things are possible, of course, to the Lord—but it is impossible for us with all the means that we have at our command and the means at our command have increased wonderfully in the last few years—but we cannot reach every soul living upon the face of the earth. They are dying off every day. They are being born every day into the world.

However, the word of the Lord being true, the time must come when the message of salvation will reach every soul. How is that to be done? We do the best we can with all the facilities at our command, through the preaching of the gospel, disseminating the truth by word of mouth, by the many facilities that are at our command, through the magazines that are published, through the press and every other means. But it is impossible for us with the facilities such as they are, to reach every soul.

Furthermore, there have been millions upon millions of people who have lived in this world who never had the opportunity to hear of Christ, never heard his name, they lived at a time and in a place where his name was not known, where the gospel did not reach them, not because of any fault on the part of our Father in heaven nor of his servants to reach the peoples of the earth, but because from the beginning of time men have loved Satan more than they loved God and they have turned away and refused to receive the truth, have raised their children in darkness and they have died in darkness, so far as the gospel of Jesus Christ is concerned.

Promises to Be Fulfilled

Nevertheless, the promises of the Lord must and will be fulfilled. From the very beginning of this dispensation just a few months after the organization of the Church, the Lord gave a revelation in which he foreshadowed the salvation of the human family, all of those who would repent and believe. I shall read to you this part of the Lord's Preface to the book of his commandments; the words of Jesus Christ, himself.

> Hearken, O ye people of my church, saith the voice of him who dwells on high, and whose eyes are upon all men; yea, verily I say: Hearken ye people from afar; and ye that are upon the islands of the sea, listen together.

Now, that is to all those who are living. But the Lord goes on to enlarge this thought. And he says:

> For verily the voice of the Lord is unto all men, and there is none to escape; and there is no eye that shall not see, neither ear that shall not hear, neither heart that shall not be penetrated.

The Lord has not limited that to any dispensation or any age upon the face of the earth. He has made that just as broad as the history of mankind, and he adds:

> And the rebellious shall be pierced with much sorrow; for their iniquities shall be spoken upon the housetops, and their secret acts shall be revealed.[2]

It seems so strange to me that the peoples of this world since the days of the great apostasy, when the apostles of old were removed and those who held the priesthood were destroyed, that the world could fall into that awful condition which today prevails, which denies salvation to every soul born into this world who never heard the name of Jesus Christ, or never had an opportunity to repent and be baptized or receive the gift of the Holy Ghost. They have held out no hope for all of these people of the nations, pagan or otherwise, who have dwelt upon the face of the earth without the knowledge of the gospel of Jesus Christ.

Lord Is Just

The Lord is just and he has made it clear that the time will come when every soul shall have an opportunity to hear the truth. That does not mean that every soul has had the opportunity or will have that opportunity in this mortal world. Millions have died without that opportunity. It has been no fault of theirs, but the fault lies with their fathers before them, who turned away from the truth which truth was given in the beginning to Adam who was commanded to teach these things to his children. The scriptures say that Adam did teach these things to his children, but that they loved Satan more than they loved God and Satan came among them and said, "I, too, am a son of God, believe it not, and they believed it not and from that time forth men became carnal, sensual and devilish," and so darkness spread over the face of the earth.

In his justice, the Lord has revealed to The Church of Jesus Christ of Latter-day Saints, just as he revealed it in the days of the apostles, that there is a salvation even for the dead, and the time must come when every soul must have an opportunity to hear it. Those who did not get the opportunity to hear it in this world will have that opportunity in the world of spirits. Peter made that very clear in his epistles, and it is only fair that those who died without a knowledge of the gospel should have the opportunity to hear. The Lord revealed that great truth to the Prophet Joseph Smith, that the time would come when the gospel of the kingdom would be declared to the dead. They who never had the opportunity to hear it should have that opportunity given to them, and if they would repent in that spirit world then we could go into the temples of the Lord and perform the ordinances for them vicariously, being saviors upon Mount Zion, and thus give unto the dead the opportunity to hear the truth, to repent of their sins. If they will repent and turn away from evil and accept the truth we can go into the temples of the Lord and perform the ordinances for them which will be valid unto them just the same as if they were living upon the face of the earth.

A Vicarious Work

The gospel of Jesus Christ is a vicarious work. Christ came into this world and died for mankind. He did not die just for those who repented of their sins and received his gospel. His death upon the cross brought salvation to every living soul, so far as the resurrection from the dead is concerned. Every soul born into this world shall receive the resurrection from the dead because they were not guilty of bringing death into the world, and man is not penalized because death came into the world. Naturally he has to die —that is part of the mortal life—but he will be raised again in the resurrection no matter who he is, no matter when he lived, no matter what he believed or what he failed to believe. That is a universal gift from Jesus Christ to every soul.

It is a different matter, however, so far as the kingdom of God is concerned, and no soul is going to enter into that kingdom until he has received either in this life in person or by proxy because he was not here to do it for himself, baptism for the remission of his sins and the laying on of hands for the gift of the Holy Ghost. What a wonderful gift it is the Lord has placed into our hands, to bring salvation to the dead, to those who are willing to repent and receive the truth.

I have no idea in my mind that every soul that has lived upon the face of the earth, who has died and gone to the spirit world, is going to repent and receive the gospel. There will be many that will not do that. Our scriptures point to that fact. They are not going to receive the gospel in the spirit world, when their souls are full of bitterness and hate towards the truth, but they have a right to have it taught to them.

One Great Family

The Lord went into the spirit world, himself, and turned the key for the salvation of the dead. Our elders when they pass to the next world, go into that world to continue their labors of preaching the gospel, bringing to repentance all who are willing to repent and receive the truth, that they might come into the kingdom of God, or as Paul calls it, the family of God in heaven and on earth. For it is the family of God. The kingdom of God will be one great family. We call ourselves brothers and sisters. In very deed we become joint heirs with Jesus Christ through the gospel of Jesus Christ, sons and daughters of God, and entitled to the fulness of the blessings of his kingdom if we will repent and keep these commandments.

In conclusion I want to read to you some statements dealing with our responsibilities towards the dead:

> The greatest responsibility in this world that God has placed upon us is to seek after our dead.[3]
>
> This doctrine was the burden of the scriptures. Those Saints who neglect it in behalf of their deceased relatives, do it at the peril of their own salvation.[4]

Again he said:

> It is one of the greatest and most important subjects that God has revealed, that he should send Elijah to seal the children to their fathers and the fathers to the children. . . . Without us they could not be made perfect nor we without them; the fathers without the children or the children without the fathers.—From the Prophet Joseph Smith.[5]
>
> We have a work to do just as important in this sphere as the Savior's work was in his sphere. Our fathers cannot be made perfect without us and we cannot be made perfect without them. They have done their work and now sleep. We work now, are called upon to do ours which is to be the greatest work man ever performed on this earth. The ordinances of sealing must be performed here, woman to man and children to parents, until the chain of generations is made perfect in the sealing ordinances back to father Adam.—President Brigham Young.[6]

Required at Our Hands

Brethren and sisters, lay these things to heart. Let us go on with our records. I pray God that as a people, our eyes may be opened to see, our ears to hear, our hearts to understand the great and mighty work that rests upon our shoulders and that the Lord of heaven requires at our hands.—President Wilford Woodruff.[7]

This is the day in which the Lord expects his Church to inaugurate the great work of turning the heart of the fathers to the children and the heart of the children to their fathers. What about your ancestors who never heard the name of Jesus Christ. You have the opportunity of gathering the names of your ancestors and by their being baptized for by proxy, they may become members of the kingdom of God in the other world as we are members here.—President David O. McKay.[8]

Now, brethren, these are our responsibilities and the Lord requires this work at our hands. The Church has gone to great expense endeavoring to gather the records of the dead and I want to say to you, has been very, very successful in that labor to gather in the records of your ancestors so that we could go into the temples of the Lord and perform these labors for them so that all who are willing to repent and receive the gospel of Jesus Christ may be brought into his kingdom and into that great family of God, which is both in heaven and on earth.

And I humbly pray that this spirit will take hold of the members of the Church.—(*Conference Report,* April, 1959.)

---

[1]John 3:5.
[2]D&C 1:1-3.
[3]*Teachings of the Prophet Joseph Smith,* p. 356.
[4]*Ibid.,* p. 193.
[5]*Ibid.,* p. 337.
[6]*Discourses of Brigham Young,* pp 406-407.
[7]*The Utah Genealogical and Historical Magazine,* Vol. 13, p. 152.
[8]*Gospel Ideals,* p. 19.

The greatest punishment that can come to any individual in this world is punishment that will come to those who have received the light and truth of the gospel of Jesus Christ, who have passed through the waters of baptism, who have had hands laid upon their heads for the gift of the Holy Ghost, and then turn away from the truth, for the Lord will not hold them guiltless.

Take Heed and Pray Always . . . Lest You Fall into Temptation

This morning we listened to a wonderful discourse addressed to friends and businessmen, prominent individuals outside of the Church, which I think was most timely, but I wish to address my remarks to the members of the Church, and more especially to those who are wayward and indifferent, and who do not seem to realize the value of their membership. I would like to read you a covenant which is taken by each individual who enters the waters of baptism.

> And again, by way of commandment to the church concerning the manner of baptism—All those who humble themselves before God, and desire to be baptized, and come forth with broken hearts and contrite spirits, and witness before the church that they have truly repented of all their sins, and are willing to take upon them the name of Jesus Christ, having a determination to serve him to the end, and truly manifest by their works that they have received the Spirit of Christ unto the remission of their sins, shall be received by baptism into his church.[1]

Now, baptism into the Church is not enough to save us. It is for the remission of sins, that is true, but there is another baptism which is just as essential, and that is the baptism of the spirit, or the bestowal of the gift of the Holy

Ghost. After we are baptized we are confirmed. What is that confirmation for? To make us companions with the Holy Ghost; to have the privilege of the guidance of the third member of the Godhead—companionship, that our minds might be enlightened, that we might be quickened by the Holy Spirit to seek for knowledge and understanding concerning all that pertains to our exaltation in the kingdom of God.

Man May Fall

In this same revelation from which I read, the Lord has also said:

> And we know that justification through the grace of our Lord and Savior Jesus Christ is just and true:
>
> And we know also, that sanctification through the grace of our Lord and Savior Jesus Christ is just and true, to all those who love and serve God with all their mights, minds, and strength.
>
> But there is a possibility that man may fall from grace and depart from the living God;
>
> Therefore let the church take heed and pray always, lest they fall into temptation;
>
> Yea, and even let those who are sanctified take heed also.[2]

Baptism and confirmation into the Church does not necessarily insure our exaltation in the kingdom of God. They do provided we are true and faithful to every covenant and obligation required of us in the commandments of our Eternal Father. It is he who endures to the end that will be saved, and there is a danger that confronts us through the temptations of the adversary if we yield to those temptations that we may lose it all.

The greatest punishment that can come to any individual in this world is punishment that will come to those who have received the light and truth of the gospel of Jesus Christ, who have passed through the waters of baptism, who have hands laid upon their heads for the gift of the Holy Ghost and then they turn away from the truth, for the Lord will not hold them guiltless.

Sons of Perdition

I think I am safe in saying that no man can become a son of perdition until he has known the light. Those who have never received the light are not to become sons of perdition. They will be punished if they rebel against God. They will have to pay the price of their sinning, but it is only those who have the light through the priesthood and through the power of God and through their membership in the Church who will be banished forever from his influence into outer darkness to dwell with the devil and his angels. That is a punishment that will not come to those who have never known the truth. Bad as they may suffer, and awful as their punishment may be, they are not among that group which is to suffer the eternal death and banishment from all influence concerning the power of God.

Now, I say I want to talk to those who are indifferent and a little wayward sometimes, those who do not appreciate the privileges and the opportunities that are given unto them to serve God and keep his commandments. If they are not here I hope they are listening to what is going on in this building today, but they are not here at this conference. They do not come to the conferences—at least, not very many of them. But after receiving the light and the knowledge and the information which the Spirit of the Lord can give, it is an awful thing to turn away.

Gift Never Received

However, it is my judgment that there are many members of this Church who have been baptized for the remission of their sins, who have had hands laid upon their heads for the gift of the Holy Ghost, who have never received that gift, that is, the manifestations of it. Why? Because they have never put themselves in order to receive these manifestations. They have never humbled themselves. They have never taken the steps that would prepare them for the companionship of the Holy Ghost. Therefore they go through life without that knowledge, and they have not the understanding. Therefore when those cunning and crafty in their deceit come to them they disturb them in their faith, if they have faith left.

They criticize the Authorities of the Church. They criticize the doctrines of the Church, and these weak members do not have understanding enough, information enough, and enough of the guidance of the Spirit of the Lord, to resist the false doctrines and teachings of those who come to them, the wolves in sheep's clothing, and they listen to them. They think that perhaps after all they have made a mistake, and first thing you know they find their way out of the Church, because they do not have understanding.

I get letters frequently from people, members of this Church, who have been disturbed principally by those of two organizations which seem to have dedicated their lives to the destruction of The Church of Jesus Christ of Latter-day Saints. These people go into the homes of our weak members, disturb them in their faith, get them all riled up, and they do not know whether they did the right thing when they were baptized, or whether they did not, but if they had lived as they should and had received the guidance of the Holy Spirit, they would not be moved. They would not be influenced by the false teachings and the false statements regarding our doctrines that these people present to them.

Simplicity of Gospel

The gospel is simple. There is nothing difficult about it. There are mysteries, no doubt. We do not need to bother about the mysteries, but the simple things pertaining to our salvation and exaltation we can understand.

Now let me refer to another passage of scripture.

> But ye are commanded in all things to ask of God, who giveth liberally; and that which the spirit testifies unto you even so I would that ye should do in all holiness of heart, walking uprightly before me, considering the end of your salvation, doing all things with prayer and thanksgiving, that ye may not be seduced by evil spirits, or doctrines of devils, or the commandments of men; for some are of men, and others of devils.[3]

So the Lord has given us a warning.

> Wherefore, beware lest ye are deceived; and that ye may not be deceived seek ye earnestly the best gifts, always remembering for what they are given;
>
> For verily I say unto you, they are given for the benefit of those who love me and keep all my commandments, and him that seeketh so to do; and all may be benefited that seek or that ask of me, that ask and not for a sign that they may consume it upon their lusts.
>
> And again, verily I say unto you, I would that ye should always remember, and always retain in your minds what those gifts are, that are given unto the Church.[4]

Now the Lord would give us gifts. He will quicken our minds. He will give us knowledge that will clear up all difficulties, and put us in harmony with the commandments that he has given us, and with a knowledge that will be so deeply rooted in our souls that the knowledge can never be rooted out, if we will just seek for the light and the truth and the understanding which is promised to us, and which we can receive if we will only be true and faithful to every covenant and obligation pertaining to the gospel of Jesus Christ.—(*Conference Report,* October, 1958.)

---

[1]D&C 20:37.
[2]*Ibid.,* 20:30-34.
[3]*Ibid.,* 46:7.
[4]*Ibid.,* 46:8-10.

It is a fact beyond successful dispute that no unclean thing can inherit the kingdom of God and obtain what is known as eternal life.

No Man Can Disobey God without Paying for It

When I was a small boy, too young to hold the Aaronic Priesthood, my father placed a copy of the Book of Mormon in my hands with the request that I read it. I received this Nephite record with thanksgiving and applied myself to the task which had been assigned to me. There are certain passages that have been stamped upon my mind and I have never forgotten them. One of these is in the 27th chapter of 3rd Nephi, verses 19 and 20. It is the word of our Redeemer to the Nephites as he taught them after his resurrection. It is as follows:

> And no unclean thing can enter into his kingdom; therefore nothing entereth into his rest save it be those who have washed their garments in my blood, because of their faith, and the repentance of all their sins, and their faithfulness unto the end.
>
> Now this is the commandment: Repent, all ye ends of the earth, and come unto me and be baptized in my name, that ye may be sanctified by the reception of the Holy Ghost, that ye may stand spotless before me at the last day.[1]

The other passage is in the 10th verse of Chapter 41, in the Book of Alma, and is as follows:

Do not suppose, because it has been spoken concerning restoration, that ye shall be restored from sin to happiness. Behold, I say unto you, wickedness never was happiness.[2]

Scriptural Passages Have Proved a Guide

These two passages I have tried to follow all the days of my life, and I have felt to thank the Lord for this counsel and guidance, and I have endeavored to stamp these sayings on the minds of many others. What a wonderful guide these teachings can be to us if we can get them firmly fixed in our minds. These thoughts are of course not peculiar to the Book of Mormon. They are fundamental teachings of the gospel of Jesus Christ and have been expressed many times by the prophets of old and our Redeemer when they were upon the earth.

It is a fact beyond successful dispute that no unclean thing can inherit the kingdom of God and obtain what is known as eternal life. This is to say the Redeemer of this world, through the great sacrifice which he made, opened the graves and restored all mortal things, both mankind the fowls of the air, fishes of the sea, and every creature that partook of death through the "fall" of Adam. In the 5th chapter of John, verses 28 and 29, we have the definite statement of our Redeemer proclaiming this truth as follows:

Marvel not at this: for the hour is coming, in the which all that are in the graves shall hear his voice,

And shall come forth; they that have done good, unto the resurrection of life; and they that have done evil, unto the resurrection of damnation.[3]

Other Scripture Given by Divine Decree

Permit me to quote some other passages of scripture from the revelations that have come to us by divine decree in this dispensation. This is from the Doctrine and Covenants, Section 29, verses 22 to 25:

And again, verily, verily, I say unto you that when the thousand years are ended, and men again begin to deny their God, then will I spare the earth but for a little season;

And the end shall come, and the heaven and the earth shall be consumed and pass away, and there shall be a new heaven and a new earth.

For all old things shall pass away, and all things shall become new, even the heaven and the earth, and all the fulness thereof, both men and beasts, the fowls of the air, and the fishes of the sea;

And not one hair, neither mote, shall be lost, for it is the workmanship of mine hand.[4]

Again the Lord spoke to the Prophet Joseph Smith in a revelation in answer to the question:

Q. What are we to understand by the four beasts spoken of in the same verse? (Rev. 4:6.)

A. They are figurative expressions, used by the Revelator, John, in describing heaven, the paradise of God, the happiness of men, and of beasts, and of creeping things, and of the fowls of the air; that which is spiritual being in the likeness of that which is temporal; and that which is temporal in the likeness of that which is spiritual; the spirit of man in the likeness of his person, as also the spirit of the beast, and every other creature which God has created.[5]

Strange Doctrine in the World

There is a strange doctrine in the world concerning the resurrection even among those who believe there will be reuniting of the spirit and body, which is to the effect that only the righteous will come forth, to receive rewards of exaltation. This, however, is a misunderstanding. Through the atonement wrought by the Son of God, our Savior, the resurrection is a complete restoration of all things mortal, even of this earth itself, on which we stand. The earth is to be purified and become the abode of the righteous. Peter understood this doctrine and in his second epistle made the following statement:

But the day of the Lord will come as a thief in the night; in the which the heavens shall pass away with a great noise, and the elements shall melt with fervent heat, the earth also and the works that are therein shall be burned up.

Seeing then that all these things shall be dissolved, what manner of persons ought ye to be in all holy conversation and godliness,

Looking for and hasting unto the coming of the day of God, wherein the heavens being on fire shall be dissolved, and the elements shall melt with fervent heat?

Nevertheless we, according to his promise, look for new heavens and a new earth, wherein dwelleth righteousness.[6]

A New Heaven and a New Earth

Let us not misunderstand this expression. The new heaven and new earth will be the same heaven and the same earth on which we now sojourn, for this earth is to receive the resurrection after this day of mortality and be the abode of the righteous in eternity. Without the revelations of the Lord given to men, this truth would not be made known. Neither would we have knowledge of the final glory to which this earth will be assigned. Even now, where men are without the divine guidance and revelation, this truth is unknown.

I am very grateful to my Father in Heaven for the privilege that has been granted to me to come into this world in this dispensation when once again the fulness of the gospel has been revealed. I have been grateful and have thanked the Lord many times for the privilege which came to me to live in the present dispensation and that I was not born two or three hundred years ago, or the great period when the fulness of the gospel was not had among men and they were running as the scriptures say "to and fro," seeking for the truth which could not be found because of the deep spiritual darkness which covered the entire earth.

This condition was not the fault of the Lord but the fault of mankind for they had been offered the fulness of the gospel but in course of time they refused to have it and their teachers turned away and caused to enter into the Church false doctrines, and false ordinances, and worse than all, a false conception in relation to God our Eternal Father and his Son Jesus Christ.

A Time without Authority

It was a day when there was not one left in mortality with the divine power to officiate in the vital and saving ordinances of the gospel. A day when false teachings, false ordinances, and false instructors came upon the scene. This condition left the entire Christian world in a state of confusion, without divine inspiration so that the notion prevailed universally that the heavens were closed. Contact with the Father and his Beloved Son had ceased and the angels for a long long past had ceased to visit mortal man on the face of the earth. Under such conditions it was a natural thought encouraged by clergy that our Eternal Father had ceased to commune with his children on the earth. Moreover the false notion became prevalent that mortal man was left with the teachings of the Bible and that it contained all of the revelation that mankind needed to insure his salvation in the kingdom of God.

Under such conditions and practice no doubt Satan rejoiced; false teachers arose and the people, no matter how devout they were, found themselves in spiritual darkness. Moreover, for a long time the edict went forth that mortal men who had not been prepared for the clergy should not seek for knowledge or search the scriptures for this was the sole responsibility of the clergy. Therefore I am exceedingly grateful for the Prophet Joseph Smith and the coming of the Father and the Son to him and directing him in the course he should take. Moreover, that the time came for the restoration of divine truth and the power of the Holy Priesthood that the inhabitants of the world could find the path to eternal life and the ordinances of the Holy Priesthood could again be exercised in behalf of the salvation of all mankind.

Joseph Smith's Statement

On January 22, 1834, the Prophet Joseph Smith said:

The great plan of salvation is a theme which ought to occupy our strict attention, and be regarded as one of heaven's best gifts to mankind. No consideration whatever ought to deter us from showing ourselves approved in the sight of God, according to his divine requirement. Men not unfrequently forget that they are dependent upon heaven for every blessing which they are permitted to enjoy, and that for every opportunity granted them they are to give an account. You know, brethren, that when the Master in the Savior's parable of the stewards called his servants before him he gave them several talents to improve on while he should tarry abroad for a little season and when he returned he called for an accounting. So it is now, our master is absent only for a little season, and at the end of it, he will call each to render an account; and where the five talents were bestowed, ten will be required; and he that has made no improvement will be cast out as an unprofitable servant, while the faithful will enjoy everlasting honors. Therefore we earnestly implore the grace of our Father to rest upon you, through Jesus Christ His Son, that you may not faint in the hour of temptation, nor be overcome in the time of persecution.[7]

I would like to quote a few remarks of divine truth from the lips of President David O. McKay, taken from *Gospel Ideals*.

No man can disobey the word of God and not suffer for so doing.

No sin, however secret, can escape retribution. True, you may lie and not be detected; you may violate virtue without it being known by any who would scandalize you; yet you cannot escape the judgment that follows such transgression. The lie is lodged in the recesses of your mind, an impairment of your character that will reflect sometime, somehow in your countenance or bearing. Your mortal turpitude, though only you, your accomplice, and God may ever know it, will canker your soul.[8]

I will close my remarks by reading a poem which I think is very appropriate, entitled: "The Guy in the Mirror."

When you get what you want in your struggle for self,
And the world makes you king for a day,

Then go to the mirror and look at yourself and see what that guy
has to say,
For it isn't a man's father, or mother, or wife,
Whose judgment upon you must pass;
The fellow whose verdict counts most in his life
Is the guy staring back from the glass.
He's the fellow to please, never mind all the rest
For he's with you clear up to the end.
And you've passed your most dangerous, difficult test,
If the guy in the glass is your friend.
You may be like Jack Horner and "chisel" a plum,
And think you're a wonderful guy,
But the man in the glass says you're only a bum,
If you can't look him straight in the eye.
You can fool the whole world down the pathway of years
And get pats on the back as you pass,
But your final reward will be heartaches or tears
If you've cheated the guy in the glass.

—(*Conference Report,* October, 1964.)

---

[1]3 Nephi 27:19-20.
[2]Alma 41:10.
[3]John 5:28-29.
[4]D&C 29:22-25.
[5]*Ibid.,* 77:2-3.
[6]2 Peter 3:10-13.
[7]*Teachings of the Prophet Joseph Smith,* p. 68.
[8]*Gospel Ideals,* p. 383.

How will a young married couple feel when they come to the judgment and then discover that there were certain spirits assigned to them and they refused to have them? Moreover, what will be their punishment when they discover that they have failed to keep a solemn covenant, and spirits awaiting this mortal life were forced to come here elsewhere when they were assigned to this particular couple?

The Blessings of Eternal Glory

My dear brethren and sisters, I hope and pray that what I might say may be uplifting to one and all. I have many letters cross my desk in regards to the subject I would like to discuss, "The Blessings of Eternal Glory."

Nothing should be held in greater sacredness and honor than the covenant by which the spirits of men—the offspring of God in the spirit—are privileged to come into the world in mortal tabernacles. It is through this principle that the blessing of immortal glory is made possible. The greatest punishment ever given was proclaimed against Lucifer and his angels. To be denied the privilege of mortal bodies forever is the greatest curse of all. These spirits have no progress, no hope of resurrection and eternal life! Doomed are they to eternal misery for their rebellion! And then to think that we are not only privileged but commanded to assist our Father in the great work of redemption by giving to his children, as we have obtained these blessings for ourselves, the right to life and continue on even to perfection! No innocent soul should be condemned to come into this world under a handicap of illegitimacy. Every child has the right to be well born! Every individual who denies them that right is guilty of a mortal sin.

The importance of these mortal tabernacles is apparent from the knowledge we have of eternal life. Spirits cannot be made perfect without the body of flesh and bones. This body and its spirit are brought to immortality and blessings of salvation through the resurrection. After the resurrection there can be no separation again, body and spirit become inseparably connected that man may receive a fulness of joy. In no other way, other than through birth into this life and the resurrection, can spirits become like our Eternal Father.

Since the kingdom of God is built upon the foundation of marriage and the unity of the family circle, there can be no satisfaction where the family circle is broken. Every soul is entitled to the right to come into this world in a legitimate way—in the way the Father has willed that souls should come. Whosoever takes a course contrary to this is guilty of an almost irreparable crime. Is there any wonder then, that the Lord places the violation of this covenant of marriage and the loss of virtue, as second only to the shedding of innocent blood? Is there not, then sufficient reason for the severity of the punishment which has been promised those who violate this eternal law? The demand for personal purity is made by the Church upon both men and women, equally. There is no double standard of judgment. "If purity of life is neglected," President Joseph F. Smith said once, "all other dangers set in upon us like the rivers of water when the flood gates are opened."

Sexual impurity is a most deadly sin. There are sins unto death John informs us, and this is one of them: John 5:16-17.

President Brigham Young said, the world is fast coming to its destruction because of it. "Learn the will of God, keep his commandments and do his will, and you will be a virtuous person."

How wonderful is the peace and joy which fill the soul of the virtuous person! How terrible are the torments of the unvirtuous! They shall have no place in the first resurrection. When the final judgment comes they are they who remain "filthy still." They cannot enter the Holy City, they are the "dogs, and sorcerers, and whoremongers, and murderers, and idolators, and whosoever loveth and maketh a lie," who are cast out.

When a man was first placed upon this earth he was given the commandment to "be fruitful and multiply." No more important commandment was ever given to man, for, through honorable marriage are the spirits brought to earth. "There are multitudes of pure and holy spirits waiting to take tabernacles, now what is our duty?" said President Young. Then he answered his question: "To prepare tabernacles for them; to take a course that will not tend to drive those spirits into the families of the wicked, where they will be trained in wickedness, debauchery, and every species of crime. It is the duty of every righteous man and woman to prepare tabernacles for all the spirits they can." "Instructions to mothers of the Church" by President Joseph F. Smith.

I think it is a crying evil, that there should exist a sentiment or a feeling among any members of the Church to curtail the birth of their children. I think that is a crime wherever it occurs, where husband and wife are in possession of health and vigor and are free from impurities that would be entailed upon their posterity. I believe that where people undertake to curtail or prevent the birth of their children that they are going to reap disappointment by and by. I have no hesitancy in saying that I believe this is one of the greatest crimes of the world today, this evil practice.[1]

When young people marry and refuse to fulfill this commandment given in the beginning of the world—and just as much in force today—they rob themselves of the greatest eternal blessing. If the love of the world and the wicked practices of the world mean more to a man and a woman than to keep the commandment of the Lord in this respect, then they shut themselves off from the eternal blessing of increase. Those who wilfully and maliciously design to break this important commandment shall be damned. They cannot have the Spirit of the Lord. Small families are the rule today. Husbands and wives refuse to take upon themselves the responsibilities of family life. Many of them do not care to be bothered with children. Yet this commandment given to Adam has never been abrogated or set aside. If we refuse to live by the covenants we make, especially in the house of the Lord, then we cannot receive the blessings of those covenants in eternity. If the responsibilities of parenthood are wilfully avoided here, then how can the Lord bestow upon the guilty the blessings of eternal increase? It cannot be, and they shall be denied such blessings.

Now I wish to ask a question: "*How will a young married couple feel when they come to the judgment* and then discover that there were certain spirits assigned to them and *they* refused to have them?" Moreover, what will be their punishment, when they discover that they have failed to keep a solemn covenant, and spirits awaiting this mortal life were forced to come here elsewhere when they were assigned to this particular couple.

In the next world we are to be judged by the things we do. We will also be punished for the things we should have done and did not do. May I make this personal remark: I am the father of eleven children and to this day every one is a faithful member of the Church and all active, for that is the way they were taught and they were obedient. *They will belong to me forever, and are the foundation stones of my kingdom.* My posterity reaches today over the one hundred mark.

Couples Will Answer for Their Crimes

I regret that so many young couples are thinking today more of successful "contraceptives" than of having a posterity. They will have to answer for their sin when the proper day comes, and may actually be denied the glorious celestial kingdom.

The world is rapidly coming to its end, that is, the end of the days of wickedness. When it is fully ripe in iniquity the Lord will come in the cloud of heaven to take vengeance on the ungodly, for his wrath is kindled against them. Do not think that he delayeth his coming. Many of the signs of his coming have been given, so we may, if we will, know that the day is even now at our doors.

> And it shall come to pass, because of the wickedness of the world, that I will take vengeance upon the wicked, for they will not repent; for the cup of mine indignation is full; for behold, my blood shall not cleanse them if they hear me not.[2]

May all Latter-day Saint fathers and mothers see to it that they teach their children the sacredness of the marriage covenant. Let them impress upon their children that in no other way than by honoring the covenants of God, among which the covenant of eternal marriage is one of the greatest and most mandatory, can they obtain the blessings of *eternal lives*. If they refuse to receive this ordinance and other blessings of the house of God, then shall they be cut off from these higher blessings. They shall wear no crown; they shall have no rule and sway no sceptre; they shall be denied the fulness of knowledge and power, and like the Prodigal Son, they may return again to their Father's house, but it will be as servants, not to inherit as sons and daughters. If they will be true to these commandments, their glory and exaltation shall have no bounds, "all things are theirs."[3] May we all be blessed with the Spirit of the Lord so we may be directed in his ways, and may the Lord bless the young people starting out in life so they may keep every commandment, is my prayer, in the name of Jesus Christ, our Redeemer. Amen.—(*Conference Report,* October, 1965.)

[1]*R.S.M.,* 4:318.
[2]D&C 29:17.
[3]*Ibid.,* 76:59-60.

God has instructed us to use only the finest materials. He cannot look upon sin with the least degree of allowance, because he knows its terrible destructiveness in people's lives. The Lord has provided that every man should carry within himself the very things he seeks—faith, courage, and love—and we can develop that with which we have already been endowed. We should develop the ability to do the right thing instead of allowing ourselves endlessly to do as we please. The Lord has told us that if we keep ourselves clean we may become joint heirs with Jesus Christ, possessing all that the Father hath.

Diligence and Love

The saying "Light the way to MIA" is something to be remembered. If we have enough love of our Father in heaven in our hearts, we will always be blessed.

In the Doctrine and Covenants, Section 86, it says: "He that seeketh me early shall find me, and shall not be forsaken."[1]

Procrastination as it may be applied to the gospel is the thief of eternal life, which is the life in the presence of the Father and the Son. There are many among us who feel that there is no need for haste in the observance of the gospel principles and the keeping of the commandments. We are living in the last days. Bad habits are easily formed. They are not so easily broken. Are we yielding to evil habits, thinking they are only trifles after all and we will get rid of them in the grave? Do we expect that our bodies will be cleansed in the grave and we shall come forth with perfect and sanctified bodies in the resurrection? There are some among us who teach this thing and excuse themselves for their practices, saying that they will be cleansed in the grave.

Doctrine Taught by Alma

Alma taught a very different doctrine. He said to Corianton, his son, "Behold, I say unto you, wickedness never was happiness."[2] The Savior said, ". . . with what measure ye mete, it shall be measured to you again."[3] Some think that a little punishment will not be so bad, and they are willing to take a chance and suffer for the offenses rather than keep the commandments of the Lord as we are instructed. Who could be happy in suffering, all the while thinking that the suffering had come because of a wilful or persistent breaking of the commandments of God when knowledge and counsel to walk in righteousness had been given?

No person can begin too early to serve the Lord. Parents are instructed to teach their children from infancy with the warning that they will be held accountable if they fail to do so. And young people follow the teachings of their parents. The child who is taught in righteousness from birth will most likely follow righteousness always. Good habits are easily formed and easily followed.

Apostle Paul said to the Corinthians, ". . . ye are God's building.

". . . But let every man take heed how he buildeth. . . ."[4]

Responsibility to Build Personality

One of the greatest responsibilities that is ever entrusted to any human being is that of building his own personality. The chief business of our lives is to build a house that will bear the weight of eternal life. In Grenville Kleiser's book *Training for Power and Leadership,* he writes,

> Nothing touches the soul but leaves its impress. And thus little by little we are fashioned into the image of all we have seen and heard, known or meditated upon. If we learn to live with all that is fairest and purest and best, the love of it will in the end become our very life.

God has instructed us to use only the finest materials. He cannot look upon sin with the least degree of allowance, because he knows its terrible destructiveness in people's lives. The Lord has provided that every man should carry within himself the very things he seeks—faith, courage, and love—and we can develop that with which we have already been endowed. We should develop the ability to do the right thing instead of allowing ourselves endlessly to do as we please. The Lord has told us that if we keep ourselves clean we may become joint heirs with Jesus Christ, possessing *all that the Father hath.*[5] I am sure that we all want to live so that we may receive this blessing. There is nothing in the commandments of the Lord that is difficult to keep. With the guidance of the Spirit of the Lord we will find contentment and happiness in doing his will. The divine law declares that we may obtain the fulness of his kingdom through our faithfulness and obedience. Our Eternal Father cannot offer more. He has placed his greatest gift within the reach of all, but it is based upon obedience to his divine commandments.

Greatest Waste in Mortal Life

The greatest waste in mortal life is that men love evil instead of righteousness. We come to this world to be tried and proved to see if we will keep the commandments when we are shut out of the divine presence. Most human beings live below their possibilities. Mortal life is short at best. It is, however, the life in which we prepare for eternity.

We are told that "the fear of the Lord is the beginning of knowledge: but fools despise wisdom and instruction."[6] True knowledge and wisdom come through prayer and wise fasting and through diligent study. Let us not forget the words of Alma:

> For behold, this life is the time for men to prepare to meet God; yea, behold the day of this life is the day for men to perform their labors.[7]

This important statement is taken from the teachings of the Prophet Joseph Smith:

> We consider that God has created man with a mind capable of instruction, and a faculty which may be enlarged in proportion to the heed and diligence given to the light communicated from heaven to the intellect; and that the nearer man approaches perfection, the clearer are his views, and the greater his enjoyments, till he has overcome the evils of his life and lost every desire for sin; and like the ancients, arrives at that point of faith where he is wrapped in the power and glory of his Maker and is caught up to dwell with Him. But we consider that this is a station to which no man ever arrived in a moment: he must have been instructed in the government and laws of that kingdom by proper degrees, until his mind is capable in some measure of comprehending the propriety, justice, equality, and consistency of the same. For further instruction we refer you to Deut. xxxii, where the Lord says, that Jacob is the lot of His inheritance. He found him in the desert land, and in the waste, howling wilderness; He led him about, He instructed him, He kept him as the apple of His eye, etc.; which will show the force of the last item advanced, that it is necessary for men to receive an understanding concerning the laws of the heavenly kingdom, before they are permitted to enter it: we mean the celestial glory. So dissimilar are the governments of men, and so diverse are their laws, from the government and laws of heaven, that a man, for instance, hearing that there was a country on this globe called the United States of North America, could take his journey to this place without first learning the laws of governments; but the conditions of God's kingdom are such, that all who are made partakers of that glory, are under the necessity of learning something respecting it previous to their entering into it.[8]

One Must First Learn Laws

So it is with the kingdom of God as now established in the earth. One must first learn something concerning the nature of its laws, how far reaching they are in relation to the temporal as well as the spiritual salvation of the individual.

We have been taught that a soul cannot be saved in ignorance of the saving principles of the gospel of Jesus

Christ. Moreover, he is under the necessity of being loyal and obedient to them. The Lord is always merciful and kind. If we draw near to him, he will draw near to us. ". . . seek me diligently and ye shall find me; ask, and ye shall receive; knock, and it shall be opened unto you."[9] Our chief trouble is we do not seek diligently. Our seeking is superficial. We seem to think that the Lord is bound to hear us without our putting forth much effort. Let diligence and love be our guides, and we shall find the path to eternal life; and let us one and all remember the theme of the Mutual Improvement organization:

> He that hath my commandments, and keepeth them, he it is that loveth me: and he that loveth me shall be loved of my Father, and I will love him, and will manifest myself to him.[10]—(Address delivered at 1965 MIA June Conference.)

---

[1]D&C 88:83.
[2]Alma 41:10.
[3]Matt. 7:2.
[4]1 Cor. 3:9-10.
[5]See Rom. 8:17 and D&C 84:38.
[6]Prov. 1:7.
[7]Alma 34:32.
[8]*Teachings of the Prophet Joseph Smith*, p. 51.
[9]D&C 88:63.
[10]John 14:21.

I appeal to you, my dear brethren and sisters, husbands and wives, fathers and mothers, to take advantage of every opportunity the Church affords to have your children trained in the various organizations provided for them by the revelations of the Lord: the Primary, the Sunday School, the Mutual Improvement organizations, and the quorums of the Lesser Priesthood under the direction of our bishoprics.

Entrusted to Our Care . . . the Youth of Israel

I will address my remarks to the fathers and mothers of The Church of Jesus Christ of Latter-day Saints, likewise to those who are engaged in the organizations of the Church looking after the youth of Israel.

Some few months ago I read in the paper that the majority of crimes committed in the United States were committed by those who were of teen ages. That was a shock to me and I think to thousands of others, many thousands throughout this land, for it seemed to be so unusual and a trend that boded only evil for this country. We have been troubled even in our own city, and this trouble has existed in all parts of the land, with vandalism, the wanton destruction of property, crimes by children and teen-agers, which show a tendency that will lead only to serious trouble within the borders of our country in years to come.

So I appeal to you, my dear brethren and sisters, husbands and wives, fathers and mothers, to take advantage of every opportunity the Church affords to have your children trained in the various organizations provided for them by the revelations of the Lord: the Primary, the Sunday

School, the Mutual Improvement organizations, and the quorums of the Lesser Priesthood under the direction of our bishoprics.

I hope that you are teaching your children in your homes to pray. I hope that you are having family prayers, morning and evening, that your children are taught by example and by precept to observe the commandments that are so precious and so sacred and mean so much to our salvation in the kingdom of God.

Teach Children Light and Truth

The Lord said in a revelation given to the Church in 1831:

> And again, inasmuch as parents have children in Zion, or in any of her stakes which are organized, that teach them not to understand the doctrine of repentance, faith in Christ the Son of the living God, and of baptism and the gift of the Holy Ghost by the laying on of the hands, when eight years old, the sin be upon the heads of the parents.
>
> For this shall be a law unto the inhabitants of Zion, or in any of her stakes which are organized.[1]

And I think I could add with equal truth in any branch of the Church in any mission or any other place outside of the stakes of Zion. The Lord requires this at our hands. I am reminded of a statement that was made in a discourse by President Brigham Young one time which I am not able to quote correctly, but the substance of it is this:

> You say this is my wife. You say these are my children. That all depends upon your keeping the commandments of God.

That is the substance of it. In other words, the Lord can take away from you this wife. He can take away from you these children. He has not relinquished his claim upon any of the children that have been entrusted to our care.

So I make this appeal because the tendency in this country today, as you all know who read the papers, is towards nuclear energy, traveling to the moon, getting off the earth, and going somewhere else. But people have forgotten God. We cannot afford to do that.

We Must Keep Our Feet on the Ground

Let us as members of the Church, no matter what else we may think about space travel, keep our feet on the ground, spiritually and in the home.

One thing, too, that I would like to call attention to—young people, when they marry, are not satisfied to begin with a little and humbly, but they want to receive just about as much as their parents have at the time they, the children, get married. They must have an automobile; they have to have a television set, a radio, all kinds of conveniences, many of which, of course, are very helpful. But they want to start out with every convenience under the sun to make them comfortable. I think this is a mistake. I think they should begin humbly, putting their faith in the Lord, building here a little and there a little as they can, accumulating piecemeal, until they can reach a position of prosperity such as they wish to have.

Now this condition of wanting everything leads to this great trouble: Both the mother and the father find employment. That means that children are left either to run the streets or somebody has to be called in to take care of them in the absence of the parents, and generally, it is my opinion that these children are left to wander the streets, to get into mischief, and they do not have the proper attention that ought to be given to them by the mother in the home.

Let us try humbly to keep our families intact, to keep them under the influence of the Spirit of the Lord, trained in the principles of the gospel that they may grow up in righteousness and truth. I think the Lord requires that at our hands. He has said, as I have read to you here, that he will hold the parents responsible for the acts of the children and they are given unto us that we might train them in the ways of life, eternal life, that they might come back again into the presence of God, their Father.

Important to Train Children in the Home

Now, some may think I am a little extreme but I think that the training of the children, the watching care over the children in the home by the mother, is worth far more than to have her seek employment, even if it is a matter of pinching a little in order to keep going in the home.

Again, we have throughout the Church, wherever it is possible for us to have this opportunity, seminaries and institutes which our children who are old enough to go to the public schools or even to the colleges may attend. Brethren and sisters, send your children to these seminaries. Those who are going to college will be old enough, if they have the proper training in their youth, to attend the institutes of the Church. They are old enough to take care of themselves. But help your children in every way you can to grow up with a knowledge of the gospel of Jesus Christ. Teach them to pray. Teach them to observe the Word of Wisdom, to walk faithfully and humbly before the Lord so that when they grow up to manhood and womanhood they can thank you for what you have done for them and look back over their lives with grateful hearts and with love for their parents for the manner in which those parents cared for them and trained them in the gospel of Jesus Christ.—(*Conference Report,* April, 1958.)

---

[1]D&C 68:25-26.

At no time in the history of the world has it been more necessary for the children of men to repent. We boast of our advanced civilization; of the great knowledge and wisdom with which we are possessed, but in and through it all, the love of God is forgotten!

The Signs of the Lord's Coming

My dear brethren and sisters, I am very thankful to be here with you at this, the 136th annual general conference of The Church of Jesus Christ of Latter-day Saints, and I pray that I might say something that will be for the upbuilding of the kingdom of our Father and for the benefit of those who are listening. I would like to speak of "The Signs of the Lord's Coming," and I pray that he will direct me in what I say.

Many things have taken place during the past one hundred and thirty-six years to impress faithful members of the Church with the fact that the coming of the Lord is near. The gospel has been restored. The Church has been fully organized. The priesthood has been conferred upon man. The various dispensations from the beginning have been revealed and their keys and authorities given to the Church. Israel has been, and is being gathered to the land of Zion. The Jews are returning to Jerusalem. The gospel is being preached in all the world as a witness to every nation. Temples are being built and ordinance work for the dead, as well as for the living, is performed in them. The hearts of the children have turned to their fathers, and they are seeking after their dead. The covenants which the Lord promised to make with Israel in the latter days have been revealed and thousands of gathered Israel have entered into them. Thus the work of the Lord is advancing, and all these things are signs of the near approach of our Lord.

Prophecy on Jews Has Been Fulfilled

Jesus said the Jews would be scattered among all nations and Jerusalem would be trodden down by the Gentiles until the times of the Gentiles were fulfilled.[1] The prophecy in Section 45:24-29, of the Doctrine and Covenants regarding the Jews was literally fulfilled. Jerusalem was trodden down by the Gentiles but is no longer trodden down, but is made the home for the Jews. They are returning to Palestine, and by this we may know that the times of the Gentiles are near their close.

The words of the prophets are rapidly being fulfilled, but it is done on such natural principles that most of us fail to see it. Joel promised that the Lord would pour out his spirit upon all flesh; the sons and daughters should prophesy; old men should dream dreams and young men should see visions. Wonders in heaven and in the earth should be seen, and there should be fire, blood and pillars of smoke. Eventually the sun is to be turned into darkness and the moon as blood, and then shall come the great and dreadful day of the Lord.[2] Some of these signs have been given; some are yet to come. The sun has not yet been darkened. We are informed that this will be one of the last acts just preceding the coming of the Lord.

One wonders if we are not now seeing some of the signs in heaven? Not all, for undoubtedly some of them will be among the heavenly bodies, such as the moon and the sun, the meteors and comets, but in speaking of the heavens, reference is made to that part which surrounds the earth and which belongs to it. It is in the atmosphere where many of the signs are to be given. Do we not see airships of various kinds traveling through the heavens daily? Have we not had signs in the earth and through the earth with the radio, railroad trains, automobiles, submarines and satellites, and many other ways? There are yet to be great signs; the heavens are to be shaken, the sign of the Son of Man is to be given; and then shall the tribes of the earth mourn.

Among the Signs of the Last Days

Among the signs of the last days was an increase of learning. Daniel was commanded to "shut up the words, and seal the book" of his prophecy, "even to the time of the end." And in that day, "many shall run to and fro," said he, "and knowledge shall be increased."[3] Are not the people "running to and fro" today as they never did before in the history of the world? Go to the Bureau of Information and ask there, how many tourists visit the Temple Block each year. Make inquiry at the various national parks, at the bus, railroad and steamship companies; learn how many are running to Europe, Asia, and all parts of the earth. Are we not, most of us, running to and fro in our automobiles seeking pleasure? Is not knowledge increased? Was there ever a time in the history of the world when so much knowledge was poured out upon the people? But sad to say, the words of Paul are true—the people are "ever learning and never coming to a knowledge of the truth."[4]

Have you ever tried to associate the outpouring of knowledge, the great discoveries and inventions during the past one hundred and thirty-six years with the restoration of the gospel? Do you not think there is some connection? It is not because we are more intelligent than our fathers that we have received this knowledge, but because God has willed it so in our generation! Yet men take the honor unto themselves and fail to recognize the hand of the Almighty in these things. America was discovered because the Lord willed it. The gospel was restored in America, rather than in some other land, because the Lord willed it. This is the land shadowing with wings spoken of by Isaiah,[5] which today is sending ambassadors by the sea to a nation scattered and peeled, which at one time was terrible in the beginning. Now that nation is being gathered, and once again they shall be in favor with the Lord.

The Whole Earth Is in Commotion

Have we not had numerous rumors of wars? Have we not had wars, such wars as the world never saw before? Is there not today commotion among the nations, and are not their rulers troubled? Have not kingdoms been overturned and great changes been made among nations? The whole earth is in commotion. Earthquakes in divers places are reported every day.

I took the liberty to call Dr. Melvin Cook and have him get for me some facts about how many earthquakes we have now. He quotes from a recent book by John H. Hodgson, from Ottawa, the following: "The way the numbers (of earthquakes) go up as the magnitude goes down makes it easy for us to accept the estimate that, if all earthquakes down to zero magnitude could be detected, the number would be between one and ten million each year." Then he goes on to say, that there are about 2,000 earthquakes each year with the magnitude between 5 and 6 and about 20,000 between 4.0 and 5.0, therefore it looks like there are around 20,000 earthquakes a year that could be damaging if they occurred in populated areas.

The other signs given by the Lord have been seen, or are at our doors. We know this to be the case, both from observation and from the predictions of the prophets. Elijah, one hundred and thirty-six years ago, told Joseph Smith that the great and dreadful day of the Lord was near, "even at the doors."[6]

Give Heed to His Warnings

Yet the old world goes on about its business paying very little heed to all the Lord has said, and to all the signs and indications that have been given. Men harden their hearts and say "that Christ delayeth his coming until the end of the earth."[7] They are eating and drinking, marrying and giving in marriage" according to the customs of the world, not of God, without one thought that the end of wickedness is near. Pleasure and the love of the world have captured the hearts of the people. There is no time for such people to worship the Lord or give heed to his warnings; so it will continue until the day of destruction is upon them. At no time in the history of the world has it been more necessary for the children of men to repent.

We boast of our advanced civilization; of the great knowledge and wisdom with which we are possessed, but in and through it all, the love of God is forgotten! The Lord, as well as Elijah, gave us warning; also Joseph Smith. The Lord said:

> For behold, verily, I say unto you, the time is soon at hand that I shall come in a cloud with power and great glory. And it shall be a great day at the time of my coming, for all nations shall tremble. But before that great day shall come, the sun shall be darkened, and the moon be turned into blood; and the stars shall refuse their shining, and some shall fall, and great destructions await the wicked.[8]

There Shall Come Another Cleansing

If the great and dreadful day of the Lord was near at hand when Elijah came, we are just one century nearer it today. But some will say: "But no! Elijah, you are wrong! Surely 136 years have passed, and are we not better off today than ever before? Look at our discoveries, our inventions, our knowledge and our wisdom! Surely you made a mistake!"

So many seem to think and say, and judging by their actions they are sure that the world is bound to go on in its present condition for millions of years before the end will come. Talk to them; hear what they have to say—these learned men of the world. "We have had worse times," they say. "You are wrong in thinking there are more calamities now than in earlier times. There are not more earthquakes, the earth has always been quaking but now we have facilities for gathering the news which our fathers did not have. These are not signs of the times; things are not different from former times."

And so the people refuse to heed the warnings the Lord so kindly gives to them, and thus they fulfill the scriptures. Peter said such sayings would be uttered and he warned the people.[9] In this warning Peter calls attention to the destruction of the world in the flood, and says that at the coming of Christ—which scoffers would postpone, or deny—there shall come another cleansing of the earth; but the second time by fire.

Is not the condition among the people today similar to that in the day of Noah? Did the people believe and repent then? Can you make men, save with few exceptions believe today that there is any danger? Do you believe the Lord when he said 136 years ago:

> For I am no respecter of persons, and will that all men shall know that the day speedily cometh, the hour is not yet, but is nigh at hand, when peace shall be taken from the earth, and the devil shall have power over his own dominion?[10]

> And behold, and lo, I come quickly to judgment to convince all of their ungodly deeds which they have committed against me, as it is written of me in the volume of the book.[11]
>
> Prepare ye, prepare ye for that which is to come, for the Lord is nigh;
>
> And the anger of the Lord is kindled, and his sword is bathed in heaven, and it shall fall upon the inhabitants of the earth.[12]

> Verily, I say unto you, this generation, in which these things shall be shown forth, shall not pass away until all I have told you shall be fulfilled.[13]

Shall we slumber on in utter oblivion or indifference to all that the Lord has given us as warning? I say unto you,

> Watch therefore: for ye know not what hour your Lord doth come.
>
> But know this, that if the good man of the house had known in what watch the thief would come, he would have watched, and would not have suffered his house to be broken up.
>
> Therefore, be ye also ready; for in such an hour as ye think not the Son of Man cometh.[14]

Be Prepared for Lord's Coming

May we heed this warning given by the Lord and get our houses in order and be prepared for the coming of the Lord, I humbly pray, in the name of Jesus Christ our Redeemer. Amen.—(*Conference Report*, April, 1966.)

---

[1]Luke 21:24.
[2]Joel 2:28-32.
[3]Daniel 12:4, 9.
[4]2 Timothy 3:7.
[5]Isaiah 18:1.
[6]D&C 110:13-16.
[7]*Ibid.*, 45:26.
[8]*Ibid.*, 34:7-9.
[9]2 Peter 3:3-7.
[10]D&C 1:35.
[11]*Ibid.*, 99:5.
[12]*Ibid.*, 1:12-13.
[13]P. of G. P., Writings of Joseph Smith 1:34.
[14]Matt. 24:42-44.

I know absolutely that Jesus Christ is the only Begotten Son of God, the Redeemer of the world, the Savior of men insofar as they will repent of their sins and accept the gospel. . . . I am grateful for my membership in this Church, for the opportunity that has been mine to serve. My desire is to prove true and faithful to the end.

A Personal Testimony

My dear brethren and sisters: We are here assembled, as we assemble at every conference, for the purpose of being instructed, built up, and encouraged so that when we return to our homes, we will be able to teach our people and keep them in the path of truth. We may even be admonished, if that is necessary.

This afternoon I wish to bear testimony to the restoration of the gospel, to the mission of our Redeemer, to the call of the Prophet Joseph Smith and the establishment of this work in the dispensation in which we live, known as the dispensation of the fulness of times. I know absolutely that Jesus Christ is the only Begotten Son of God, the Redeemer of the world, the Savior of men insofar as they will repent of their sins and accept the gospel. Through his death he redeemed all men and took upon him that sacrifice which would relieve us of our sins that we may not answer for them if we will accept him and be true and faithful to his teachings.

I am just as fully satisfied, because I know, that the Father and the Son appeared to Joseph Smith and revealed to him the great truth which had been lost because of the wickedness of the world; that they are separate distinct

Personages; that the Father and the Son, together with the Holy Ghost, constitute the Godhead, the great ruling power of the universe; that Jesus Christ volunteered to come into this world to redeem it; that John the Baptist came to the Prophet, as did Moroni before him, and Peter, James, and John later, to give authority and to usher in the kingdom of God anew in this dispensation in which we live, because men had turned away from the truth. Through darkness which covered the earth they had lost the knowledge of God; they had transgressed the laws and changed the ordinances; and instead of teaching the simple truths of the gospel of Jesus Christ, they taught the commandments of men just as the Lord Jesus Christ declared to the Prophet Joseph Smith.

I am grateful for my membership in this Church, for the opportunity that has been mine to serve. My desire is to prove true and faithful to the end. I realize that this is the dispensation of the fulness of times; that we live in perilous days; that men's hearts are failing; that contention prevails; nations stand in opposition to nations; and there is no peace.

I realize, because I discover it, that there is commotion not only among men, but also in the elements pertaining to this earth; that they too are becoming angry. The judgments of the Almighty are being poured out upon the inhabitants of the earth by earthquakes, by flood, by famine and pestilence, and in many other ways, and all of these are signs that have been given by our Lord Jesus Christ to convince men upon the face of the earth that his coming is near, even at our doors.

When you return to your homes, teach the people. Call upon them to repent wherein they need to repent, to get on their knees before the Lord, to remember their covenants, and their obligations to keep them, and to walk faithfully and humbly in the sight of their Eternal Father.

That is one of the most important missions that we have. Let us carry it out, I humbly pray in the name of the Lord Jesus Christ. Amen.—(*Conference Report*, April, 1956.)

Index

—I—

—J—

—K—

—Q—

—R—

—S—

—T—